D1188263

HOMECOMING HEROES

By the same author:

OUR SERGEANT:
The Story of the
Corps of Commissionaires

HOMECOMING HEROES

An Account of
the Reassimilation of
British Military Personnel
into Civilian Life

by
PETER REESE

LEO COOPER
LONDON

To my grandson
Henry Peter Reese.
May he too have the courage
and humanity of so many who went to war

First published in Great Britain in 1992 by L C
190 Shaftesbury Avenue, London WC2H 8JL
an imprint of Pen & Sword Books Ltd.
47 Church Street, Barnsley, S. Yorks S70 2AS

copyright © Peter Reese, 1992

A CIP catalogue of this book is available
from the British Library

ISBN: 0 85052 329 X

Printed in Great Britain by:
Redwood Press Limited, Melksham, Wiltshire

CONTENTS

ACKNOWLEDGEMENTS

This book, the result of an abiding interest, has been long a' coming. That it has been completed at all owes much to the kindness and generosity of many people. Most notable are my wife Barbara who over the years has taken on a plethora of responsibilities which should have been mine and my publisher, Leo Cooper, who is willing to take up projects he considers might have some inherent virtue although they are unlikely to bring major financial rewards.

As for the writing itself, despite his many other concerns, General Sir Edward Burgess gave me priceless time and encouragement when it was sorely needed and subsequently made most telling observations on the script; my valued friend and mentor Dr Leslie Wayper was there, as before, for me to bounce my unformed ideas upon and give me his unparalleled powers of analysis (he then corrected serious factual errors in the script); another long-time friend, Mrs Jennifer Prophet, magically reduced the original solecisms and assisted with the index. The early draft was also read with immense care by Lord Haig and Colonel Mike Wellings who both made valuable observations. Finally it was given the editorial treatment by Tom Hartman.

As one would expect, the great voluntary institutions concerned with veterans gave major assistance; among these were The Royal Hospital Chelsea, The Royal British Legion (both North and South of the border), SSAFA, The Soldiers' and Sailors' Help Society, the American Legion, The Royal Star and Garter Home, St Dunstan's and the Regular Forces Employment Association. In all cases I was privileged to find the controllers (or their equivalent) eager to help, but particular assistance 'on the ground' was given by Jeremy Lillies and Denis Yorke (RBL), David Lawson and George Smith (RBL Scotland), Mike Wellings (SSAFA), Ella

Linder and Anne Finley (SSHS), Joe Hovish and John Hanson (The American Legion), Ian Lashbrooke (The Royal Star and Garter Home), David Castleton (St Dunstan's) and at many times in past years General Pat Claxton and Mollie Tew (RFEA).

Among the sources held by academic institutions, those in the Department of Sound Records of the Imperial War Museum were vital, as were the Haig Papers held in the National Library of Scotland.

Most of the actual writing was done in the unique location of the Prince Consort's Library, Aldershot. Its two librarians, Paul Vickers and Tim Ward, have given endless help. From daily acquaintance all its staff have become part of my extended family and, I hope, in some way I am now part of theirs.

Writing this book has been a remarkable experience. As I might have expected, I have found veterans and their sponsoring organizations generous, warm-hearted, unafraid either of expressing emotion or voicing their fierce patriotism, people of inexpressible courage and humour. In this respect it is difficult to think one could have chosen a better subject, but, despite the great help, when trying to cover such a wide canvas in relatively few pages there must be some inexcusable omissions and errors. Responsibility for these rest with the author alone.

CHAPTER ONE

Gone for a Soldier

"Our God and soldiers we alike adore
Ev'n at the brink of danger; not before;
After deliverance, both alike requited,
Our God's forgotten,
and our soldiers slighted."

Francis Quarles, 1592–1644

DURING the recent military operation to recapture the Falkland Islands, many classic lessons of war were relearned by Britain's latest generation of fighting men. Among them was the demonstration of what has become increasingly appreciated by both ordinary observers and medical experts alike, namely the shock experienced by men in combat.

Sergeant Peter Naya, talking of the bombing of the *Sir Galahad*, expressed the emotions of all front-line soldiers who have faced death: "I feel humble, and lucky, that I survived. But it still comes back, it plays on your mind, especially at night. You see the experience was so traumatic that it hurts to talk about it, so I just clammed up. I couldn't talk about it to anyone." [1] Other participants in that war expressed other traditional soldiers' reactions. One was relief after screwing up one's resolution. As Flight-Lieutenant David Morgan said, "And when we came back home . . . we were all standing, lining the deck and everyone had tears streaming down their faces. At long last we could actually let it all go". For another officer, Captain Samuel Drennan, the relief was in the fact that they had come through morally intact: "I don't want to do it again but I've looked inside myself to see what was there and I wasn't too ashamed of what I found."

All realized they were changed; some saw themselves as more mature, others expressed it as valuing their lives and families more than previously. There was the same feeling of pride in the more thoughtful Army of the 1980s as in the earlier ones. Captain Ian Gardiner analysed it in the following way: "I believe I have had a glimpse of the sort of moral strength that made our forbears continue despite knowing the chances were poor," while Major John Kiszely exclaimed that "Courage caught on – it was absolutely contagious," attributing it to the great filial traditions of the foot guards. It was that same resolution which Lord Moran in his book on courage has talked of in terms of a man's will-power as a finite quality. "If it is used up he is finished . . . The call on the bank may be only the daily drain of the front line or it may be a sudden draft which threatens to close the account."[2]

Fittingly, it fell to Major Chris Keeble, who had assumed command of 2 Para at a crucial stage after its Commander had been killed, to express his belief in the great counterpoint to fear, the unique sense of comradeship born of adversity which comes to the best units, together with the eternal regret of the soldier that it is a transient thing: "I miss the brotherhood of that gang of folk who were called 2 Para who are now dispersed to the four winds."[3] Particularly for men who have consciously faced death, but probably, in a lesser degree, for all those who have been members of the British armed forces, however safe their billet might have been, there is a common consciousness. Like Shane in Jack Schaefer's great Western of that name, they will always be apart from those who have never had to stand up and be counted.

The separation of serving men from their own societies represents a clear historical pattern. The extreme case in modern memory of fighting men being separated from normal society surely applied to infantry soldiers in World War One, when, returning home on leave from that awesome and violent demiworld of the trenches, they found society at home virtually untouched by war. An ex-school mistress, Becca Macauly, speaking of the irrevocable changes brought by the Great War to the men from a small Highland township, said that, while "many young men did not come back, those who did were not the same. They had seen things we could not believe and therefore would not tell us about."[4] The unique bonds which had existed within such Highland communities were broken and, in their new rootlessness, many men turned subsequently to seek the wider pastures of the colonies, particularly Canada and New Zealand. In the Second World War there were soldiers who, after serving in the Far East for over three years, virtually lost touch with affairs in their mother country.

Exceptionally with nations in arms like ancient Sparta or modern Israel no separation between soldier and civilian occurs. All male Spartans were imbued with martial values from birth and were potential soldiers; all able-bodied Israelis, both men and women, stand ready to answer the call to arms. This has hardly been the pattern with most western states, either when a war has been fought by their regular armies or when it required further mobilization of manpower. The traditional lot of fighting men through the ages, not just those battle-broken in body or spirit, is not only for them to be separated from normal society but to experience major difficulties when they attempt to rejoin that greater community of citizens they are pledged to protect. In this respect British ex-servicemen, especially soldiers, have been no exception. Quite the opposite, for British ex-soldiers have traditionally received less official help than those any other major European nation.

Apart from Sparta, the Greek states kept their fighting men apart. More than four centuries before Christ they used mercenary soldiers to conduct their wars, leaving their citizens free to use their talents and energies on what they did best, conducting the administrative and commercial affairs of normal life. During the Peloponnesian war most citizens were soldiers, but after the defeat of Athens by the Persian King, Cyrus the Younger, he sought to control the Greek States by replacing them with mercenaries. These came to know nothing but war and became virtually incapable of being reassimilated into normal society. The rough régime of the camp and the fighting line, the excitement, danger and above all the comradeship of military life marked them irrevocably. When they laid down their arms special arrangements were therefore needed to help them settle down, as far as possible with their comrades of many campaigns beside them.

Ancient Greece demonstrated another perennial problem for men trained in war, namely the fears which national leaders always harbour for standing armies once the threat to their state has diminished. In the *Anabasis* Xenophon wrote about a Greek mercenary army, ten thousand strong, bereft of its great king-leader, Cyrus. Its sufferings are graphically described. Repeated attempts to find a new national leader failed as it passed through different but universally hostile regions where it was feared by all. Shiftless and lacking purpose, its members too often found themselves betrayed by those who no longer had a use for their swords.

After close on 1000 years of feudalism, the emergence of the nation state in the fifteenth century led to the redevelopment of professional armies in the modern world. The political tradition of each state directly affected both the structure and use of these armed forces and its relationships with them. For most civilians, though, their attitudes to the military have not been without a certain amount of apprehension.

Unsurprisingly, the experiences of Cyrus's veterans have been repeated in the annals of later regular armies, including the British after the French Revolutionary Wars, for instance, or at the end of the First World War. The main danger over, they found that state and society had other priorities and rewarded them by cutting their establishments to the bone and starving them of funds.

They tended in consequence to stagnate militarily. Like all victors, confidence in their past successes inclined them to reject novel tactics and financial restrictions led to delays in receiving the latest weapons. As a result it has been the pattern of British military history that at the start of major wars those regulars who have been deprived of resources during the balmy days of peace have to pay an initially high and disproportionate price in blood and debilitating exertion until larger forces have been raised and new weapons and tactics are adopted.

As for those discharged, both the regulars and those recruited

4

for the duration of wars which traditionally prove more protracted than most expected, their fate has been to rejoin a hostile and adverse environment bedevilled by the economic and social convulsions which follow major conflicts. The services of the soldier are then forgotten, but the suspicion in which he has traditionally been held is not, and retiring veterans have been at a perennial disadvantage. This was particularly serious for those discarded in 'extra' cutbacks soon after the main ones. For all such veterans, their military exploits favoured them little and they had to readjust to a changed world or suffer the penalties of the 'outsider'.

Apart from a lack of experience of contemporary developments in civilian society and the different values of military life, British soldiers in general have tended to suffer from fear on the part of civilians both of their chosen calling and their continued potential to use force. The figure of Cromwell, regicide and national leader of a fearsome and dedicated army, who brought fire and sword to a country not accustomed to such an experience, still overshadows British attitudes to its military. Since Cromwell soldiers have been seen as potential *agents provocateurs*, men with the capability and, if thwarted, the desire to take power into their own hands. After the Napoleonic Wars, for instance, in 1819, ex-soldiers were reported to be drilling working men and one of the Six Acts passed to preserve public order during that year expressly banned the practice. Over fifty years later men who had completed short-service engagements experienced major difficulties in finding civilian jobs because of their continued liability for reserve training and their possible embodiment at times of crisis. Employers' apprehensions were not confined to their annual absences at the fortnightly training camp or to the possibility of losing them in time of war but, in part, because such men continued to preserve their military values and skills. At the end of the First World War demonstrations by soldiers disgruntled with the chaos of demobilization arrangements, although quickly put down, led an alarmed Government to make rapid adjustments.

After all wars the classic civilian reaction is that soldiers need to be brought back to the realities of life. At the end of the First World War there was a universal feeling, captured by Lloyd George's rhetoric, that the time for fighting was over and national reconstruction should be the first priority. After a war, politicians, intent on new objectives, can always cite the Christian attitude to the different states of peace and war. The famous text from Ecclesiastes that there is "A time to kill and a time to heal . . . a time of war and a time of peace"[5] is regularly dusted down and quoted. And in Britain, an island nation enjoying that extra security given by the sea and relying on international trade for survival, the need to resume business as usual within the shortest possible time has tended to put her retiring veterans at an even greater disadvantage.

Different national attitudes can be seen in the subsequent treatment of great wartime leaders, men who captured the public imagination in wartime. In the circumstances they must frequently represent a potential or actual challenge to the current hierarchy, as their humble followers do when they return expecting to get their jobs back. Apart from his strong personal antipathy to Haig, who stood for so many things which Lloyd George opposed, it was, after all, only traditional political tactics for Lloyd George to diminish him after the Great War. Such actions are not, of course, confined to leaders of Liberal Democratic states. In Communist Russia after the Second World War, where the Party leadership was intent on preserving power, Marshal Zhukov personified victory to most Russian citizens and was second only in public veneration to Stalin himself. By July, 1946, though, he found himself transferred to Odessa Military District. There he took up a relatively minor military post and was expelled from the Central Committee of the Supreme Soviet. Zhukov was subsequently transferred to even greater obscurity, a post in the Ural Mountains, before his partial re-emergence in 1952.[6]

In Germany, on the other hand, with its more militaristic tradition, the old Field-Marshal Paul von Hindenburg was elected President of the Republic in 1925, and no civilian leaders, including others on the National Resistance Council (or for that matter the President of the United States), could stop the progression of General Charles de Gaulle in 1944 from gaining supreme power in France. Nor did the average Frenchman want it otherwise. While in the United States, where the careful checks and balances imposed by its constitution reduce fears about control by ex-military men, the progression in 1953 of Dwight Eisenhower, ex-Supreme Commander during the Second World War, to the Presidency was directly in line with the tradition set by America's first soldier President, George Washington, and continued by Jackson and Grant.

In Britain, with the unique position of its monarchy after the Restoration, the tradition has always been different. Since Oliver Cromwell, the accession of a senior military leader to a high political position has proved repugnant, the exception being the Duke of Wellington. But his short term as Prime Minister of a high Tory administration thirteen years after the Napoleonic Wars constituted no threat whatever of a military takeover. In any case, by the mid-Victorian Age the combined strength of Parliament and the British constitutional monarchy made the chances of an ex-soldier again becoming titular head of state virtually negligible. The showering of honours on Britain's military leaders at the end of wars has usually presaged their neutering as far as political power is concerned. The partial exception in recent years was the royal sailor Earl Mountbatten, but his major political responsibilities were in British India rather than in the United Kingdom.

Opinions vary as to how much the election of wartime leaders to the highest offices of state benefits their veterans. Yet the veterans' organizations in France, Germany and the United States have developed quite differently from those of the United Kingdom and have always tended to exercise more political power. Much, therefore, depends on the nature of a state's military tradition, and more attention will be paid to Britain's unique tradition subsequently, but the difficulties experienced by her veterans at the end of great wars and at other times is an indisputable and inglorious legacy of it.

In fairness it must be said that the problems encountered by British veterans have not always been due to blind civilian bias against ex-soldiers. In the past such men tended to be held in low esteem by reasons of their background. Unlike their officers, they were deliberately recruited from the lowest stratum of the population. The Duke of Wellington, comparing the British and French armies in 1835, said, "The officers of the French Army live a good deal more with their men than ours do: they are the same class of persons to a greater degree. As an Army raised by conscription, the French contained men of all classes but British soldiers are taken entirely from the lowest orders of society."[7] This was not all. When such men took the Queen's shilling and joined that hard-drinking, hard-swearing brotherhood in arms, many humble families felt it was the crowning disgrace. Even when first engagements were reduced in length and men returned to civilian life relatively young, the image was largely unchanged. Tim Carew, writing of the pre-1914 'Regular', said that, "like the archetype Tommy before him he frequently joined for *economic*, *alcoholic* or *amatory* reasons. Work was scarce in the early 20th century and not infrequently men could say, 'I joined to get three square meals a day and a pair of trousers with an arse in them'. Others, often men of greater education, joined to escape from the Police or other members of the establishment."[8] Out of such unpromising material some men rose to be outstanding leaders and to perform remarkable feats across a worldwide Empire. The young Wullie Robertson, who, by 1915, had become Sir William Robertson, Chief of the Imperial General Staff, was one of these. But when he joined as a trooper of 17 in 1875 his mother was scandalized and wrote to him, "What cause can you have for such a low life? I shall name it to no one for I am ashamed to think of it . . . I would rather bury you than see you in a red coat."[9]

This low opinion of the military does not apply to the soldiers of the two World Wars, when a true cross-section of young men joined the colours. In the case of these veterans, or those from post-1945 military engagements, what happened during their service was surely more important than their early background. It was probably equally important for the Tommies who served in earlier times.

Much is due to the fact that fighting men bow to the yoke of military discipline, the instant obedience which is vital to retain cohesion in the face of ultimate danger when facing stresses unknown to civilians. More than any citizen, including those in the Second World War, servicemen consciously place their very lives in pawn. To offset the common danger, though, they achieve a degree of comradeship and exclusiveness impossible in normal life, based, as Russell Braddon put it, on, "the knowledge that their courage and physical grandeur can rise above any physical stress".[10] One has only to witness reunions of the Desert Rats, the 14th Army or the Falklands veterans to see the accuracy of this statement.

During military service all men are obliged to adopt military ethics, some of which are antipathetic to civilian ones. Soldiers are compelled to lose touch with civilian life by the very nature of their calling. Uprooted from former associations and cast into an entirely new environment, they can view things from a wider perspective and with more critical eyes. With the likely prospect of death or injury before them, they often take the opportunity of discussing with men from different backgrounds the basic issues, including questions about how to eliminate the deficiencies as well as recognizing the advantages of their former existence. This rough university, the free interchange of thoughts and opinions during barrack-room debates, applied just as much to successive intakes of National Servicemen. Inevitably such discussions help to change attitudes and arguably none are unaffected. Thus changed, they return to a society also changed.

In certain men the flaring of the human spirit in the face of death has tempered their subsequent ambition and self-assurance. Possibly the 'grit' in Harold Macmillan's oyster which fed his determination and led him on the ruthless path to the Premiership owed as much to his wartime experiences as to his later marital difficulties. Others lack such stoicism. Like Henry Williamson after the First World War, they find themselves unable to reconcile their patriotic duty with the grotesqueness, suffering and illogicality of war. His battle experiences led Williamson to pacifism. Desperately clutching any unlikely straw for peace, even when Germany was patently re-arming, he described Hitler as "the great man across the Rhine whose life symbol is the happy child".[11] For many who were neither noticeably inspired nor repelled by such experiences there was a sense of anticlimax on their return. Captain John Wedderburn-Maxwell, looking back 70 years to the end of the Great War, said that his and other officers' reaction was of being absolutely lost. "Our main thing in life up to then had been killing Germans . . . Our reaction may seem strange but I heard afterwards that others had felt the same sense of bewildered depression. It was a puzzle."[12] Just 20 at the start of the war, he was 24 at its close. Never again, though, would any cause during the succeeding years of his long life be pursued with such intensity of purpose.

The problems are not confined to those who returned at the end of great wars nor to those Tommies of past centuries who returned after long years abroad to a society which had long ago written them off. After the Second World War the Korean and Malayan conflicts went largely unregarded, as did the lesser conflicts associated with the ending of Empire until the re-emergence of the Northern Ireland question from 1969 onwards. Today soldiers injured by terrorist action might justly feel that more compassion and publicity is given by contemporary society to student protesters in China or even to animal victims of medical research campaigns than to themselves. Second-Lieutenant D. J. Hollands, a National Serviceman who subsequently wrote a novel about his service in Korea, expressed the age-old attitudes which still applied to those civilian soldiers who fought there:

"For a day they might be the heroes of the Hook, but they were not heroes – the heroes of the nation were a bunch of men who had climbed Everest, or sportsmen, or film stars; they were simply the latest edition of Tommy Atkins, the men who in time of peace were treated as the scum of the land, laughed at, sneered at, and generally held in ridicule by the public and who in time of war were taken for granted."[13]

Servicemen returning from the Falklands, although warmed by their delirious reception, were subsequently bewildered to witness the political wrangling about the advisability of conducting the war at all and the endless furore about the sinking of the Argentinian cruiser, *General Belgrano*.

For those demobilized in the late 1980s, men who in many cases returned to civilian life with more universally recognized qualifications than any previous generation, there were still major difficulties of reintegration in civilian society. It is difficult, whatever technical qualifications you may possess, to explain to a potential employer that your past role was to kill people.

The recent hero of so many British citizens, Mikhail Gorbachev, was admired partly because he preached disarmament and troop reductions. This charismatic leader of a faltering Empire, whose fundamental power base was still the largest military machine ever assembled, caused many Britons, particularly those who were not involved in the great conflicts earlier in the century, to question their own soldiers' role in Western deterrent strategy and even the use of force in any circumstances whatever.

It goes without saying that for one class of men in particular retiring from war, the maimed and injured, there have always been particular and grievous problems. Largely unregarded in terms of their subsequent employability until the end of the nineteenth century, such men returned in unparalleled numbers after the two World Wars; a lesser, although continuous stream still emerge today to face the additional hazards of civilian life due to their injuries. These, in justice, require special assistance, traditionally given late, sparingly and grudgingly by the state. Happily in this century better arrangements are available and the service charities continue both to protect them and to press their cause. A proportion of them suffer from mental breakdowns and here sympathy from society at large has always been noticeably absent. To many, the warrior whose spirit has been broken by his experiences is a contradiction and embarrassment. Most difficult of all are those with 'delicate nerves' who, with misplaced shame, are reluctant to seek help in their later years.

Too often disregarded in the past have been the widows of fighting men, including those still surviving from the First World War whose lives were blighted irretrievably by the early loss of their husbands. The long neglect of First World War widows by respective Governments has been a cause for shame and frustration on the part of the ex-servicemen's organizations which has only recently been removed.

The special difficulties facing British ex-servicemen, particularly soldiers, both at the point of retirement and subsequently, have been long recognized and, in the British way, limited official provisions have been supplemented by a number of relatively long-standing, proud, voluntary organizations. For the most part these were set up by ex-officers concerned about the deleterious effect which impoverished ex-soldiers and their families would have on the military image. Some were established to help one particular group, like the disabled, while the British Legion from its foundation assumed a broader role. Today these many bodies, while retaining their independence, form a loose partnership where common interests are concerned. Together they act with the Ministry of Defence, which itself has a number of departments with partial responsibility for ex-servicemen, and with other departments of central Government.

This book is concerned with the traumatic and sombre story of the British ex-serviceman through the ages, his neglect and many sufferings and the evolution of that particular diffuse and overlapping system created by our unique military tradition to assist him both on his retirement and afterwards. The story does not end here. The mandate remains awesome, and in the next few years ex-service organizations face a massive challenge at a time when many of their experienced voluntary helpers must yield to the advancing years. Even now, when most of the First World War generation have passed away, there are eight and a half million ex-servicemen and women, together with their families, who fought both in the Second World War and during the post-war campaigns associated with a contracting empire. These are joined by approximately 35,000 servicemen who retire annually and about the same number of dependants.

This category is now providing a sharply increasing number of distressful cases, particularly among those who took part in the Second World War, men and women who stood up when it mattered and are now experiencing problems, some directly attributable to their wartime service, others more difficult to pinpoint, but who as members of that great body of ex-service personnel now deserve the consideration of a caring state.

Put another way, some 50% of the over 60s have some connection with the Armed Forces, either personally or through their friends and families. This generation, born as part of the birth bulge at the end of the First World War, is of particular concern, for, with lower casualty levels than in that earlier war, there are far more elderly survivors. It is unique in that it was the last to spend its tender years under the shadow of the workhouse when, during the slump of the interwar years, it suffered privations unknown to those born after the Second World War. It fought to keep its individual pride and self-sufficiency in a climate of large numbers on the dole, means tests stringently applied and the humiliations of public assistance committees. Within its ranks are a good proportion who have never enjoyed occupational pensions, and those who saved to safeguard their old age have seen their life savings hit by inflation, particularly during the early 1970s.

In a 'peacetime' society where interest in the services and the ex-service community runs at its traditional low level, it is up to the voluntary ex-service associations to target those needing help. This will be made less easy because, as a group, the men and women of the Second World War tend to be fiercely proud and independent, anxious to conceal their problems just as the majority are reluctant to talk of their war experiences. By now the eldest of those National Servicemen and regulars who joined after the Second World War are nearing their sixties but in the main this younger group has different needs. A premier one is surely obtaining and maintaining employment at the appropriate level. For many contemporary veterans the option will be self-employment, a risky process without sufficient information, early guidance and adequate capital.

For the coming challenge the ex-servicemen's organizations have recently been examining and revising their structures. To achieve the level of efficiency needed, there must surely be some further streamlining of role. The besetting problem with a comparatively large number of voluntary bodies raised in the first place by individual benefactors is threefold: continued adherence to original objectives now partly obsolete, lack of financial flexibility and repetitive, overlapping services. Their great strength surely lies in the large numbers of dedicated and caring people long identified with them. The final part of the book discusses some necessary rationalization here.

In an age of unsurpassed affluence, but one where clear evidence of need is required before official aid is forthcoming, the service charities (all charities for that matter) have new obligations to investigate the needs of those coming within their sphere of responsibility. There are, too, aspects of caring which go beyond material assistance. Old soldiers uniquely suffer from a special loneliness, the need to exchange tales of past derring-do which can only take place with men and women who have also served and understand their vulnerability. Having required men to endure terrible experiences on behalf of their state, there is a continuing need to assist those inevitably marked by such exertions. When so much attention is properly being paid to environmental issues, ecological balances and the preservation of animal life, in plain justice equal attention should be given to the needs of a generation who with their very lives gave society the luxury to consider such concerns.

Unless the service charities in conjunction with central agencies are vigilant and effective, the 'senior' old soldiers of past world conflicts – which we hope can never be repeated – stand to suffer the traditional fate of British ex-soldiers: indifference and condescension from a generation absorbed in other contemporary, predominantly selfish issues.

CHAPTER TWO

Traditional Attitudes to British Veterans

"On becoming soldiers we have not
ceased to be citizens."

*Representation addressed to Parliament by
the soldiers of Cromwell's Army, 1647.*

In the ancient empires of Greece and Rome, which have severally bequeathed so much towards modern Western civilization, professional soldiers were generally well provided for. Dionysius of Syracuse, for instance, who owed his considerable power and success to a picked body of mercenaries, loyal to him alone, rewarded them by giving generous bounties when they succeeded in battle and by the promise of rich, empty land at the fringes of his Empire, where they could settle and form their own communities when their fighting days were over.

With Rome, the immense size of the Empire and its very duration (Roman soldiers campaigned for virtually 1000 years) make it exceedingly difficult to summarize prevailing attitudes towards them. The Roman equivalent of the Greek mercenaries owing allegiance to particular leaders were the Praetorian Guard. These men protected a specific emperor against all comers and were highly rewarded both during and after their service. They had to be. On his accession a new emperor usually appointed his own contingent and the previous Guard were compelled to seek their fortunes elsewhere.

15

The professional Roman soldiers were different. Recruited from Roman citizens or from her subject peoples, they owed allegiance to Imperial Rome rather than to individual emperors. As Roman civilization was founded by, and maintained its power through, military force, legionnaires were well regarded and there were detailed resettlement arrangements made for them. They could expect gratuities (or land grants in lieu) at the end of their service, although these were sometimes given on condition their sons enlisted. This was by no means all the story. In a militaristic Empire they often assisted with civilian projects during their service, constructing public buildings, canals or roads. Their technical and administrative skills, together with their martial qualities, were usually highly regarded by the communities they rejoined. However, all was not always rosy for them; there is evidence that some experienced serious health problems within a relatively short time, a legacy arising from the harshness of their previous life. Once free from its iron regime, a proportion tended to deteriorate rapidly. In the late years of the Empire many legions came to take on definite geographical responsibilities. They served, married and settled afterwards in the same location, thus virtually eliminating problems of reintegration but, like some localized units of the present Chinese and Soviet Red Armies, this reduced their military effectiveness too.

After the break-up of the Roman Empire in the West a further millennium was to pass before regular soldiers were again seen there, men who were separate from and who needed to rejoin civilian communities at the end of their service – ample time for the main Roman tradition to be long forgotten. Generally speaking the European feudal system had no room for professional soldiers. Society revolved around martial values and military service in time of danger was the duty of every vassal to his lord. They were peoples in arms if not yet separate nation states. In Britain to combat external threats all men were assembled in the great fyrd, the brotherhood of active men. Once the threat had passed they returned immediately to their homes. It was the fyrd, or local levies, which made up the bulk of Harold's Saxon army at the Battle of Hastings. In parallel with the duty of the vassal was the duty of the mounted knight who owed chivalric allegiance to his supreme feudal leader. While some of the castle knights became semi-professional soldiers or house-carls, and formed protective bodies akin to the earlier Praetorian Guards, these were the exception.

The system was to change both in Britain and Europe during the fourteenth century with the rise of separate nation states. In Britain by paying an agreed sum a knight (and his retainers) could now avoid their annual obligation to serve, and the king, by using the money he received, could assemble a permanent or semi-permanent army for overseas wars. At the start of the Hundred Years' War against France in 1337 there is ample evidence that a professional army was assembled. A Parliament at Westminster imposed a tax on wool for the duration of the war and laid down that every knight and soldier of the Royal Army should draw pay. This was in no sense a standing army; it would have been far too expensive for the Crown at that time and would, in any case, have gone against Magna Carta which a century earlier had required King John to dismiss his standing bodyguard of (foreign) mercenaries.

On their return from France the men of the King's Army were quickly disbanded and it is likely that the characteristic attitude of British civilians to returning soldiers was developed at this time. The Royal Armies in France were filled by men who were far from the cream of contemporary society and their ranks were further swelled by foreign mercenaries and freebooters. Many of these came across the channel not with the intention of becoming civilians but of chancing their luck with whoever would still employ them as soldiers. The whole complement was described in terms equally applicable to soldiers of succeeding centuries:

"The adventurous, the ambitious, the romantically-minded nobles carrying forward a family tradition, the mercenary-minded, the discontented, the ne'er do well, the outlaw."[1]

But other types of 'old soldier' soon became apparent. There was the boaster, that same vainglorious storyteller satirized centuries before by Aristophanes. He was mocked in *Piers Plowman*:

"A boaster who has nothing;
A teller of tales in towns and taverns
He says what he never saw and means to his honesty;
He devises deeds that were done by no man."

Sometimes the boasters were civilians masquerading as ex-soldiers. There was also the maverick – pardoned criminal or not – who found the habits he had acquired, including pillage, irreconcilable with normal life. Some of the mavericks formed outlaw bands still arrayed for war.

The net result of such unwelcome freebooters was a series of repressive measures instituted by those powerful new local officials, the Justices of the Peace. These decreed savage punishments for all felons and loiterers, many but not all of whom were plainly ex-soldiers of the French wars, half-forgotten and starving during the later stages of the conflict. The problems caused by men returning to Britain at this time were as nothing compared with those in Europe. The relatively few outlaw bands were easily dispersed by the local shire levies, but in an island where memories tend to be long-standing the seeds of suspicion and antipathy were sown against ex-professional soldiers.

Henceforth the British military tradition took a different path from the other major European powers. In mainland Europe the existence of Free Companies of mercenaries offering their swords to the highest bidders was widespread. Some of these had been used by both the British and French during the Hundred Years' War. In peacetime such men were no more than bandits; their one security lay in legalized warfare. Moving to Italy, the Condottieri (literally mercenary captains who had signed condottas or written contracts with the Princes of the cities which hired them) became involved in a century and a half of warfare which only ended when the Italian Condottieri triumphed over their foreign challengers. After their martial successes they were able to establish themselves as Dukes and leading men, supported, of course, by their own standing armies. In France the challenge of the mercenaries was solved when Charles VII (1403–61) took them into his pay and legitimized them by forming the first regular national army in Europe.

In Britain things seemed to be going much the same way. Many of the returning soldiers from the Hundred Years' War joined the great nobles, who, with the disappearance of a common enemy, turned their swords against each other, thus bringing home the horrors of warfare on one of the very few occasions in our history. In a most important way the Wars of the Roses were different from the European conflicts as both sides continued to recognize the unity of the Kingdom under the threefold governmental system of King, Council and Parliament. By 1485 Henry Tudor had triumphed, but the fighting cost 100,000 lives and in the process the country as a whole had been roused against warring nobles and their professional soldier retainers. In this climate the King dared not rule through a standing army and emphasis turned to consolidation at home and colonization abroad, a policy largely achieved by naval forces. Under Henry VIII the navy was expanded further and with its defeat of the Spanish Armada in 1588 it became the world's premier fleet and the main instrument by which the homeland was made safe.

The Tudor monarchs fostered this new military tradition; external threats were met by the navy while land forces were strictly circumscribed and the part-time militia favoured. This revised version of the select fyrd now came under the authority of the county Lords Lieutenant. It had clear affinities with the county territorial forces which were to develop almost 200 years later. The militia was of most variable quality, although the trained bands of London were the most formidable, and the costs of this policy were repeated failures in the successive, if limited attempts, at overseas aggression. Queen Elizabeth continued the pattern of favouring the trained bands, but for overseas service additional elements of professional troops were required. When this human flotsam returned from France, after suffering many privations on behalf of its monarch, it was treated, like the Royal Army of Edward III, with cold severity and ingratitude.

During the later years of Elizabeth's reign no returning soldier was allowed to gather with other soldiers. He was compelled to obtain a testimonial signed by the Justice of the Peace nearest his place of disembarkation. This recorded his home location and the time permitted him for his journey there. For the most part, the footsore and hungry soldier was hardly welcome when he reached his native parish as he was rightly seen as an unexpected and exceptional drain on the hard-pressed local rates. Parishes even avoided looking after the wounded or disabled by giving them licences "to beg", usually for up to a twelve-month period only. To complicate matters, many imposters feigned wounds and these led to still less sympathy being felt for the unfortunates of foreign wars. Against such an unpromising climate professional soldiers, especially the perennial soldiers of fortune from Ireland and Scotland, forsook this country, taking their swords abroad. The Irish 'Wild Geese' were to find fame in France and Flanders during the late sixteenth century.

After the early Stuarts, a relatively short and exceptional period followed, a major 'blip' on the strikingly consistent flow chart of British military history. The Civil War between King and Parliament brought fighting back to this country and the Commonwealth period gave Britain a regular army again and no ordinary army at that. Macaulay, admittedly never an unbiased historian, observed that the ordinary soldiers of the New Model Army were different – they had a moral purpose. "They were . . . freeborn Englishmen, who had, of their own accord, put their lives at jeopardy for the liberties and religion of England, and whose right and duty it was to watch over the welfare of the nation which they had saved."[2] Strictly speaking, impressment had continued until 1651 to bring the New Model Army up to strength, but the religious purpose, discipline and sheer efficiency of it compared with other military bodies of the time became legendary. This God-fearing, self-confident machine of a Regicide beat all before it and left a trail of deliberate destruction not at all to the liking of the ordinary Englishman. In the historic pattern of Roman rather than British military history, Cromwell relied on the Army both for his power and continued survival. It was only to be expected that, even after his death, this formidable instrument of his policy, still 65,000 strong, should receive better treatment at the end of their service than was normal for other British armies before or after. Under the Commonwealth, injured soldiers were treated in special hospitals converted to their needs, and pensions were given both to disabled soldiers and, by a historic measure, to their families as well (4/- a week was the maximum payment for a family whatever its size).

This practice swiftly ended at the Restoration. Disabled soldiers (and sailors), together with 1500 widows and orphans, were given twelve weeks' pay each and returned to the far from tender care of their parishes. Yet in other respects faith was kept with the men. General Monk organized an order of disbandment determined by lot for the regiments of horse and foot and by great efforts all arrears of pay were made good. Equally, or more important, an Act was passed which followed Cromwell's historic Ordinance of September 1654 (in parallel with Roman custom) to help healthy old soldiers regain worthwhile employment. This laid down that any man who had served for a period of not less than four years should be free to practise his trade or occupation, in spite of the restrictions imposed by several Trade Corporations against partly-qualified members. This was keenly appreciated by the New Model's relatively high-grade soldiers, men of a calibre probably not equalled until the twentieth century. The measure appeared to succeed, for successive disbandments between 1652 and 1660 went off smoothly, something which was not achieved at the end of many later wars.

A friend remarked to Samuel Pepys in 1662:

"Of all the old Army you cannot see a man begging about the streets. You shall have this Captain turned shoemaker, the Lieutenant a baker, this a brewer, that a haberdasher; this common soldier a porter; and every man in his apron and frock etc as if they had never done anything else."[3]

The idealized account given to Pepys was far from the whole picture, even in the New Model Army. Many soldiers lacked trade skills altogether and others by reason of their experiences would not be able to pick up the threads of civilian life easily.

Attention was drawn to such men as these in contemporary ballads like *The Disbanded Soldier*:

"In Red-coat rags attired I wander up and down,
Since fate and foes conspired thus to assay me

Or betray me to the hard censure of the town.
Alas, poor soldier, where wilt thou march?"[4]

On the negative side, too, the Commonwealth period served to increase the British public's suspicion about, as they saw it, the privileged and dictatorial position held by standing armies. By Cromwell's Ordinance the powerful Trade Guilds, forerunners of Trade Unions, were alienated from helping ex-soldiers.

Once more in the British way memories tended to be long. That doyen of Army historians, John Fortescue, writing about the war with Spain which opened in 1739, some eighty years later, said:

"The nation had not yet ceased to rail at the iniquity of a standing Army . . . the attitude of the ordinary citizen towards the soldier was unfriendly even to aggression."[5]

At the Restoration in 1660 anti-militaristic feeling was such that it was decided to restrict the Regular Army to the traditional Royal Bodyguard. The decision had to be amended, though, when an insurrection by 'fifth monarchy men', a fanatical sect, was not suppressed until Monk's Regiment of Horse, the next to be disbanded, put it down. This outbreak demonstrated the need to retain a small permanent force, but its numbers were to be kept to a minimum.

From the time of the Restoration until the 1870s, when among other things the reforms of the Liberal Secretary of State for War, Edward Cardwell, led to the development of a more professional Officer Corps and introduced a shorter period of initial engagement for soldiers, the pattern for Britain's land forces remained broadly the same. This was despite a situation where British military involvement grew steadily throughout the eighteenth and early nineteenth centuries.

Under the unreformed system essential security needs were met by a core Army manned by long-term regular soldiers, most of whom came to know nothing else than military life. This was remarkably small in peacetime and it was ever starved of funds. Between 1756 and 1775, for instance, the Army totalled just 48,000 men, for duties which included the garrisoning of a large overseas empire, not forgetting North America. When war broke out rapid recruitment would be undertaken and particular emphasis paid to the traditionally fertile recruitment areas of Ireland and Scotland. At the war's end an equally or even more rapid disbandment would follow. When necessary, the British ranks were swelled by professional troops from other countries, like the Hanoverians. Towards the end of the eighteenth century, during the war against Revolutionary France, so great was the requirement for men that, Fortescue observed, "every agent of the British Government on the continent of Europe was on the watch to bring in recruits of every nation".[6] A German Legion, mainly composed of Hessians, served under the British flag during the Crimean War in the mid-nineteenth century and in the same war Swiss and Italian legions were also used.

Another traditional policy practised throughout the period was to construct alliances whereby a significant or even major part of the land fighting would be taken on by other countries.

This British military tradition caused a distinctive pattern of arrangements for its regular fighting men both during and after their service. The relationship between officers and soldiers in the unreformed British Army was far different from that of its predecessor, the New Model Army. After the Restoration there was a clear determination that never again would another Cromwell be allowed to emerge. To prevent this the Army's leadership was kept deliberately amateur, despite determined efforts by the Duke of York when he was Commander-in-Chief to amend it. One of Britain's greatest soldiers, the Duke of Wellington, was in no doubt that it was the very absence of military professionalism that safeguarded the constitution and prevented another Cromwell. He thoroughly approved the fact that:

"There came into the service men of fortune and education – men who had some connection with the interests and fortunes of the country besides the commissions they held."[7]

In the enigmatic way of British institutions, some of these officers, including Wellington, became masters in the art of war, more skilled even than the most seasoned European professional. This firmly-held belief that an officer should be a man of substance had a direct effect on both the military establishment and upon his prospects when returning to civilian life. The long-time Royal

Commander-in-Chief during the nineteenth century, the Duke of Cambridge, went further when he said that an officer should be a "a gentleman first and an officer second". He was of course only echoing the Duke of Wellington's beliefs here. But given this prevalent attitude among the Army's leaders towards the officer class it was perfectly understandable that any special arrangements to help their re-entry to civilian life should be long delayed. In the unreformed Army they were hardly required.

As a man of substance, a man of property, an officer would leave the Army with capital enough to re-establish himself. As a gentleman he would be welcomed back to civilian society. Indeed, he was unlikely to have lost touch with it. Generous allowances of leave enabled him to retain control of his home affairs. There were cases of officers being away for up to 250 days each year and Wellington, while struggling against a more numerous enemy in the Peninsula, complained bitterly about the amount of home leave taken by certain of his officers. An officer could even be a Member of Parliament while serving.

If he had no other source of capital (and in most cases this was unlikely) an officer on retiring would always have the residue from the sale of his commission. Commissions were purchased up to the rank of Lieutenant-Colonel and the sums were not inconsiderable. At the time of the Crimean War a Captaincy might cost £2,400 and a Lieutenant-Colonelcy £7,000. With the 'smart regiments' the figures were much higher. In 1836 Lord Cardigan paid over £40,000 for the Colonelcy of the 11th Light Dragoons.

Even those promoted from the ranks, like John Shipp, while not enjoying the financial security of their better-connected seniors, were still eligible for posts in the public service. Although he was dismissed the service, John Shipp, a man of great courage and spirit, became an Inspector with the newly formed Metropolitan Police and was later elected Governor of Liverpool Workhouse. Shipp served for more than 30 years, the Army was the core of his being, and as he said the thought of leaving it "bowed him to the earth."[8]

This was the situation right up to the Cardwell Reforms. Although the Royal Military Academy (for technical officers) had been established as far back as 1741 and the Royal Military College (for the cavalry and infantry) in 1802, the majority of officers still purchased their commissions. Between 1860 and 1867 3,167 commissions were obtained through purchase and just 836 through the free entry arrangements offered by the Academy and the College.[9]

The abolition of purchase and the substitution of a competitive examination for all aspiring officers hardly led to the results which the reformers expected in the years up to the First World War. With the exception of the Indian Army, it was still almost impossible for an officer to live on his pay and Regiments carefully vetted their applicants accordingly. Despite the necessary cramming needed for entry and the greater competition experienced at the training establishments, the old, unreformed way of life was preserved to a remarkable degree and the percentage of officers from the lower-middle class remained very small, while those from the working class were minimal. Most of these officers had no difficulty in returning to civilian society, indeed the prestige of having held their commissions was often a powerful aid. It was not until the multiplication of the Officer Corps during the First World War and the admittance to it of many more who were promoted from the ranks that it was felt necessary to set up any machinery to help them find employment. Field-Marshal Haig, in a number of addresses to the London Livery Companies in 1920, specifically identified this class of officer as being in particular need of assistance. The officer, therefore, because he experienced relatively few difficulties on retirement, was reckoned to need no special arrangements until the early twentieth century. For the soldier the case was very different.

In contrast to their officers, the rank and file came from the lower orders of society. Once they had joined, and not infrequently they were inveigled into joining by persuasive recruiting sergeants armed with plentiful quantities of strong liquor, they were given up by their relatives for lost. To have gone for a soldier was a disgrace for most working-class families. While a proportion joined for the adventure, more entered because they were starving. The men of the old Army, certainly until the advent of the Crimean War, were consistently held in low regard by the population at large.

That keen observer of military life, Robert Jackson, who as a doctor examined successive waves of recruits and who later became Inspector-General of Army Hospitals, wrote in 1803 that "Military service does not bring distinction in England as it does in many parts of Europe . . . The better class of peasantry do not leave the plough and shuttle for the sword; consequently the recruits of infantry regiments are not on a level with the mass of the nation. They are often drawn from the refuse of manufacturing towns; for instance from destitute workmen who enrol themselves in the Army through necessity or want of bread, not a love of arms . . . . The military character of the British nation is not therefore fairly judged as estimated by the qualities of recruits who may be drawn from the refuse of its population."[10]

In the previous century Edmund Burke had coined the description of soldiers as "brutal and licentious" and Wellington, speaking of the same men as those observed by Robert Jackson, was hardly less damning in the early nineteenth century. He said his "Army was composed of the scum of the earth . . . a band of men who terrified their leader if not the enemy." His remarks were hardly without foundation. With the storming of Badajoz, admittedly after a long and costly siege, his Army gave themselves up to an orgy of rape, drunkenness and pillage. They sacked every house and fired upon officers who tried to restrain them, even firing a drunken *feu de joie* about Wellington himself.[11]

One can well understand such men experiencing difficulties when attempting to rejoin civilian life, although, in fairness, at the time of Badajoz the Army was so desperate for men that many serving were not 'typical' soldiers. They had been forcibly swept into it from the ne'er-do-wells who thronged the fairgrounds or even from men awaiting prison sentences. Even if one dismisses Edmund Burke's description as an orator's flourish, it is more difficult to dismiss the evidence of the Duke of Wellington and Robert Jackson, admittedly both referring to a desperate time of recruitment, and not to conclude that the average soldier before 1870 was not well equipped for civilian life. Spending most of his time abroad, he became a stranger to his own country, and when at home the all-embracing bonds of military life effectively kept most from normal social intercourse with ordinary civilians.

Whether drink had, or had not, been used as a persuasive agent in their recruitment, most serving soldiers drank hard even by the standards of their day. They were also inveterate gamblers. To subdue them a wide range of draconian punishments, particularly the widespread use of the lash, were used. Not until 1836 was the number of lashes awarded by a General Court Martial limited to 200 and after 1856 to 50. Even from then onwards the Judge Advocates' Records show that the humiliating and excruciatingly painful sentence of 50 lashes continued to be awarded for quite minor offences, including insubordinate language. Floggings were always administered publicly before one's own assembled colleagues and a proportion usually fainted at the spectacle. The Duke of Wellington and others giving evidence before the 1836 Commission on Military Punishments maintained energetically that discipline could not be maintained without flogging. Twenty years earlier he had signed the order for a soldier who had passed a counterfeit two-franc piece at Versailles to be given 999 lashes. Significantly in the French and Prussian Armies of the day there was no equivalent to the cat o' nine tails, no corporal punishment at all in the French Army and such punishment was only for the incorrigibles of the Prussian Army.

One has to admit that, whatever the cost, and many men were never the same after such punishment – some even died as a result – it worked in retaining the cohesion of an Army whose prevailing vice was drunkenness. It helped to cow men even when their officers were absent. It kept an Army under control when there were very few diversions and when, until just before the Cardwell Reforms, living conditions were bad by any standard.

During its investigations the 1857 Royal Commission on Army Health found that soldiers' living conditions were bad, even by contemporary standards: barracks were generally overcrowded, ventilation was almost non-existent and sanitation primitive. Fuel for fireplaces was usually in short supply and, to retain the heat, soldiers invariably closed up all the ventilators and windows. Wooden urine tubs were left in the rooms all night and in the morning merely rinsed out. By then, as one soldier recalled, the smell was nearly overpowering. In some cases soldiers washed in the tubs or they were used to carry in the day's rations. Food consisted of a never-ending routine of one pound of bread and three-quarters of a pound of meat per day; anything extra had to come from their meagre pay. For the married soldier conditions in barracks were, if possible, worse still. Separate married quarters were virtually non-existent; instead wives were given a bed in the corner of the room shielded only by a blanket hung from a cord. Of the Army's 251 stations at this time only twenty provided separate quarters.[12]

In the late eighteenth and early nineteenth centuries rates of desertion and sickness were ruinously high. Sickness levels were higher than those for the population as a whole, despite the initial weeding-out of unfit men on enlistment. *The Times* of 6 February, 1858, wrote, "There can be little doubt that the chief cause of the evil [prevalent sickness] is deficient accommodation and the consequent overcrowding of barracks . . . the closeness, the dirt, the indecency spoken of remind one of a slave ship more than a place for English soldiers to inhabit."

Punch observed wryly, "Those who survive [life in Army barracks] are the bravest of the brave and we may add too the toughest of the tough."

In full knowledge of public sentiment towards the soldier, William Thackeray, as Michael Angelo Titmarsh, pilloried the military profession in *Punch*: "It is not like other professions which require intelligence. As to the men they get the word of command to advance or fall back, and they do it; they are told to strip and be flogged, and they do it; to murder or be murdered, and they do it; for their food and clothing and twopence a day for their tobacco."[13]

When the Army was not engaged in a major war, and particularly during the long years of peace after Waterloo, many civilians, like Thackeray, were not slow in viewing it at home as an irrelevance. Others were antipathetic because, prior to the establishment of Police Forces from 1829 onwards, it was used on a number of occasions to support the civil authorities.

Unlike their officers, soldiers had every reason to experience

28

difficulties when returning to civilian life. Within this context one can better consider how different arrangements came to be made when one realizes that there were three different groups: the long-term regulars, men recruited for the duration of wars only and those whose health had broken down either through wounds or disease. For all three classes of old soldier one common yardstick applied, namely that economic considerations would be paramount where arrangements for them were concerned.

CHAPTER THREE

Men from the Unreformed Army

"Hack'd, hewn with constant service,
thrown aside,
To rust in peace, or rot in hospitals."

Thomas Southerne
1660–1746

On the formation of his standing Army in 1661, small though it might be, Charles II took on full responsibility for its career soldiers, the main category considered for resettlement in civilian life. Having already served in the Parliamentary forces, many of the men he inherited were reaching the veteran stage. They had shared the brotherhood of arms through many famous battles and there had been a strong tendency to retain them for as long as they remained effective. It was hardly surprising that, given the prevailing antipathy to ex-soldiers, they should, in the autumn of their lives, experience severe difficulties when re-entering civilian life. Their problems were soon brought home to the King by the many letters and petitions sent him on their behalf. Like Elizabeth before him, Charles II found himself hounded by such appeals. One letter, received from a lady on 30 June, 1666, put the situation very clearly:

"There is now I perceve severall commissions to raise men, but if Your Majesty did but heare the slite and scopes that is mad; for, saie the people, be a soulder, now, we have presedents daily in the streets, we will fight no more, for when the wars is over we are slited like dogs."[1]

By any standard such old soldiers were poor examples for the would-be recruits he so urgently needed.

However much the King might sympathize with his old warriors and whether or not, as legend would have it, he was influenced by Nell Gwynne on their behalf, any plans he might have had to assist them were hampered by a chronic shortage of funds which dogged him throughout his reign. After unsuccessful attempts to re-saddle Parishes and Counties with the relief of veterans, his thoughts turned towards a National Hospital for old soldiers. This was in line with current thinking, for in 1670 Louis XIV had founded the Hotel Royale des Invalides in Paris designed to house all 5000 ineffectives of the French Army. Apparently, like Charles's Nell Gwynne, his current mistress, Madame de Maintenon, had been a strong influence on this project. It seems as if mistresses felt a natural affinity with old soldiers, perhaps because their own profession involved constant, if different, sorts of risk, although the rewards were usually higher. They too attracted the antipathy and scorn of normal citizens and were particularly vulnerable when age dulled their powers. In Ireland the Marshal General of the Army, the Earl of Granard, had decided to build a hospital at Kilmainham in the Curragh Park at Dublin. This was to house "ancient, maimed and infirm officers and soldiers of the Army of Ireland who were rendering the Irish Army inefficient." The problems which faced the old soldiers of the day were well summed up in the charter of this institution: "The Army living without action produced in about 20 years old soldiers, who having honestly served the King from the time of their youth and being arrived to old age which rendered them incapable of further service therein, having neglected all other ways of procuring a livelihood of Arts or Trades, must of necessity starve if dismist."[2]

In July, 1679, Charles II approved the erection of Kilmainham Hospital. It was named after him but the necessary funds came not from Royal sources but through a deduction of 6d in the pound from the pay of all soldiers serving on the Irish establishment. From this time compulsory deductions from serving soldiers became the accepted price for their old comrades' security.

A combination of financial difficulties, coupled with Parliament's residual hostility to military forces, delayed the establishment of a National Hospital in London. In 1681, though, the King acted, instructing the first Paymaster to the Forces, Sir Stephen Fox, to find a site and attend to its building. It was to be a Hospital "for the relief of such land soldiers as are, or shall be, old, lame or infirm in ye service of the crown."[3]

Despite the shortage of funds, Sir Christopher Wren drew up a grandiose design for the hospital. (He had earlier designed Kilmainham.) Once more, like Kilmainham, the main source of funding came from serving soldiers, although it was their Paymaster who made the actual sacrifice by surrendering his 'commission'. Two-thirds of the poundage fund was thus allocated. (A Paymaster was eligible for poundage at the rate of 1/- in the pound from all soldiers as a recompense for paying them weekly and on time.)

Eleven years were to elapse before Chelsea was ready for occupation and during the interim the problems caused by the numbers of old soldiers grew. In recognition of this the King instituted a temporary pension scheme, chiefly relating to soldiers, but including the widows and orphans of men killed when fighting. The widows received 11 months' pay and soldiers' orphans a third of this. Under the scheme, daily subsistence payments were made to soldiers awaiting admission. Wren's plans for Chelsea were based on the requirement for a Hospital housing 422 men or 5% of the remarkably small Army of the time. Due to subsequent increases in the military establishment, the original specifications for Chelsea (and Kilmainham) were inadequate for all the deserving men.* The numbers of outpensioners continued to increase at such a rate that any thoughts about expanding the hospitals to accommodate them were dismissed on both practical and financial grounds. Initially the outpensions could be paid from Chelsea Hospital's own resources, notably from the contributions of serving soldiers, but after 1692 the increased numbers rendered this no longer possible and henceforth they were paid from central funds.

* Kilmainham housed less than 300 pensioners.

National policy towards its land Army at this time was taking on a pattern familiar to later generations of soldiers. On the one hand there was growing military involvement both on the continent of Europe and in the increasing British dependencies overseas. This compelled increases in the establishment which were given most grudgingly by Parliament. Yet, when military activity lessened, the maximum economies were imposed in double quick time.

As for the commitments to those who had left the ranks, their pension levels were always kept as low as possible. In 1713 they were actually reduced to 5d a day and remained at that level for almost a century, till 1806. During the years 1832–59 they were still only 1/4d a day, well under half that earned by the average semi-skilled civilian at the time.[4] Under this system, which operated until 1870, except for men released in the rapid reductions following wars, it was never expected that regular soldiers would re-enter civilian life in the normal way. Despite their unquestioned sacrifices they were not welcomed back by civilians, who must have viewed them in the same way as some twentieth century shopkeepers react to marauding soccer supporters. Only in the last two decades before 1870 were some able to find worthwhile employment because by this time public opinion had shifted somewhat in their favour.

During the eighteenth century, after men had spent their best years in the Army, they were generally happy to extend for as long as possible. In the main deserters, and there were many of them, came from the young soldiers who were unable to reconcile themselves with the hardships and iron routine of military life. The chilling prospects awaiting middle-aged men in civilian life were just too much. This suited the military establishment because throughout the period the losses due to both desertion and disease were ruinously high.

Even in the final years of the old system, when wastage rates had much improved, the discharge documents of a single regiment demonstrate the hard physical demands on infantry soldiers and the inevitable results these had on their future job prospects after release. In the fifteen years 1855–70, 707 men left the Royal West Surrey Regiment. Of these over two-thirds were discharged on medical grounds. The average age of the medical discharges was 27 years, compared with 40, or over, for those who had completed their full engagements. But of these men in their twenties, 22% suffered from heart disease or tuberculosis, 18% from insanity, chronic rheumatism or blindness, while a further 8% suffered from a number of diseases simultaneously. On enlistment 53% had been classed as labourers but they were hardly in any condition to resume such activities. In any case, as the Regiment had been out of the country for a large proportion of the fifteen-year period, its members would have lost touch with normal society in Britain.[5]

It is true that old soldiers had a measure of security when they left the unreformed Army. A small proportion could enter the sheltering walls of Chelsea Hospital, while the majority received their small pensions, large enough to avoid actual destitution and its terrible humiliations, but not sufficient for even a modestly comfortable existence. In fact, imbued as they were with military lore, relatively few chose to try their luck with the community at large. Needing some means of topping up their pensions, a good proportion turned to the haven they knew, with those who understood them. They took up instructional and other more humble jobs with militia units. Because they were in receipt of pensions, the rates paid by the military authorities for such duties were normally set at suitably low levels.

Broadly similar arrangements were made for naval veterans. James II had started preliminary enquiries about a home for old sailors but it was Queen Mary who selected the site of the old Royal Palace at Greenwich and set in motion plans for the building of a great institution there, far larger than the Hospital at Chelsea catering for the larger Army establishment. The building of Greenwich Hospital, like Chelsea, featured grandiose building plans on the one hand and financial restrictions on the other.[6] Like Kilmainham and Chelsea, it was designed by the same remarkable architect, Christopher Wren, although in its final stages it was 'adorned' by Sir John Vanbrugh. Under Queen Anne (and Vanbrugh) the building itself became pre-eminent, assuming a magnificence beyond Wren's original concept and quite beyond the needs of the pensioners who were to be housed there. For instance its old inmates never used the Painted Hall as a dining room (its original purpose) as it was too draughty and overpowering.

By 1705 just eighty-one men had been admitted and no less than fifty-four years were to elapse before it was finished. By then Greenwich had cost over £400,000 and had taken four reigns to complete. The hospital was not filled to capacity until the great exodus from the Navy after the Napoleonic Wars, but from 1814 to 1850 its complement stood at 2700 men.

The necessary funding came from a number of sources, but central were the deductions of 6d a month from all seamen and the prize monies which men had forfeited. Due partly to Greenwich's greater size and the Navy's smaller complement, its Governors were always heavily against granting outpensions in lieu of residence. Until 1798, when the Treasury assumed responsibility for payment, Naval outpensioners were paid a miserable £7 a year, compared with the Army's £13, which itself was little enough.

During the long period of peace after the Napoleonic Wars the Hospital languished. With the increase in merchant shipping, men who had completed their naval service could still get sea-going posts. Others, with that hardiness characteristic of sailors, found civilian employment long before many Army veterans did. There developed a marked reluctance to enter Greenwich and, although the standards of admittance were steadily lowered, it finally closed in 1869.

While ex-sailors generally found employment more easily than old soldiers, in the years prior to 1870 both services had adopted the policy of institutionalizing their veterans (admittedly many of the old salts in Greenwich Hospital carried serious wounds) or, as an alternative, granted them small pensions on the understanding that they, too, would not re-enter civilian life in the full sense.

In the Army's case the chances of an old soldier obtaining worthwhile civilian employment were very low, not just because he might be out of touch and have anti-civilian values but because of the military's assumption that pensioners were still a legitimate part of the military establishment. This was demonstrated by their re-embodying such old men at times of need. By any standard one would have thought they had already made their full contribution to the state.

The first embodiment occurred in the late seventeenth century, during the relatively early days of Chelsea. It was instigated by the rapacious Treasurer of the Hospital, the Earl of Ranelagh. His principal motive was to reduce the cost of outpensioners. Yet the rates of pay for the so-called Invalids' Companies at this time were only equivalent to those received by outpensioners. Few considerations were made for their age and frequent breakdowns in health occurred, some of which led to deaths.

After this precedent, instances of re-embodiment continued. In the early eighteenth century Invalid Companies were used to guard marshes on the Medway where the old men had to stand in water up to their knees, unprotected from the wind, at posts up to three miles from the nearest shelter. By 1718 there were no less than 28 companies of Invalids but the gravest doubts must have been raised concerning the effectiveness of such men. Forty years later the position had hardly improved. An inspection in 1767 required a regimental return, which showed a Major Edward Grode aged 82, Lieutenant Lawson 80 and Ensign Chase 71. Both subalterns were stone blind and a further ensign called Stopworth was 79 years of age. In 1779 an order gave permission for Invalids to ride on horseback or to be placed in carts if they were unable to march. After the Treaty of Amiens in 1802 100 companies of Invalids were disbanded but quickly reformed into the less ardous Royal Garrison Battalions which remained in existence until the end of the Napoleonic Wars.

With the threat of civilian disorders following the end of the Napoleonic Wars all Pensioners were required to present themselves for medical examination and, if considered fit, for re-incorporation into veterans' battalions. 15,026 outpensioners reported, of whom 8,957 were proclaimed fit and a proportion were quickly sent for service in Ireland. In Britain they were used to counter civil unrest during 1830, were active against the Plug Plot disturbances of 1842 and especially when the Chartist troubles arose in 1843–4 and 1848.[7] There were still 14,000 men enrolled eight years before the Cardwell Reforms abolished the practice.

The successive re-embodiments of old men who had already given long and valuable service to the Crown was a ruthless and ignominious page in Britain's military history. That it happened was to some extent an illustration of the military authorities' desperate shortage of men but also a clear indication of the low priority in which the old soldier was held by them. In 1819, for instance, the Commandant of Hospitals, Colonel Christie, spoke most unflatteringly about the veterans. The system at the time, no doubt for reasons of economy, was to pay pensions quarterly, in advance, from a limited number of appointed agents. To collect them pensioners had to travel some distance from their homes and with three months' pay in their pockets the temptations were obvious. According to Colonel Christie, "With what they squander with their old companions and the necessary expense of their journey [they] frequently return without a shilling and, with their families, become a burden on the parish. They are habitually idle, and from want of practice must now be generally bad workmen . . . and thousands of them are at this moment mingled in the mobs in the manufacturing districts."[8] Whatever their predilections, with the possibility of re-embodiment always in their minds, they were tempted to be feckless and there was virtually no incentive to settle into a fixed occupation. The military authorities of the time would have had distinctly mixed feelings if their veterans had landed good jobs. Such successes might have persuaded others to buy themselves out or decide not to extend. Ambivalence towards the successful resettlement of returning soldiers is inevitable when an Army like the British one relies on long-term voluntary recruitment. At the least it brings about a marked reluctance to devote central funds towards such a marginal purpose. Sometimes it goes further; when recruiting is difficult there is a tendency to softpedal any arrangements which would help men to succeed after their retirement. The cost of maintaining British security both in the face of external threats and internal disturbances fell particularly heavily upon its long-term veterans in the period up to 1870.

An essential part of the British military tradition after the Restoration was to keep military establishments as low as possible and, in the light of this, forces raised for war purposes were rapidly disbanded when peace was restored. This occurred after the early eighteenth century wars with Spain, the Seven Years War, the American and French Revolutionary Wars and after the Crimean War of the mid-nineteenth century. The return of large numbers inevitably brought special problems regarding their re-integration. In the eighteenth and nineteenth centuries they could not be treated with the callousness practised by the Elizabethans but before the founding of Police Forces they would rightly be seen as a potential menace to public order if they were not quickly settled and, like Colonel Christie's pensioners, were to mingle with those who were already unemployed. Special arrangements, quite apart from those made for the regular retirements, were called for.

One notable initiative was to grant land to the men of the great disbandments far from their home country. This owed much to the exemplars of Greece and Rome. It was also in tune with one of the sociological tenets of late Georgian and early Victorian Britain that, within the population, was a 'criminal class' and the best solution to restore the health of the body politic was to extract this class and transport it to Australia. Jeremy Bentham was an arch-critic of the theory whereby men with criminal dispositions were considered to be "a set of *animae vires*, a sort of excrementitious mass that could be projected, and accordingly was projected – projected, and as it should seem purposely – as far out of sight as possible."[9]

After major wars the unemployed, feckless ex-soldiers, that excrementitious mass from the Army, were ripe candidates to join the criminal class. Some came from it in the first place. If they could be sent to the colonies, or better still persuaded to stay in those countries away from the homeland, they might achieve a fresh start impossible in Britain, help provide the colonies with a trained reserve in times of threat and, above all, save the military authorities a great deal of money.

Following the 1745 Peace of Aix-La-Chapelle, in 1749, 4,000 men and their families were settled in Nova Scotia. Fortescue was in no doubt why this scheme was instituted; "The number of men disbanded from fleet and Army was so large that it was deemed prudent to make some provision for them."[10]

In 1763, at the end of the Seven Years War, a further settlement programme concerned lands in Quebec, East Florida, West Florida and Grenada. The *London Gazette* of the time explained that the measure "served to prevent many officers and soldiers from unemployment and it gave new immigrants to the newly ceded territories in America."[11] The markedly different treatment of officers and men was illustrated by the respective areas of land allotted them: a field officer (major) qualified for 5,000 acres, a private soldier for 50.

The largest settlement in the eighteenth century was for those loyal Americans, many who had served in the militia, who during the War of Independence remained faithful to the mother country. 40,000 men, women and children were assisted in emigrating to Nova Scotia and the detailed plans here formed a framework for later military schemes.

Unfortunately, three important factors clouded the success of these schemes, particularly in the eighteenth century: the rushed and incomplete nature of the arrangements (symptomatic of the relatively low priorities given them), the parsimonious attitude of the authorities and the inability of many soldiers to meet the massive challenges they presented.

In the succeeding century guidelines were much more carefully formulated, but the parsimony continued. In 1829 a War Office scheme of emigration for pensioners, most of whom were bound for Canada, required them to commute their pensions and even showed the greatest reluctance over granting an initial free passage.

"The question of free passage is the most doubtful part of this proposition . . . . I do not apprehend [the Treasury] will agree to it as, though the object is important to remove the pensioners at once from the country and the pension list, I do not see how the public can be expected to promote it further."[12]

The parsimony rebounded. Although by 1830 the scheme was taken up by 3,944 men, in a large number of cases the results were most disappointing. This was partly due to administrative blunders which caused great hardships. Many men were allowed to emigrate before they had been given their balance of pay, which resulted in them congregating at the port of disembarkation waiting for the balances to come through and in the meantime getting into debt and starving for want of money which was rightfully theirs.[13] Many of the emigrants should not have been sent in the first place; the climate was undoubtedly harsh and many were not up to the punishing labour needed to develop virgin land. Some were just too old. Sixteen of the men had served for over 30 years and one had completed 39 years 270 days. Others had acquired debauched habits during their service, particularly hard drinking.

At the request of the Canadian authorities the system of commutation was suspended three times, yet the War Office was most reluctant to end it because of the economies it offered. In the end, while pensions were not restored, limited and grudging relief was given. Because of the continuing hardship, this had reached the very considerable sum of £14,098.15.8½ in the two years to March, 1843.[14] The War Office's false economy had blown up in its face.

An emigration scheme to Australia which operated during 1832–3 brought few serious complaints from pensioners who were required to commute but they felt bitter resentment at having to pay their own fares out.

After the Crimean War new, carefully formulated schemes were devised. The model ones related to the Foreign Legions which had aided the British cause. The German Legion was settled in Cape Colony, while the Swiss and Italian ones were given generous terms and placed outside the Empire in the territories of the Argentine Confederation. The Argentine Government offered to pay each man of the Swiss and Italian Legions for three years and allocated them both agricultural implements and building materials. It was a far cry from the Canadian experience.

On the whole, settlement never lived up to the expectations of the authorities nor of the participants looking for a new life. During the eighteenth century schemes were usually ill-conceived, the Canadian venture being undoubtedly the most costly in both financial and human terms. Far from reducing the cost of pensions, it involved the War Office in widespread subsidies for indigent men, men who had already received capital sums from the commutation of their pensions and it helped to debase the reputation of old soldiers among colonists. In human terms, after years of unquestioning obedience, the average soldier lacked the knowledge, capital or initiative to develop the land allocated, itself often of indifferent quality.

Edward Costello, a veteran of the Napoleonic Wars, gives a chilling account of his friend Tom Plunkett, an ex-corporal, who returned to England within a year of settling in Canada. "By way of apology to his friends [he] stated his grant of land was so wild and swampy that it made him so melancholy . . . looking at it in the morning out of the chinks of a wretched log hut he had managed to erect upon his estate."[15] The last time Costello saw Plunkett he was in rags selling matches.

Although later in the nineteenth century schemes were generally more carefully drafted, circumstances still weighed against their success. Some men were often exploited by the colonial authorities and many just did not have the qualities needed for such pioneering work. In 1855 the War Office bemoaned vigorously the fact that British pensioners set down in the Cape of Good Hope, close to the border, had almost all got themselves killed at great cost to the authorities. "Not less than £200,000 [was] required to settle a body of 100 pensioners at the Cape."[16]

With the exception of those organized for the Foreign Legions, the settlement schemes which did succeed were offered in the last quarter of the nineteenth century. These were for soldiers and citizens alike and offered at regular intervals, not just at the end of wars. The War Office did no more than publicize them through official channels. Most soldiers likely to take them up were now short-service men not in receipt of pensions whose settlement in the colonies would therefore not reduce the War Office's annual pension lists. Ironically, being younger and not so imbued with military customs, their chances of success were considerably greater.

At home a proportion of the large numbers of men discharged with the greatest swiftness at the end of wars succeeded in finding worthwhile civilian jobs long before the regular time-expired men. They usually possessed the rare advantage of being younger. Some, while still genuine job-seekers, were lucky enough to qualify for pensions after just twelve years due to a temporary relaxation of enlistment regulations when wartime recruiting was desperate. In any case, from the 1830s onwards new opportunities were beginning to appear within the developing public services, the Police Forces, the Post Office and particularly, after the late 1840s, with the Railways. In a few instances even the long-term regulars were to find such positions.

The numbers taken on at this time were never high, however. The Police were choosy and, while favouring ex-soldiers in the initial stages, the physical standards they set often debarred them. Some 440 ex-soldiers were recruited for the new Metropolitan Force, but in the early years a very large turnover of personnel occurred, with many ex-soldiers being dismissed for drunkenness, their prevalent failing. The same picture was repeated in the new County Forces, drunkenness being the main cause of military expulsions. Yet by 1866 there were 640 soldiers in the Metropolitan, one twelfth its total strength.[17] The Post Office recruited just 2% of its employees from ex-soldiers or sailors in the years 1857–61 following the Crimean War; it was to become a larger employer towards the end of the century.[18] The main problem for ex-servicemen here was the age limit of 26 years, too young for pensioners or many shorter-term men and too strenuous an occupation for soldiers who had been medically discharged.

The Railways were developing at a very fast rate during the 1840s but they did not become large employers of ex-servicemen until twenty years later, just prior to the Cardwell Reforms. By then they were the major employer from public utilities. Henry Pringle Bruyeres, Superintendent of the London and North-West Railway Company, giving evidence before the 1866 Dalhousie Commission on Military Recruiting, said that a fifth of his employees from the south division were ex-soldiers. They had limitations, though. He preferred to use them as pointsmen or signalmen, not sorters, because he considered "they were not fond of work but intelligent men who were obedient to orders". As soon as they were no longer capable of carrying out such duties they were discharged.

Generally speaking, throughout the period few special arrangements were made for a third category of returning soldier, those who had broken down on account of wounds or disease. If not too incapacitated, they could be accepted by Chelsea or Greenwich or given modest pensions often of a temporary nature, but foremost, despite their serious additional handicaps, they had to find some occupation within their home communities, however humble or ill-paid it might be.

During the long period of peace after the end of the Napoleonic Wars and before the Crimean War, things continued much in the pattern of the previous century and a half. A change in the public attitudes came as a result of a war which was still fought by the old Army but which revealed the need for a new force in which men would complete far shorter regular engagements, followed by reserve liability. During the Crimean War there developed a new intimacy between the nation as a whole and its Army. The great *Times* war correspondent W.H. Russell described the campaign in graphic terms and his despatches were transmitted through the influential pages of that newspaper with a new immediacy made possible by the invention of the electric telegraph. A Select Committee reporting on the Army before Sebastopol wrote in uncompromising terms: "The patience and fortitude of the Army demanded the admiration and gratitude of the nation on whose behalf they have fought, bled and died. Their heroic patience under suffering and privations have given them claims upon their country which will long be remembered."[19]

Florence Nightingale, who became a strong influence on senior politicians of the day like Lord Panmure and Sidney Herbert, wrote after the war, not about brutal and licentious men, but about "the innate dignity, gentleness and chivalry of men . . . amidst scenes of loathsome disease and death".[20] Before their deeds could be forgotten the Indian Mutiny occurred and the swift and successful actions of British soldiers under General Havelock were again material for W.H. Russell to report for *The Times*.

The Crimean War helped to persuade people that soldiers were worthy subjects for civilian assistance, indeed a forgotten and fruitful area for Victorian charitable work. Led by the Queen's example, every parish in England sent free gifts to the troops in the Crimea and the attitude of the religious public changed dramatically towards the Army. The evangelical *Memorials of Captain Hedley Vicars*, published in December, 1855, sold 70,000 copies in its first year. It demonstrated that a professional soldier could also be an ardent Christian, and that stern, indeed eccentric, Baptist, General Henry Havelock, who died in India while conducting the relief of Lucknow, was made a national hero on his death.

From the late '50s onwards the Army was to become a productive area for missionary work and Soldiers' Institutes, Reading Rooms and Temperance Societies were set up in garrison towns. In 1862 an Army Officer's widow, Mrs Louisa Daniell, established a mission hall in the great new camp at Aldershot and opened further Soldiers' Homes and Institutes at Weedon, Colchester, Manchester, Plymouth and Chatham.[21] Some soldiers were even to become known for their Christian voluntary work. The term Christian soldier was adopted and the contrast with the hard-swearing pagan soldier of Napoleonic times became marked. Chaplains were made members of the Officer Corps and, in the specifications for new barracks, chapels were provided in the same way as gymnasia and schools. Religion was now to play a part in the Army unknown since the Commonwealth period, partly through an evangelical revival that was taking place in civilian life reminiscent of Cromwellian times. Given the Victorians' passion for respectability, a practising, or even a nominal, Christian would be more welcome in the Victorian workplace than one who was not.

It was during the Crimean War that the third category of returning men, the sick and wounded, began to attract new consideration from a public whose compassion had been awakened to their cause. When rapid communications were able to reveal not just the glory but the horrifying costs of war to the ordinary soldiers who took part this was inevitable. The next great battles of the late 1850s on the European mainland at Magenta and Solferino led to the foundation of the International Red Cross movement which in turn led to better provisions for the sick and wounded and improved treatment for prisoners of war. Even a Bonaparte, Napoleon III, writing to the Emperor of Austria after Magenta, revealed how he was sickened by the battlefield spectacle, saying,

"It is on the battlefield, amid the sufferings of vast numbers of wounded men, surrounded by 15,000 dead bodies, that I adjure Your Majesty to listen to the voice of humanity."[22] All was working towards a greater consideration for the ordinary combatant, the man who exposed his blood and sinews to the withering fire of increasingly hostile battlefields and was cut down in increasing numbers. From the Crimean War onwards, after Roger Fenton had carried out his pioneering work there, photographs portraying the horrors and savagery of warfare also became available.

In Britain since the Restoration this third category had received scant regard. Shortly after 1660 Charles II had the Savoy Hospital of Parliamentary times re-opened to treat them but, once they had partially recovered, their subsequent treatment was hardly bountiful. Florence Nightingale highlighted as never before the primitive conditions at Scutari Hospital, little better than those in the old Savoy almost 200 years before. Her missionary zeal and the particular eloquence of W.H. Russell were lent power and persuasion through the new communication media; together they captured the public's imagination by detailing the sufferings, while at the same time stressing the courtesy, patience and indeed the nobility of ordinary soldiers. Were these men, it might be asked, the same drunken animals who previously had to be cowed by the lash and were incapable of rejoining normal life, itself rent by all the inconsistencies and hypocrisy of Victorian society? In point of fact, floggings were still an almost daily occurrence at Balaclava and the lash was not abolished from home service until 1868.

Even before public sympathy had been aroused, practical help for the streams of men already returning to Britain, either wounded or with their health broken down by the rigours of the campaign, was being organized. The main impetus came from retired officers and Lieutenant Loyd-Lindsay, the future Lord Wantage, who had been awarded a VC in the Crimea, became a key figure in the establishment of the British Red Cross Organization. Machinery was even being set up to help them find subsequent employment.

Such arrangements benefited the healthy ex-servicemen as well. For most of these some form of civilian work was essential. In past times many officers had been accustomed to employ one or more of their old soldier comrades on their estates or to recommend them to their friends. Generally they did not display the immense generosity of that dashing cavalryman, the Marquess of Granby, who, at the end of the Seven Years War, dispensed so many purses to help his men in after life that he beggared himself. His monument, though, remains in the number of pubs which were named after him. But other good officers were not uncaring.

With the increasing job market of the 1850s something more than alerting one's immediate friends was possible. A group of ex-senior officers and 'other men of substance' met on 18 July, 1855, with the purpose of establishing an employment society for all men of good character from the Army and Navy who had qualified for a pension, with particular emphasis on those who had been wounded. On the one hand the new organization collected together all offers of employment for ex-servicemen, and appealed for more, while on the other it sent the ex-soldiers and sailors who had registered with it details of those posts which appeared to suit their qualifications. This matching process marked the creation of the first Employment Agency in Britain, fully half a century before Lloyd George's National Employment Exchanges. (While some Civilian Exchanges appeared in the 1880s, they were regarded with marked suspicion by the trade unions; doubtless this suspicion would have been far greater for the military-inspired bodies created fully 25 years earlier.)

Life membership of the organization (and the privilege of recommending men for situations) cost five guineas, annual membership one guinea. All regiments or ships who wanted the opportunity to recommend their men were required to pay £2 annually. Support was quickly given by Her Majesty the Queen, who pledged an annual subscription of £50, as did the Prince Consort. Support for the society also came from the Royal Commander-in-Chief, the Duke of Cambridge, and from many other influential people. It marked the commencement of another tradition, the enthusiastic support by the Royal Family for voluntary bodies designed to assist the returning soldier or sailor, sick or healthy, in the absence of official arrangements on his behalf. It marked an acknowledgement that the bulk of soldiers returning from a mid-nineteeth century war needed subsequent employment in Britain and could no longer be shunted off to the colonies on emigration schemes.

Formed in the heat and fervour of war, it was hardly surprising that enthusiasm for the organization should cool once the war was over. In any case, the intractable problem of finding suitable jobs for ex-servicemen against the long-held prejudice of the public could not be ended by a body established for the short term. This did not prevent larger numbers of men approaching it for employment than the founders had ever expected. Some of these were thrown up by a second rapid augmentation and subsequent rundown brought about through the Indian Mutiny. Although support dwindled, men continued to come for help and the organizers who struggled on in adverse circumstances found, by 1859, that the society had fallen into considerable debt.

It was bailed out by a man who, among those who had come together in 1855, possessed the most modest military credentials. Edward Walter was a Captain in the Eighth Hussars who retired in the year preceding the Crimean War. More important than his lowly Army seniority, though, was his membership of a family which founded the pre-eminent newspaper of the age, *The Times*, and whose brother, John Walter III, was its outstanding proprietor for 47 years. After his retirement Edward Walter set himself on a personal crusade to compel governments to give worthwhile assistance for old soldiers and sailors and to induce such men to become a valued and reliable commodity for the civilian job market. It was a crusade which was to last almost 50 years until his death in 1904.

Although laudable, the achievements of the society during the first four years of its life were quite limited. The great majority of the employers who used it wanted servants and many of the situations offered were temporary ones which paid inadequately. Equally disappointing, the donations from ships, regiments and battalions remained at a low level.

While Edward Walter thought it worth saving – his one stipulation for rescuing it was that its ruling body would henceforth be composed solely of Officers from Her Majesty's Services – it did not go nearly as far as he desired. The revised rules included a strong moral commitment towards the cause of the ex-servicemen, particularly those whose health had been affected. Whether in peace or war, the Society's Charter was to act as a means of raising the men's characters by demonstrating to the soldier or sailor that "in the decadence of his powers, whether from wounds, climate, accident or long service he was still cared for".

Yet, by offering men an inadequate number of poorly paid and humble jobs, it was hard to see how they would either be overjoyed or even regain their self-respect. Most importantly, such an agency, through its own efforts, could never break down the deep-seated civilian prejudice against the old soldier.

Walter therefore set up a body to effect the changes which he considered necessary. France not only offered the example of reserving Government posts for ex-servicemen, it gave him the idea and title for his organization. Attached to every French hotel were *valets de place* and *commissionnaires*. The former conducted a traveller to all places of interest in a neighbourhood, while the latter got baggage safely through the customs, carried letters and ran errands. He called his new society The Corps of Commissionaires, anglicizing the word *commissionnaire* by taking out the second n. The Corps of Commissionaires was the result of Edward Walter's analysis of the assets possessed by ex-soldiers in civilian terms and how best these could be exploited. Ex-soldiers of good character had the military bearing, integrity and trust-worthiness to carry out commissions. Such men could guard a bank or office block "using no weapons save the authority of a suitable uniform and their own purposefulness and courtesy".[23] In their role of guarding and message-carrying ordinary unqualified soldiers and sailors could well serve London or any other great city and, by doing so, transform the low opinion held by the public about ex-soldiers in general. On the platform of a successful Corps and aided by *The Times*, Edward Walter could persuade the authorities to grant reserved posts for ex-servicemen in such establishments as the Customs or the Post Office, in the same way as France or Prussia.

From the outset Walter aimed for a corps d'elite composed of mature, scrupulously honest and sober men, the flag-bearers of all ex-servicemen in his struggle for general civilian acceptance. The first eight recruits were all wounded men. His private army, for it was no less than that, led by himself as Commanding Officer, with an Adjutant and a Sergeant Major, required men of notable self-reliance. They had to pay for their distinguished uniforms, modelled on those of the Rifle Brigade, by weekly stoppages. There were other stoppages too, towards a health fund in the event of sickness, and into the Corps Savings Bank against the time they would be unable to continue working. In addition to these sub-scriptions there was a substantial risk that commissionaires would be fined for misdemeanours (absence from church parade warranted a fine of 1/-).

No wonder, then, that many ex-soldiers were unable to live up to the standards set. The main reason for dismissal was for the soldiers' besetting weakness, that of drunkenness. By 1880 over 4,000 men had joined but only one man in four remained in the Corps for any length of time, although many of those who stayed were to serve happily for a remarkably long period. In the process less emphasis was now paid on recruiting wounded men, since it was found they were not up to the tasks required. Special employment arrangements for them would not be reinstated until the beginning of the twentieth century.

Sadly, by the time of the Cardwell Reforms the revolution which Edward Walter hoped for in the public's reaction towards ex-servicemen had not taken place. The two original societies dedicated to help provide civilian jobs were still in existence but their degree of success was strictly limited. During 1859 and 1873 the Pensioners' Society had found employment, of some sort or another, for 7,573 of the 9,000 eligible pensioners who had regis-tered with it, while by 1873 just over 600 men were on the roll of the Corps of Commissionaires, but his initial stress on finding posts for wounded men was less evident. The limitations of his work can be appreciated when annual outflows from the Army alone during the years 1859–73 averaged around 19,000 men and totalled some 293,000 over the whole period.[24] Despite his energetic campaign for the allocation of minor Government posts to ex-servicemen and the loyal support given him by *The Times*, virtually none were forthcoming. The major instance came about in 1873 when the Post Office offered jobs as rural messengers, but these were quite unsuitable for men of ambition. No less than 103 of the original 220 nominees from the War Office declined the messenger appointments for this reason. Unfortunately this only confirmed some of the public in their belief about the unreliability and poor quality of servicemen for jobs in the public sector.

Just prior to Edward Cardwell's great Army reforms, notwithstanding the slow progress of the job-finding organizations, the situation for ex-servicemen was more favourable than before the Crimean War. The Services themselves were better appreciated. Despite the public's traditional disregard, it now became enthusiastic to know more about its fighting men. After 1855 the newspaper stamp tax was removed and papers who found that their circulations had been stimulated by wartime events responded accordingly. New ones appeared and the Armed Forces gained their share of the increased publicity. They also benefited from the strong patriotism and sentimentality in the Music Halls. During the war their audiences sang with massive enthusiasm such refrains as 'Alma's Heights', 'The Midshipmite' and 'England's Queen to England's Heroes'.

At the same time reforms which resulted from the plethora of Commissions and Committees following the Crimean War were tending to reduce the deadening monotony and absence of personal initiative in military life compared with that of civilian society. Attempts to improve the health of soldiers came after 1858 with a greater variation in their diet and the installation of modern kitchens in army barracks. In the same period the Army Sanitary Commission outlined proposals for improved water supplies, the better ventilation, heating and lighting of barracks and for better hospital accommodation. From 1861 literacy improved when Army Certificates of Education were instigated which were linked directly to promotion and through the increase in the number of Army Libraries.

Such reforms, culminating with the major ones in 1871, were, of course, designed to make the British military machine more efficient. How far they also assisted British soldiers and sailors for their return to civilian life we shall consider in the next chapter.

CHAPTER FOUR

The Short Service Era, 1870–1914

"A man o' four-an-twenty that 'asn't
learned of a trade
Beside "Reserve" agin' him—'e'd better
be never made."

Rudyard Kipling,
1865–1936.

BRITISH military reforms from 1870 onwards aimed to create an adequate reserve in the growing likelihood that Britain would in due course take part in a major continental war. The method adopted, a period of short service with the colours followed by a further commitment to the reserves, necessitated a reintegration with civilian society radically different from any such need of the old Army. The number of men re-entering civilian life each year was now much larger than before and the men were far younger than the soldiers of the pre-Cardwell Army. They had greater needs and often greater expectations of a full civilian career after their military service.

Under the voluntary system, because of the much larger numbers of men required annually, the disincentives to recruiting caused by men suffering employment problems at the end of their regular service could no longer be ignored. This was particularly the case since the reforms assigned Regiments to particular county locations. Not only were men required in larger numbers, but many would have to come from hitherto untapped areas and they would need to be of a higher quality than their predecessors. To accommodate them it seemed that henceforth the Army would have to become a more liberal and popular institution, less divorced from civilian life and with less rigid classifications of rank. Edward Cardwell stressed this fact on the second reading of his bill: "You are invited to give [the recruiting authorities] additional power, and to enable them to attract to the standards a class of men who will not now join . . . . . Everything that tends to make the Army more popular, and to create a good feeling between it and the community at large cannot fail to be beneficial to both."[1]

This was one of the reasons behind his plan to professionalize the officer cadre by abolishing the purchase of commissions and adopting the continental practice of a competitive examination as the normal means of officer entry. By such means it was hoped to diminish the hitherto irremediable division existing between commissioned and non-commissioned ranks, which, it was realized, had in the past discouraged the better class of working men from joining up. Cardwell emphasized that soldiers should be allowed greater personal freedom and the chance to exercise individual initiative.

It seemed reasonable to hope that such changes would reduce civilian prejudice against ex-soldiers as employees. Hopes ran high when, in 1870, a Director General of Recruiting was appointed who, in his first Annual Report, gave successful resettlement a prominent place. He hoped that, after a short period of service, a soldier "could retire with advantage to himself [by which] a great benefit would arise to the state and also to the soldier, who could thus resume his place among the civil classes."[2] Such language was unprecedented. He followed it by looking to the employment of all deserving men on their discharge by "Government, commercial companies and the public generally". The new stress laid on the *right* to civilian employment was fully in accordance with the systems relating to recruitment and the organization of the reserves which operated elsewhere in Europe at the time. Representatives from the War Office discovered that, after twelve years' service, French soldiers were offered employment in the civil departments of the state and their military service was allowed to count towards the number of years necessary to qualify for an occupational pension. In Prussia and Austria after twelve years men had similar claims to jobs in the Police, the Post Office and allied organizations.

The level of interest, however, was not sustained; subsequent Directors General of Recruiting addressed themselves to what, in their opinion, were more direct incentives, notably levels of pay. There were pious hopes for easier re-settlement rather than tangible measures towards its attainment. The only advances occurred in 1884 when two registers were introduced into Regimental Districts, one to record the number of recruits belonging to each parish, the other to hold the names of soldiers in need of civilian employment.

Despite the rhetoric which accompanied Cardwell's great debate on Defence and the appointment of Directors General of Recruiting, virtually nothing practical was done to assist the short-service soldier's return to civilian life. It is true that a Committee on the Employment of Soldiers & Sailors had been convened in 1877 but, in the nature of so many such committees, little came of it. Official disregard of the problem was demonstrated when the War Office authorized recalling the reserve for the Egyptian War of 1884/5, thereby convincing many employers of the foolishness of taking on men with reserve commitments. Some officers were incensed and risked their own careers by openly pointing out the dire effects of re-embodiment. One Commanding Officer wrote to the Duke of Cambridge with remarkable candour: "No employer of labour will submit to their men being taken away from their manufactories because a few naked savages are to be punished. And I am sure if these persons were asked whether they would employ reserve men, they would answer that they would not engage reserve men if they knew them to be as such."[3] It took far more than comments like this to move the old Duke, although re-embodiments for small wars now became rarer.

By the mid-1880s the great majority of ex-soldiers, though younger than those of the old Army, were still experiencing problems in finding permanent civilian employment. After some six years in the Army, for the most part with neither technical accomplishments nor relevant experience, many employers considered them less than attractive material. With the possibility of recall hanging over them, they had to display exceptional qualities to land worthwhile jobs. Even the Duke of Cambridge, in his role as Manager of the Royal Parks, told the Secretary of State for War that he would not employ reservists who might be recalled: "I am compelled to say I cannot take such men [they must be permanently at their posts]."[4]

As a result many reservists were faced with destitution, both for themselves and their families, within a few weeks of their release. In a letter to the Duke of Cambridge Sir Donald Stewart, when Commander-in-Chief, India, cited "the uncertainty of employment entertained by men who have no trade or calling" as a powerful reason for them extending their service.[5] Doubtless the Duke, while concerned about the reservists' personal misfortunes, would have strongly approved of their signing on. There were cases where desperate men faced with starvation re-enlisted under assumed names, often encouraged and abetted by the recruiting staff.

In typical British fashion further positive initiatives to help with civilian employment were to come not from official but from voluntary sources, although Directors General of Recruiting were quick enough in their reports to mention such efforts in favourable terms. In 1885 a new employment organization for short-service soldiers was founded, its impetus coming from an Army Officer, Colonel E.F. Chapman, who was at the time Military Secretary to the Commander-in-Chief, India, General Sir Donald Stewart, who wrote on his behalf to the Duke of Cambridge and other influential figures explaining that through his proposed Association Chapman hoped "to combat the prejudices that are entertained against soldiers". The Commander-in-Chief was not disposed to help and the Duke of Connaught, Queen Victoria's third son, an ardent soldier then holding the rank of Major-General, was also reluctant to assist. His reasons were different from those of his arch conservative superior. The Duke of Connaught thought, with some justification, that more official action was necessary to improve ex-soldiers' employment opportunities and the setting up of another voluntary organization would only let the authorities off the hook. "With voluntary enlistment the government are bound either to increase the pay of the soldier or to give him a good pension, or to find him employment on completion of service . . . . A great deal can be done to help deserving men, but I don't like to see the Government shirking out of their responsibilities, leaving it to private or county agencies."[6] In many respects this is what did indeed happen over the next hundred years; voluntary bodies assumed the burden which should rightly have been borne by the state.

The Association's first meeting was held on 4 February, 1885, at the house of Lord Wantage, VC, longtime champion of both the soldier and his family. From the beginning a determined campaign was launched to publicize the aims and work of the new body, which was given the laborious title of "An Association for Promoting the Employment in Civil Life of Reserve and Discharged Soldiers", later to become the National Association. All the Army establishments were circulated, together with heads of the civil and military departments, the county authorities and large employers of labour. By the end of its first year eight county Branches had been established and three Regimental Associations were persuaded to affiliate their own embryo job-seeking activities with it.

Its first Annual Meeting was held at the Mansion House and proved a brilliant public relations exercise. The Secretary of State for War (The Rt Hon W.H. Smith) and many other important figures attended, including W.H. Russell, the noted *Times* correspondent, who moved the adoption of the First Report. Presiding over affairs was the venerable and much-respected Field-Marshal Lord Napier of Magdala. The Chairman opened by stating that successful employment after service was the most important factor in popularizing the Army and encouraging recruiting. Under the system of voluntary enlistment a short-service Army needed 35 to 40,000 men each year and these *had* to be given a good chance of employment at the end of their engagements. He gave notice that the Association would put pressure on the government to allocate a fair share of its minor public posts to servicemen.

Understandably, as yet achievements in placing men lagged some way behind the ideal. By the time the second Annual Meeting was held 576 men had been found situations, but their modest nature was hardly commensurate with the superior type of man avowedly sought by the Association. Within three years, though, a powerful pressure group had been created which gradually assumed a semi-official status. Two facts were emphasized with endless persistence, namely that ex-servicemen needed special privileges and that the Association, by reason of its national character, was the best vehicle to achieve this.

From its foundation until the beginning of the Boer War the National Association steadily increased the number of posts found annually. In 1899 these totalled 6,160, but, like those first two organizations sponsored by Edward Walter, it only assisted men of good character. No attempt was made to help the malcontents or the sick. In developing its power base as rapidly as possible it rightly concentrated on potential winners.

By the end of the century it became the practice for Inspector Generals of Recruiting to give employment placement figures in their Annual Reports. In his 1896 Report, for instance, the Inspector General noted that, from an outflow of 24,051 men, 18,246 had reliable characters. (This eliminated 25% of the total requiring employment.) Of those with reliable characters, 7,604 were found employment through all the employment organizations charged to assist them (not just the National Association), while 1,457 passed to the reserve after just three years. (By the Association's charter, and in the Inspector General's opinion, these were not eligible for assistance either.) In modern parlance, a degree of creative accounting was used in presenting the outflow statistics. Everything was designed to give the most favourable impression possible. Even so, there were still 8,064 men, or 45% of the total, about whom nothing was known. If one added those not eligible, then over 50% of the outflow were likely to be experiencing employment difficulties of an extreme nature, despite the admirable initiatives taken since the Crimean War. Because of the much increased outflow the numbers suffering difficulties were not far different from those of the old Army.

In spite of the Association's aim to find a better type of job for the superior class of men now completing their short service, its statistics showed that the largest categories were still servants, grooms, coachmen, labourers, porters and messengers. In the adverse climate of the time, though, any job was better than the stigma of poverty.

That problems still existed is evident from the emergence of a whole clutch of lesser organizations interested in finding employment. Some, like the Rifleman's Aid Society (founded 1883) and the Royal Engineers Labour Bureau (founded 1894), relied on the facilities of the National Association, but others did their own job-finding. These included the Naval Employment Agency (founded 1896) and the Irish Guards and Brigade of Guards Employment Society (founded 1891). The latter was financed through the generosity of its officers, while, in typical fashion, the Irish Guards enjoyed an exclusive arrangement for their reservists to join the Royal Irish Constabulary. The Brigade's Employment Society catered for limited numbers. In 1891 135 men were found jobs; in 1898 139 men and widows of ex-guardsmen were fixed up, but the latter total included some in temporary employment at the Olympia Exhibition Centre.[7]

The National Association had no interest in emphasizing the difficulties which so many contemporary servicemen faced; it naturally dwelt on the growing number of successes gained, especially as it had ambitions to assume responsibility for all employment-finding. It never sought to encompass the fiercely independent but small Corps of Commissionaires whose responsibilities towards its members went so much further than those of any employment agency.

The Association's achievements were recognized by a government grant of £200 annually which was subsequently increased to £500. These trifling contributions confirmed the Duke of Connaught's fears that, with its foundation, the Government would be able to discharge its responsibilities to ex-soldiers with the minimum trouble and expense. As with other arrangements for soldiers' welfare, far more financial assistance came from other sources: the Queen gave an annual subscription, as did other influential supporters, but the main contributions were made by the men themselves through subscriptions from their various batteries, regiments, corps and departments.

There were, of course, extremely good reasons why the National Association should present the most favourable picture it could of its successes in the employment field, though Directors of Recruiting had less to lose and were rather more candid in their Reports. Even so they had no predisposition to criticize organizations which were struggling to make up for official omissions.

In any case, while recruiting was difficult over these years, it was never desperate; the large numbers required, several times greater than before short service, were coming forward. But as the exodus from the countryside to the urban areas continued, the traditional recruit, a countryman used to hardship, amenable to discipline and not too clever, had to give way to the less well-nourished, under-sized, but quicker-witted youth from the great cities. Men came to the Army from the great towns because they were without work and, while it could be argued that good employment prospects afterwards might attract a better class of man, it was their uncertain prospects after service which persuaded a good proportion to extend their service. For this reason, under the British system of voluntary recruitment good resettlement arrangements did not rate high among the range of recruiting incentives.

The recruiting figures were certainly helped by reductions in the rates of wastage and desertion. Wastage was lower because the soldiers' health was better, due to improvements in diet, thanks to the amelioration of punishments, to better living conditions and because they now enjoyed a more varied lifestyle, including organized sports. The old illiterate NCOs of the past were fast disappearing with promotion now dependent upon educational success. An educated soldier, John Fraser, who, if he had served 20 years earlier, would have been mercilessly ridiculed by his barrack-room mates, described in the late 1870s the curious experience of school parade between 3.15 and 4.15 daily. He used one of the newly-established libraries as a place of personal retreat from the barrackroom, a place where he could find peace to write his letters home.[8]

When recruiting was difficult, the authorities could always lower the physical standards required for admission and the opportunity was taken on a number of occasions. As a result lighter and smaller men were enlisted, usually drawn from the great industrial areas. The costs of this policy were felt during the Boer War. Some home battalions were peopled by recruits who, as Sir Evelyn Wood noted, were the physical equivalent of schoolboys between sixteen and seventeen years of age. But, despite its disadvantages, the system worked after a fashion.

Soldiers were now joining the Army at a younger age. In 1862 only a third of the recruits enlisting were 19 or under: by 1889 this had risen to 50%. These younger men, many of whom were only committed to six years' service, had much less reason to desert. Part of the price they paid, however, was that, after the six years, which were usually spent abroad, they would need worthwhile employment at once, but would return home to find that the employment agencies provided a relatively limited service. Equally important, like all soldiers at their point of release, would come the realization of what they were giving up, the excitement of service life, the comradeship of Regiment and friends in arms, the rough but sheltering bonds of discipline, all of which had no equivalent in civilian life.

In 1885, the same year as the National Association, another major voluntary organization, the Soldiers' and Sailors' Families Association, was founded, this time pledged to improve conditions for dependants. Once more it was an Army Officer who took the initiative. Major (later Colonel) James Gildea, a militia officer with the Royal Warwickshire Regiment, had long been concerned about the great hardships suffered by service families when their soldier breadwinners went abroad, particularly in times of war. At the very moment when soldiers were called upon to risk their lives to protect their country, they were also faced with increasing worries about their families. Although the Geneva Conventions, and their implementation through the British Red Cross Society, were establishing more humanitarian conditions for the combatants themselves, servicemen's dependants were, for the most part, still ignored by the military authorities.

The British Army of the 1880s recognized only a very small proportion of wives, normally those of its senior NCOs and a number of soldiers with over 7 years' service. These were "on the strength", eligible for a separation allowance of 1/- per day, with an extra 3d for each child. This included a compulsory stoppage of 3d from the husband's pay. Most wives, including all those married to short-service men, were "off the strength". When their men went to war it spelt disaster. They were allotted no living accommodation and no allowances; no widow's pension was granted if the husband was killed in action. During their husband's foreign service, the most such wives could hope for was the 3d a day stoppage from his pay. Even those women on the strength received no pension if their husbands died in ways not directly connected with active service.

The Navy was even less caring for its families. In 1886 Admiral Sir Astley Cooper, speaking at the first meeting of the new families' body said, "Every sailor and marine we have is in the same position as a soldier who is married not on the strength of the Regiment. At the Admiralty we do not recognize a married sailor; we do not help him with his family officially."[9]

Up to and including the Crimean War, a proportion of soldiers' wives were allowed to accompany their husbands on campaign. Thereafter all were compelled to suffer the separation, uncertainty and risk of bereavement, with, for most, subsequent penury. For reasons both of economy and military efficiency, the number of families who were officially recognized were kept to the minimum. In the 1880s a blanket partitioning off part of the barrack room was no longer acceptable to house a serviceman's family; they rightly needed accommodation of their own. In the military mind, though, the typical young soldier was unencumbered by a family, happy to move with his Regiment wherever it might be sent. The cost of his physical frustrations were paid in the wards of Army hospitals, full of young men disfigured by venereal disease. In the 1890s the admissions to British military hospitals for VD were seven times greater than in the Prussian Army and four and a half times that of the French. The admissions for the British Army in India were two and a half times greater than for the home Army.[10]

The image of soldiers' families living at the edge of starvation —the gaunt mother and ragged children—did nothing to help men find worthwhile employment after service, for many employers insisted on seeing a man's family as well. Nor, indeed, did their hard drinking and sex-related diseases, stemming in many cases from the authorities' deliberate stance against marriage.

By the 1880s it was seen in many quarters as an unjust and dehumanizing policy, ripe for amendment, but it was left to James Gildea to act. Although he had earlier raised money for widows and orphans of the Zulu and Afghan Wars, it was the sending of the Expeditionary Force to Egypt which caused him to write a letter to *The Times* appealing for funds and volunteers to form an association devoted to looking after the families left behind. Its funds would provide a small allowance, where needed, for married women, whether on the strength or not, or for aged parents who were dependent on their sons. Assistance would also be given towards self-help: to find employment for those women who could take it.

Ladies were to be recruited, who, formed into permanent local committees, would look after families in need. These were established in the first place in or near the new garrison towns. In time it was hoped to have representatives not only across the face of Britain but in British possessions abroad.

Once again the Royal Family responded, the Princess of Wales (the future Queen Alexandra) becoming its first President. From the beginning she took a most active part and the Queen herself was soon enlisted as Patron.

By the end of its first year 231 women and 466 children had received grants totalling £515.10.0, while many others had been given clothing and several were found work.

In its second year Gildea decided to widen his scope of activity to include widows and children of officers not entitled to pensions. Some of the officers in the reformed Army, apart from those promoted from the ranks, were no longer wealthy men and, just before the Boer War, plans were made to establish a home for officers' widows and orphan daughters. This was completed in 1905.

In 1892 SSFA extended its practical assistance to Service families in large garrisons and seaports, both at home and abroad, by providing fully qualified nurses to attend them. This district nurse system was a pacesetter in late Victorian society. Mrs Norah Diamond, the Association's first nurse, was appointed in 1892 to Dublin's Curragh Camp. Most of her families were "off the strength", living in what she described as "huts and hovels not fit for cattle". At Aldershot it was no better, a group of tumbledown dwellings occupied by families "off the strength" huddled close to the great walls of the Cavalry Barracks there. By 1897 the Association had twelve nurses at work, one at the Curragh, three in Aldershot, one in Dover, one in York, one in Malta, two in Devonport, one in Gosport, one in Mauritius and one in Cairo. When not nursing the sick, the nurses gave general hints and advice on health and hygiene.

James Gildea was a restless, dynamic reformer, determined not to rest on his achievements. While much had been achieved through his nationwide network of dedicated ladies and through his professional nursing service, he looked forward to the challenges which would face his organization during another war. Given the increasing tension in Europe this promised to be on a large scale.

Gildea was by no means alone in his estimation of the likelihood of oncoming war. Aware of this, late Victorian society began to exhibit a new interest in and concern for their soldiers and sailors quite unusual in Britain. Among the more extreme were the jingoists, men who bragged about their country's preparedness to fight and who generally advocated a bellicose policy in dealing with foreign powers. In typical fashion, when war actually came at the end of the century it was in an unlikely place against a surprising enemy. Of one thing there was no doubt, it was a popular war. As one commentator has put it, the Boer War "was marked by an orgy of patriotism the like of which had never been seen before; men really did flock to the colours to show their involvement in the dreams of Empire".[11]

As for the regular soldiers, the men required to put the brave words into action, thousands of their families were thrown upon the hands of SSFA, many being the result of hasty marriages performed virtually at the time of embarkation as pledges were kept.

64

Within 24 hours James Gildea had acted to take advantage of this civilian enthusiasm. Supported by the Princess of Wales he made a strong appeal for contributions:

"On no previous occasion of the despatch of a large expeditionary force from this country has there been a complete organization of over *3,000 ladies and gentlemen* throughout the kingdom voluntarily undertaking to befriend the wives and families of our soldiers and sailors during their absence on active service. Additional funds are all that is now required." The level of patriotic feeling at the time guaranteed a good response. A Fund opened by the Lord Mayor of London gave SSFA the huge sum of £550,000 with which to alleviate the sufferings of soldiers' families while their breadwinners were away. The general principle adopted was for the family income to be made up to two-thirds of its normal level.[12] Allowances were paid at the rate of £50,000 a month, and when more contributions were needed, an appeal by Princess Alexandra produced a further £300,000 which was subscribed within a month. In all £1,205,877 was dispensed to 206,439 wives and dependent relatives and to 235,977 children.[13]

In 1900 the growing power of the popular press was demonstrated by a separate initiative undertaken on behalf of Service families. The *Daily Mail* launched its Absent-Minded Beggar's Fund after a poem of that title by Rudyard Kipling. Donations reached over £100,000 within three months. Part of the fund was still unspent at the end of the war and went towards the provision of a hospital at Alton, in Hampshire.

The main campaign, though, was waged by James Gildea, enthusiastically supported by the Princess of Wales and well publicized through the press. With society alerted to its responsibilities for servicemen's dependants, a major and longstanding injustice during time of war was relieved.

The preparedness of the Edwardian public to help the soldiers themselves was demonstrated by its generosity to the British Red Cross Society. This fitted out two hospital trains and a hospital ship of its own and sent vast quantities of clothing and hospital comforts to South Africa.[14] Such ways of making a man's hospitalization more effective and more comfortable were obviously welcome and no doubt his treatment had come a long way from that offered at Scutari. However, another longstanding but unquestionably major injustice remained. Even in the late 90s after medical treatment most of the men still needed extra time to recover from the traumas they had undergone. In the case of officers they were often given generous sick leave to convalesce but this was not the general practice with soldiers. In the majority of cases their home environment could hardly provide the conditions required.

For those whose health had been so seriously damaged as to render them unfit for further service virtually nothing more was done than in the seventeenth century. After the granting of a pension, often for a strictly limited time, they were released into civilian life to cope as best they could. Like the disabled, they needed not just help to reassimilate but training towards appropriate employment through which they could support their families and feel they still had something to offer. Their cause was to be taken up during the Boer War by yet another Army officer, this time of Royal lineage.

Just before he was killed, the young Prince Christian Victor, grandson of Queen Victoria, had talked to his mother about the need to help men who were returning from South Africa with disabling wounds. As a result, in 1899, another major charity, the Soldiers and Sailors Help Society, was formed with Princess Christian as its first President. On its foundation it soon incorporated two earlier initiatives for helping the disabled. The Army and Navy Invalid Training Home at Portsmouth, which had been founded six years earlier by yet another retired officer philanthropist, General M.H. Synge, joined immediately, and Lady Brabazon's workrooms for disabled soldiers in London and Dublin came over in 1904. In the workrooms wounded and maimed men had been trained to make toys and other simple articles by Lady Brabazon's secretary, Miss Jean Castleton. Both enterprises were run on a strictly limited scale.

A further major boost came from the Building Trades of England. At Bisley, on land donated by Lord Pirbright, they built, entirely at their own expense, five separate blocks which together were called the Princess Christian Homes. At the Bisley Homes and in the society's workroom at Montpelier Street, London, disabled men came to be taught ways of earning their own living, despite their injuries. Like SSFA, the SSHS constructed a network of friends across Britain. By 1902 12,048 people had offered to act in this capacity. Some provided temporary homes for sick or wounded who were expected to recover their health after a period of convalescence. 200 such homes were found for over 2000 soldiers. Alternatively, the society made grants of up to 5/- a week for single and up to 10/- for married men who preferred to recover with their own families. By current practice those who elected to stay with their families lost their separation payments. As yet what was to become the Help Society's main commitment, that of training the disabled for employment, was only conducted on a minute scale.

The cataclysm of war invariably leads to significant changes and the Boer War was no exception. Yet, even allowing for the public's greater involvement, the remarkable degree of their response to appeals made on the servicemen's behalf suggested a new level of sympathy for the British soldier.

The increased concern could not be attributed entirely to the Boer War itself; one of the chief reasons for a greater interest in the military at this time appeared to come from a new feeling of vulnerability, admittedly sharpened by the Boer War, about the country's ability to defend its large Empire, together with the growing conviction that another even larger conflict was inevitable. This could be seen in contemporary articles about teaching military virtues at school, while consideration of universal conscription led, in part, to the development of certain Christian movements of a paramilitary nature, like the Salvation Army, the Boy's Brigade and the Church Army.

At the same time professional soldiers had certainly become subjects for greater consideration. Kipling's poems about the ordinary soldier, often shamefully treated after his service, enjoyed great vogue, while a virtually insatiable demand created the spate of current military periodicals, like the *Navy and Army Illustrated*, *Under the Union Jack* and *Black and White Budget*, which included many photographs of the services on exercise or in action. The last two were started during the Boer War. These years also marked a great popular movement in military paintings. The doyenne here was Lady Butler, wife of General Sir William Butler, of whom Wilfred Meynell said, "[she] has done for the soldier in art what Rudyard Kipling has done for him in literature – she has taken the individual, separated him, seen him close, and let the world see him."[15]

In the short term all this had little effect on the large numbers of soldiers released at the war's end who, above all things, needed good employment. Admittedly most of the militia soldiers found their jobs were still there, but for many of the reservists and others who joined up for patriotic or less idyllic reasons the situation was not so favourable. It was one thing for leading civilians to support charitable appeals during the war, quite another to readmit 'soldier types' into their shops and manufactories. This was understandable when replacement staff, some with three year's seniority, were doing a good job. Most of the men still had to rely on the admirable but rather ramshackle employment arrangements developed through voluntary initiatives.

During 1902 64,445 soldiers were discharged with good characters, or above, and 45,981 were reckoned to have found employment.[16] This was a remarkable effort on behalf of the National Association and other employment societies, although the figures did not include those discharged from special Corps raised for the duration whom it was assumed would have their old jobs back. Nor did they apply to those discharged with less than good characters. The traditional employment agencies were assisted this time by the Forces' Help Society which alerted its nationwide system of friends to tackle the premier welfare need of the hour, namely that of finding jobs. Its chairman, Major-General Lord Cheylesmore, in his report for 1902 had no doubt this was the area where the greatest current need lay: "Many must go, at least temporarily, to the wall: their sufferings will be part of the price of war, not the least part of it."

On the debit side, over a third of all soldiers discharged from the war had still not found employment twelve months after it had ended. The jobs too, as in the past, were often very humble ones.

Any job was better than nothing and the average wage was only 19/-. The largest single employers were the Railway Companies who took 8,314 men during 1902.

Improvements to the employment services could not be achieved overnight but conditions appeared favourable for new developments. Leo Amery's history of the South African War, commissioned by *The Times*, made no bones about reforms being required. In particular it criticized military training, acknowledging that men showed "the greatest courage and regimental esprit de corps in South Africa but [that] their military skills were sadly lacking."[17] Amery and other commentators were agreed that in future men needed to be able to exercise their own initiative.[18]

This was considered the more difficult because Amery knew well that soldiers had traditionally been recruited from the lower ranks of unskilled labour and in physique and intelligence were, generally speaking, below the average level of the nation. He showed knowledge of the serious legacies, notably of youth and immaturity, inherited from successive Directors General of Recruiting who reduced entry standards, and observed that when many mature reservists returned to the colours they were often in poor physical condition due to unemployment. The leading commentators on the war all agreed that the future success of the Army depended upon attracting good men. If better resettlement was a genuine factor in attracting a better class of recruit, then improvements in this area could reasonably be expected as part of the postwar reforms.

Unfortunately, after the Boer War there occurred the usual prolonged debate on what shape the British military machine should assume. This was conducted against the inevitable demands for military economies after the high cost of war. Military budgets competed against a range of urgent civilian programmes. The Army had no irresistible Dreadnought programme through which it could extract substantially increased funding from politicians. Its leaders didn't even speak with one voice. They were divided on the length of a soldier's enlistment: Lord Roberts favoured a form of National Service, Garnet Wolseley was a firm champion of short service, while others like General Airey favoured longer engagements. The majority, though, acknowledged that voluntary enlistment would continue, certainly for the time being.

As one might imagine, this was a background most unlikely to produce rapid or sweeping reforms extending to employment arrangements after service. The voluntary employment bodies had performed wonders at the end of the war, despite the limitations in many of the jobs they offered and the substantial numbers who remained unemployed. When things returned to normal they could be expected to do even better in percentage terms. By their exertions they gave the authorities breathing space to consider possible improvements. (For those soldiers who had failed to find jobs there was no such respite; between 1903–8 the Help Society identified 120,602 men who were in distress and to whom it gave clothing and small amounts of money. In all £49,098 was distributed in aid, a large sum from the organization's limited funds and indicative of the widespread nature of the privations.)

Full use was hardly made of the respite. The main, almost the only, result of official concern over jobfinding after service was the setting up of a War Office Committee (the Ward Committee) in 1906, at the request of Richard Haldane, Secretary of State for War at the time. It made two recommendations, one about improving and extending employment facilities, the second on co-ordinating the existing agencies into a single organization. As a result Haldane charged the new Local Territorial and Regimental Associations with additional responsibilities for the care of reservists and discharged soldiers. In a few cases only were they beginning to assume these shortly prior to the start of the Great War. Some training in civilian technical skills was made available for long-term men shortly before their release, but the numbers taking it up were quite small compared with the total annual outflow. Its popularity was hardly helped by men having to pay their own fees. As for amalgamating all the voluntary bodies into one agency, the Ward Committee recommended that £20,000 should be allocated, £16,000 from the Army, £4,000 from Naval Funds. This proposal was not taken up. As the Secretary to the Committee put it: "The Treasury, never keen in these days, as far as my experience went, to do anything of a specific nature to help the ex-servicemen to get employment, flatly refused to grant the subsidy to form the nucleus of the Central Association."[19]

The most dramatic development in the employment field was again as a result of a voluntary initiative. Two men, James Malcolm and Major Arthur Haggard, members of an Officers' Club in Holborn, London, established "The Veterans Corps and Employment Bureau Ltd". It was a uniformed, disciplined body with a military-style rank structure and its own band. The chief executive was a Commandant who answered to a Council of distinguished officers. It was a rather more relaxed version of the Corps of Commissionaires and its members became messengers, time-keepers, caretakers, club stewards and watchmen. While hardly approximating to the new image of retired servicemen, it flourished and was just under 1,000 strong on the eve of the Great War.

During the last decade before the First World War more agencies than ever were concerned with helping ex-servicemen find employment and, at times, their functions overlapped. The most important of them were still voluntary bodies. For servicemen it was like walking through a maze, with the uncertain reward of a job at its exit. Dedicated amateurism remained the order of the day. The system was so complicated that a remarkable ex-gunner, W.G. Clifford, set himself to help soldiers interpret it. At his own expense he published a simple job-finding guide, *How and Where ex-soldiers can GET Work,* and he personally founded and edited a monthly *Soldiers' Employment Gazette* which individual units and formations supported.

The British Regular Army in the years between the Boer and Great Wars was not separated from civilians by the gulf which had existed for the hardbitten regulars of the old Army. Most of its soldiers returned to civilian life after a relatively short time. Its political chief, Richard Haldane, saw the Army in the shape of a metal cone, with the regulars making up the sharp point of tempered steel, backed by the reserves (in civilian occupations) and the Territorial Forces (civilian soldiers) from every county location. With the likelihood of a major war looming, British society was unusually militaristic at this period, although Professor Michael

71

Howard has called it militarism in "a mild solution" compared with that of the continental powers.

No one has seriously questioned the statement that the British Expeditionary Force in 1914 was, up to that time, "incomparably the best trained, best organized, and best equipped British Army which ever went forth to war."[20] While destitution was still its best recruiter, a leavening of superior men had joined it and, more than ever before, it placed great emphasis on individual initiative and self-reliance in its members.

With such professionalism, the continuing amateur nature of its job-finding arrangements were a contradiction. If the Territorial Associations had taken up their responsibilities sooner, as Richard Haldane intended, or as enthusiastically as the King's (Liverpool Regiment) "which found employment for every good man within a few days of their leaving the colours", the situation would have been very different. As it was, the different voluntary organizations struggled to find posts in a climate where trade was slack and setbacks occurred. With the establishment of Employment Exchanges in 1910, civilians, in one bound, now enjoyed more assistance in job-finding than the ex-servicemen's bodies had achieved after so much struggle. At the same time the Trade Unions, freed from liability to conspiracy by the 1906 Act, began to orchestrate national stoppages like those of 1911–12. These bodies of skilled or semi-skilled workers now flexing their powerful muscles were traditionally opposed to ex-soldiers who in the main were technically unqualified.

Soldiers, often returning from overseas, still experienced the classic problems of readjustment even after just six years away. Most employers, unless they were enthusiastic members of the Territorial Army, while they might have rather more sympathy for ex-servicemen than in the past, would hardly take the risk of employing them preferentially. Tradition and practice were still far removed from the position in France, where 65,000 minor positions had been granted to regular soldiers since 1898. The result was only too predictable – considerable hardship on release in the age-old way.

In 1910 young Winston Churchill, a notable but undoubtedly

privileged ex-soldier, talking in his capacity as Home Secretary, was only too willing to persuade himself that the placing of 20,000 men by the National Association during the previous year had solved the perennial problem: "We have always been shocked at the high proportion of soldiers who are discovered in the casual wards, men who have perhaps been injured in the course of service abroad, who have lost those previous years of life when they might have learnt a trade and made a footing for themselves . . . we ought to rejoice in the progress of the Army."[21]

Sadly the reality, as the 1909 Royal Commission on the Poor Law stated it, was depressingly familiar and in the long tradition of returning British soldiers: "It is the men who have left the permanent situation afforded by the Army and who have abandoned hope of getting employment of a permanent character who furnish the largest contingent of the floating population of the casual wards."

For all, both the misfits and those happily settled, the drums were to roll and bring them "back to the Army again". The curse on British ex-soldiers was now to fall not just upon those "traditional recruits" but on a whole generation brought in ever increasing numbers to the field of Armageddon.

CHAPTER FIVE

Soldiers All: False Expectations

"They mustered their soldiers."

Ballad of Mary Ambree.

IMMEDIATELY before the First World War more organizations than ever before existed to fight the inequalities suffered by British servicemen and their families. It was now unthinkable that families should be denied allowances while their fighting men were away or that returning servicemen should not have the benefit of job-finding organizations expressly designed to help them. Apart from an eligibility for some form of pension, those men who returned with their health damaged now had a society pledged to meet their needs, although as yet its scale of operations was very limited. In the British fashion the system, if it could be said to justify such a label, was inspired by volunteers, staffed by them and wholly dependent upon voluntary contributions. All its larger components enjoyed support from the Royal Family and frequently their enthusiastic participation as well.

This was philanthropy of a high order. However, quite soon after the First World War began, it became obvious that the numbers requiring assistance would exceed the wildest estimates. In European terms British involvement was still small. Unlike other western countries, though, it was to increase markedly right through the conflict and with it came growing numbers of fatalities and wounded with their insistent demands upon the system. During 1914 only the regular British Expeditionary Force was involved in land fighting, but this was to change. During 1915 an average of 15,000 soldiers and sailors were killed each month, creating both personal and economic distress for many parents and widows and (probably even more important to the serviceman's organizations) somewhat over double that number were wounded. By 1916 the deaths had risen to 44,000 a month and by 1917 to 56,000, with a proportionate number of wounded. By early 1918 fatalities had increased five-fold over those of three years before, to 75,000 a month. At the war's conclusion over 5 million men from Great Britain had donned uniform (the Empire contributed a further $3\frac{1}{2}$ million). Of these 900,000 died and 2,200,000 were wounded or taken prisoner – 38% of the total. From the British Isles alone the casualty figures were more horrific still. Over 700,000 were killed and 1,660,000 injured, about 48% of the total enlisted.[1] By the end of the war hardly any family in the land had escaped a bereavement and at least one of its menfolk returned with his health seriously impaired. The involvement of a whole generation meant that by 1918 the disabled alone were to number over twelve times the strength of the original British Expeditionary Force.

The political and social repercussions to the nations involved in the vast conflict are now common knowledge, but fundamental changes, too, were forced on the British system of servicemen's resettlement. Central Government was compelled to assist, to intervene and in some cases to take over existing provisions. Because of the unique British tradition and the pattern of our ascending participation, official action came much later than in other countries, attended as it always was by an extreme reluctance towards compulsion. It came largely as a result of a plethora of committees considering the many problems of national reconstruction needed at the war's close and, tragically, was too late in many cases to save the endless ranks of those returning from suffering the age-old fate of British ex-servicemen. During the war, groups of dedicated men, fearful of just this outcome, formed themselves into new pressure groups to force their political leaders to keep faith with those who fought. Yet before they had settled their own differences, in the protracted fashion of British institutions, and came to speak with a single voice, the situation for the returning millions had deteriorated beyond anyone's power, of Government or dedicated voluntary agency, to change the bleak outlook for so many.

Writing seventy years afterwards, it is easier now to see how the tragedy occurred than for those struggling with the massive and varied problems of the time. It came from a rare conjunction; just at the time that traditional arrangements had been made better than ever before, they were swamped by rapid, vast and unimaginably ascending demand. All subsequent attempts to meet such demand were hampered by the dislocation and economic convulsions caused by the monumental conflict. One might still legitimately ask why governments in Britain and other European states, together with their military authorities, were so lacking in foresight.

That a great war could come to Europe was acknowledged from 1870 onwards, that it would be fought by major armies was certain (hence even in Britain reforms were undertaken to create a large reserve force), that it would be bloody because of the greater effectiveness of modern weapons was almost joyfully accepted. To suit the mood of the time certain theories propounded by Clausewitz, the great German philosopher on war, were adopted (and adapted), notably his two basic principles that "against a strong enemy only great military force can achieve success" and that "superiority of numbers becomes every day more decisive". But Clausewitz had always viewed war as a legitimate political instrument and to the great statesmen of Europe, together with their political advisers, it was unthinkable that war, when it came, could be of such a kind as to break the chain of natural progression for the whole continent. They could not believe war would be protracted enough to lay the whole of Europe open to a mutual weakness and exhaustion, destroying the social and economic cohesion of contending countries, and that it could produce so long-lasting a stalemate.

Only a few exceptional men forecast the shape of modern war with any accuracy. Pre-eminent here was a French caricaturist and satirist, Albert Robida, who in 1883 wrote an article about the folly of humans who could develop novel weapons of great destructive power: "submarines, underwater troops, mines, torpedoes, smoke-screens, automatic small arms fire, air bombardment of cities, a chemical corps complete with poisonous shells, a bacteriological warfare company to spray the enemy with microbes and the "*blockhaus roulants*"[2]—the forerunners of H.G. Wells' land ironclads.

H.G. Wells showed remarkable prescience about land warfare, although he was quite inaccurate with regard to sea conflict. On land he foretold the stage when increased firepower would lead to a stalemate, where fronts would be held by chains of small, mutually-supporting units lying in holes and armed with self-loading rifles or light machine guns. This infantry, supported by long-range artillery, "could stop the most multitudinous attack in the world." To break the stalemate he proposed a land tractor "that could at a pinch cross a 30-foot trench". He predicted that aircraft would be used and, once command of the air is obtained, "the war must become a conflict between a seeing host and one that is blind". He even foresaw atomic power and that, in a war with "atomic bombs", the ground would be seared with radioactivity and areas rendered uninhabitable by fallout. Such forecasts were much too far-fetched and unreal to influence statesmen or conservative military experts. Equally important, they ran counter to the general desire (based on past precedents) for a decisive war.

There were other and more 'serious' prophets, but for different reasons their ideas were also dismissed. A Polish financier, Ivan S. Bloch, wrote a huge work which was published in English in 1899 with the ponderous title *The Future of War in its Economic and Political Relations. Is war now impossible?*. In this he predicted stalemate and slaughter on the battlefields and forecast these would produce domestic perturbations acute enough in some countries to overthrow the political order.

In Britain, Norman Angell's book *The Great Illusion* argued that if a militarily successful nation destroyed another it would "thereby destroy its own market, actual or potential, which would be commercially suicidal". But Norman Angell was a pacifist in an age when war was considered the natural activity both for great nations and small states seeking new economic markets.

The prophecies of science fiction writers, a German Jew based in Poland and a British pacifist, however percipient, were hardly likely to influence the chief European nations prior to 1914. The reaction of the British military authorities to Norman Angell's writings was characteristically and understandably splenetic.

Yet recent military experience should have made the British somewhat less blinkered than the rest of Europe to the limited power of the offensive. The war in South Africa had demonstrated that defended fronts were virtually unbreakable even against superior forces. It had led to improved musketry training and amendments to tactics where the individual initiative of junior commanders was emphasized. But Sir John French and Douglas Haig had successfully carried out a powerful rearguard action on behalf of the cavalry, the *arme blanche*, which assumed that Britain would succeed in a future war through speed of manoeuvre, largely dependent upon horsemen (Haig even had a proportion of lances re-introduced in 1909). While Roberts and Kitchener opposed the cavalry school and favoured artillery and dismounted fire, they still based their tactical doctrines on a future war of manoeuvre.

Unfortunately, it was unwise to take the avowed optimism of Haig and Kitchener at complete face value. Both these outwardly aloof, taciturn men gave other strong indications that they expected a long, extremely costly and debilitating contest. Haig enthusiastically taught the Army traditional cavalry tactics, but, as it approached, during his 'Staff Rides' in Aldershot, he came to emphasize the uncertainty of war "and realized that any attempt at stereotyped strategy would invite disappointment and even disaster".[3] In 1906, foreseeing the awesome responsibilities which, he hoped, would come his way, he painted the coming conflict as "a great war requiring the whole resources of the nation to bring it to a successful end", stressing that the nation's resources should be organized "for a war of several years".[4] As yet the terrible butcher's bill and the sufferings of men after war were not his prime concern. Kitchener, with his earlier struggles to bring the Boer War to a successful conclusion fresh in his memory, envisaged the Great War lasting some 3–4 years and being fought on a massive scale. In this context he despised the Regular Army, because he thought it was far too small for the part it would have to play, and the Territorial Army for its amateur spirit, which he considered was incurable. In 1911 he even told Lord Esher that the coming war would only be won with the aid of "the last million men whom Great Britain could raise, train, equip and hurl into the fight".[5]

Given the prevailing mood of the country, it would have been extremely damaging for their careers if such senior soldiers had preached such sombre predictions too enthusiastically. In any case all Army reforms, even from 1906 onwards, depended on a measure of compromise caused by the other demands upon central funds. Haldane's ceaseless and skilful lobbying had brought into being the Territorial Force, and, together with Haig, he was determined it should become an efficient military instrument, but serious shortcomings in its level of efficiency remained, due to its limited funding. As a modern observer has noted, "He had done the best he could in spite of a parsimonious government and a weak-willed nation".[6] To call the British weak-willed seems harsh indeed. Hitler made the same judgement. Undeniably, though, they have always been slow to take up their military responsibilities, to the cost of their forces in being. In any case, after the 1906 Anglo-French Staff conversations, British land forces were committed to a great continental war on the European mainland. Here France was the senior partner and her doctrine was firmly wedded to the *arme blanche*, supported as it was by her famous quick-firing, mobile artillery – artillery eminently unsuited to static warfare and a strategy of attrition.

Alone among the senior soldiers prior to the First World War Roberts, who had long been seen as the soldier's friend, took active steps to help improve conditions for returning men from the anticipated conflict. He had close connections with the Soldiers' and Sailors' Help Society and in June, 1914, he attended the last meeting of its Trustees before his death. On the way to his car he remarked that war was obviously imminent and hoped the Society would expand greatly to deal with the casualties that were bound to result. From this came the Society's much-increased concentration on helping disabled men find employment, and the title was amended to the Soldiers' and Sailors' Help Society and Lord

Roberts' Workshops. The appeal, which used Roberts' name, raised £500,000 for sheltered workshops, which was a magnificent response, but, in view of the numbers involved and the capital-intensive nature of sheltered employment, quite inadequate.

By this time central government had begun to show its willingness to become involved in a range of social reforms, often to the detriment of service budgets. This led the dedicated bodies concerned with the social well-being of the soldier on his return, and of his family while serving, to feel confident that a party which had pioneered old age pensions, health insurance and employment exchanges would not allow injustices to the returning soldier to occur. It would be unlikely, for instance, to leave to voluntary initiative alone the collection and payment of separation allowances for a vast body of men who until recently had been normal citizens themselves. While SSFA itself made all reasonable preparations, it was rightly confident that, after the precedent of the Boer War, never again in wartime would servicemen's families suffer the destitution of earlier days. As a whole, the service's charitable organizations looked forward to a new situation of partnership between themselves as the voluntary flag bearers and a more compassionate nation. Alas, they were to find themselves treated with rare insensitivity by a government which still relied on their help for much of a seemingly endless war.

Expectations of a short war were not, of course, solely a British phenomenon. Elsewhere in Europe its proponents were supreme —if soon to be disillusioned. The French, after their humiliation in 1870, turned to a reborn belief in a certain élan, in the power of the offensive carried through as Colonel de Grandmaison expressed it "à outrance". In order to balance the greater German manpower, very few military deferments were granted and 52% of French industrial establishments were closed on the outbreak of war. It was as if the whole nation paused, waiting to hear decisive news from the battlefield. In Lorraine, working to the precepts of their infamous Plan 17, massed French troops, many in their cherry-red pantalons, attacked fortified positions in massed ranks, supported by inadequate artillery. The result was only too predictable – rows and rows of corpses and groaning wounded prostrated before the defence lines. By the end of August, 1914, the French armies were engaged in that most difficult of all military operations, withdrawal. In their early ill-conceived offensives, the French lost upwards of a million men, this on top of considerable numbers of skilled men who had to be released to staff the factories as half the country's stockpile of artillery ammunition had already been consumed. 300,000 men were killed and twice that figure had been injured or captured. Where possible, men were returned from hospital for further fighting but those no longer able to fight had to be found some constructive role in civilian life. This presented France with a massive problem, occurring with terrible suddenness, which required effective arrangements. These were organized, in the French way, through a National Office for discharged and disabled men set up expressly for the purpose.

Germany was committed to the policy of the offensive out of practical necessity. Bismarck's long fear of France and Russia coming together had been realized and Germany, faced with war on two fronts, needed to destroy one enemy at a time by "a calculated risk on one front, lightning speed on the other".[7] This strategy was embodied in the Schlieffen Plan, conceived by the Chief of the German General Staff, Count von Schlieffen, in 1905, and regularly amended since. By a great encircling movement the French Army was to be destroyed in forty days, before the ponderous Russian mobilization on the Eastern Front could be completed. It was faith in the master plan which had led the Kaiser to tell his departing troops in the first week of August, "You will be home before the leaves have fallen from the trees".[8]

In the event the German thrust failed. But, desperate for success, they, like the French in Lorraine, were profligate with their troops. At Ypres, although they had outdistanced their heavy artillery, they retained close formations against accurate British rifle fire. Here they sacrificed many of their middle- and upper-class young men who, as student volunteers, flung themselves into near-suicidal attacks. The Germans, too, quickly experienced the humiliating return by thousands of young men shattered in battle for whom they had to make provision.

In 1914 Czarist Russia was no place to find accurate prophesies on the coming war. The country was only just recovering from the Russo-Japanese War of 1904/5 and its mobilization machine was cumbrous. Yet, goaded by the French, whose ambassador insisted "upon the necessity of their armies prosecuting an offensive '*à outrance* to Berlin'," they launched their attacks just a fortnight after the beginning of the war. Without adequate logistical support, the result was only too predictable, a great defeat. Schlieffen's plans of encirclement which had been frustrated on the Marne were achieved in East Prussia, at Tannenburg. Simultaneously the Russians were inflicting a great defeat on the Austrians, causing 250,000 casualties and taking 100,000 prisoners. From this initial crippling reverse Austria never recovered. After Tannenburg the Russians suffered further defeats in the next year which led to the political upheaval that culminated in the Russian Revolution and their total withdrawal from the war in 1917, a situation only too accurately foreseen by Bloch.

With the violation of Belgian neutrality, itself part of the Schlieffen plan, Britain came into the war and almost immediately the BEF was sent to France. Most of the pundits in Britain thought, like the Kaiser, that the war would be over by Christmas. By Christmas, however, the BEF, engaged not in sweeping cavalry moves but in dogged withdrawal, had virtually been destroyed, 85,000 of its men becoming casualties, and the race was now on to increase our land forces, to replace the old professionals with reinforcements from the territorials and then with Kitchener's volunteer armies.

By the end of 1914 the enormity of the national butchers' bills was clear. The French had lost 854,000 men, the Germans 677,000, the Austrians 350,000, the Russians 1 million. In the early months many of those killed were either from the cutting edge of Europe's professional armies or men who had used every means possible to be where the guns spoke. Vast numbers were killed but still more came back to their mother countries not in victory but shattered in mind or body, some to be fed back into the insatiable battlefronts. Others, whose health had been seriously impaired, needed every assistance to pick up, as best they could, the threads of an earlier existence. This was organized in different ways throughout

Europe, to some extent in accordance with long-held military tradition, but in all cases Governments assumed responsibility for their disabled men. In Germany employment was assured for those with a disability of 50% or more, whereas in France employers were compelled to take men with less than 50% disability. In Italy and Belgium industry took a set quota of disabled servicemen in accordance with Governmental instructions.

Of all the combatants Britain had come off most lightly, although, as in earlier wars, it was her professional soldiers who paid with their lives for earlier economies and long-standing national antipathies towards standing armies. For instance, eleven days after the 1st Battalion, The West Yorkshire Regiment landed in France during 1914 only five officers and 250 other ranks were left from the original complement of twenty-seven officers and 957 soldiers.[9] Anyway, was it not the lot of professional soldiers to risk death or injury?

The amateurism of the British military system had terrible implications for many of her fighting men both during and after their service and for many of the communities which provided them. In terms of recruitment, with the regular Army destroyed, the nation turned to its second line of defence, its Territorial Army. This, in many instances, was neither very well-trained nor particularly well-equipped, although its spirit was outstanding; but while Kitchener's Armies were being prepared it became the nation's spearhead. Support for it varied widely across the country, being particularly strong, for instance, in some rural areas, especially in Scotland and Wales. As a result, from the early stages of the war some rural communities found themselves practically denuded of young men, most of whom went into the Infantry, where casualties were traditionally highest. During the war 86.07% of the total war casualties among the Army's fighting arms were suffered by the Infantry. In comparison Naval casualties were relatively light, being some 2.75% of the total.

In the North-West Highlands of Scotland virtually all the men were Army territorials or Naval reservists. The local Drill Hall had both fed their martial instincts and given them opportunities for wider social pursuits, through weekly parades, annual sports contests, national musters and far-flung shooting competitions. Officered by their local aristocracy, most of these hardy, serious-minded men, who could use every fold of land when approaching a quarry and had handled guns from their childhood, went to France as private soldiers. The magnificent spirit engendered by brothers, cousins, or close neighbours fighting shoulder to shoulder could in no way justify the profligacy of using – and destroying – such natural leaders in humble roles. This often occurred in a single battle. In the case of one remote Highland parish, Gairloch, from a total population of 3,317, 507 men joined the forces and many women left to serve in the QMAAC, WRNS, or as nurses and munition workers. Of the men ninety-two were killed and about double that injured, some more than once.

The pattern of loss reoccurred across the agricultural shirelands. On one day, 9 May, 1915, during the battle for Aubers Ridge, two battalions (both approaching 1000 strong) of the Royal Sussex Regiment each suffered over 200 casualties. The Territorial Battalion lost 24 young men killed from a single small village, Wadhurst, the results of which can be imagined.[10]

In rural Wales, one day before the Royal Sussex's travail at Aubers Ridge, the loss was even greater. The 1st and 3rd Monmouths, two territorial battalions in the Ypres Salient, found themselves subjected to a tremendous bombardment in which both were virtually annihilated, their "survivors between them hardly amounted to a war-strength company".[11] After this they were re-embodied as pioneer battalions.

This melancholy pattern was repeated across Britain and the Empire, and many rural townships within the vast Canadian prairies, the Australian outback and in New Zealand were decimated. Tragically there seemed little place for disabled men in small country communities where agricultural work was too hard and there were very few, if any, industrial or retailing opportunities. For different reasons many of the fit men never returned after the war and the reduced economic activity thus lessened the chances of the disabled still further. The cost of patriotism for many such communities was the virtual destruction of their previous way of life. Some most enlightened schemes for re-integration of the wounded were undertaken in the Empire, notably by New Zealand; nothing comparable occurred in the mother country.

By the Autumn of 1915, after the Loos offensive, the Territorials had suffered the fate of the old Regular Army. Starved by Kitchener of the necessary reserves to make good their losses, they were to give way to the third influx of manpower for the insatiable battle-fields. Under Kitchener's urging, new armies of volunteers had come forward. By September, 1915, the first 100,000 had rushed to join the colours to be followed by 400,000 more. All had to be trained from scratch. A good proportion of these Kitchener forma-tions, over 300 battalions in all, came together because their men shared identical interests rather than through any centralized selec-tion system. The 'Pals' principle was adopted whereby groups of workmates or friends were induced to volunteer – the Leeds' Pals, the Grimsby Chums, the Stockbrokers' Battalion of the 10th Royal Fusiliers, the Manchester Clerks' Battalion, and the Public School Battalion of the Middlesex Regiment. Sometimes all the members of these units were of outstanding quality, like the Uni-versity and Public Schools' Brigade of the Royal Fusiliers or the Artists' Rifles. Although a constant stream of men left such units, many of whom were to be subsequently commissioned, many more elected to stay on as private soldiers among like-minded colleagues. Magnificent in its way, it was a prodigious waste of talent which was not repeated in countries operating a system of conscription. After one day's fighting, 1 July, 1916, the Leeds Pals lost 24 officers and 504 other ranks, and a sister Battalion, the 2nd Bradford Pals, numbered only 7 officers and 170 other ranks.

Under a system depending upon voluntary enlistment unfair-ness was endemic. Professions and trades varied in their levels of enlistment, partly due to uncertain Governmental policy on reserved occupations. Between August, 1914, and February, 1916, over 40% of men from the professions of finance and commerce enlisted. Before conscription was enforced, strong pressure to join up was put on men united in their failure to gain employment. In August, 1914, the Local Government Board instructed charities not to grant relief to those unemployed who were eligible for enlistment. In Bristol, for instance, 10% of the workforce had been laid off in July, 1914, and a further 26% placed on short time because of the war. As a result 9 out of every 10 men laid off joined up.[12] The difficulties such men would have in achieving employment after some years away can only be imagined.

The call was insistent in other inner city regions where unemployment was endemic. Due to limitations in diet, recruits tended to be much smaller than their big-boned country cousins, but proved themselves tough, acute and quickwitted soldiers, attributes they required to survive in the adverse environments of the great cities. Such areas were ruthlessly harvested. From the streets of North London the Middlesex Regiment was to raise its complement of men to almost 50,000, expanding from four to twenty-three front-line battalions with a further twenty-three serving in India, Ireland and at home. There was virtually a 100% turnover of personnel during the four years of war. 12,694 officers and men were killed and twice that number wounded, most of them on the Western Front. The front line units required constant infusions of young men like 2/Lt (later Lt-Gen) Horrocks who lasted six weeks before he was wounded and taken prisoner on 21 October, 1914.

The grimy brick towns on the banks of the Tyne and the bleak pit villages of its hinterland were gleaned to feed the ranks of the Durham Light Infantry. Its complement rose to 16 battalions during the course of the war and its casualties equalled those of the Middlesex, over 12,000 dead and double that number in wounded.

Recruiting parties went repeatedly into the great industrial cities and the surrounding villages of Yorkshire's West Riding where they found the men for their County Regiment. The West Yorkshires raised no less than 38 front-line battalions and suffered comparable casualties with the other infantry regiments.

After May, 1916, when universal conscription was introduced, the burden fell more even-handedly, but it was then too late to bring back the lost generation of men whose potential had not been fully utilized by an earlier, amateurish, if heroic system of recruiting. By then a disproportionate percentage of national leaders had been sacrificed, individual communities had been needlessly mutilated and responsibility had passed to less public-spirited men.

The outcome of the four different recruiting processes through four years of war was to render all able-bodied men liable to take up arms. (In the later stages they were joined by very modest numbers of women, although their roles were still ancillary ones).[13] This time, though, unlike service with the fyrds, their service was not for a number of weeks. Many of those Welshmen, Sussex Yeomen, Cockneys, Highlanders and the rest served up to four years in conditions of immense discomfort and danger. Whereas individuals varied widely in their length of service, in their different operational theatres and their particular military responsibilities, the majority had perforce taken on the stamp of the fighting man. For all there was the separation over months and years from their previous environment, a separation which the soldier returning on leave was bound to feel more bitterly as he discovered how remarkably normal civilian society was and how far remote from life in the trenches.

Putting it another way, a whole generation now faced the habitual difficulties which past professional soldiers met with on their release. These were made more serious due to the huge numbers involved, the larger numbers of seriously wounded who survived and because of the severe social and economic dislocation which attended the war.

CHAPTER SIX

The Millions Return

"A man who is good enough to shed his
blood for his country is good enough to
be given a square deal afterwards."

Theodore Roosevelt, 1858–1919

UNLIKE the Second World War with its 'phoney phase', the Great
War hardly gave anyone a breathing space. This was certainly true
in the case of the forces' welfare services. Joint military plans with
the French were for a British Expeditionary Force of six divisions
to be in France within fifteen days of the outbreak. The timetable
was followed closely and in answering the call Reservists left their
wives and families at a moment's notice, some "with virtually
nothing in the house."[1] Young women, many with sizeable families,
were faced with immediate and severe financial problems.

From 23 August, when the BEF clashed with General von
Kluck's superior forces, the casualty lists started appearing and
the wounded began to be carried back to the mother country. From
the outset responsibility for soldiers' families and for wounded
men rested very largely upon two long-established voluntary
organizations.

In the case of families whose breadwinners were away fighting,
financial help was urgently required. Here the Soldiers and Sailors
Families Association stood ready for the role it had performed so
well during the South African War. Repeating the procedure of the
past, Princess (now Queen) Alexandra, as President of SSFA,

issued an appeal for funds and simultaneously another appeal was made by the Prince of Wales to deal with distress arising out of the War. The contributions which they attracted were amalgamated into a National Relief Fund, with SSFA as its agent and distributor.

From the beginning the scale of the task was awesome. During the three years of the previous war SSFA's network of 800 branches nationwide had distributed £1¼m in relief. This time the rate of payments was tenfold that of the previous war – in the first five months alone over £1 m was paid out – but it was not only a question of payment. Before any payment, detailed enquiries had to be made about eligibility and these were hardly straightforward. Many women were married but 'off strength' and unknown both to the War Office and SSFA. Many more married at the very time of their soldier's departure on active service. There were also common-law wives. A furious discussion developed within the organization and beyond over these. Eventually it was decided, and confirmed by Lloyd George in an emotional address to Parliament, that if evidence could be found of a real home, then they should receive allowances. There were unmarried mothers with "war babies". Other dependants also needed assistance, notably mothers. But, with the enormous workload, the latter could not be catered for until the spring of 1915. The vast numbers increased, hundreds of thousands of men flocking to the colours every few weeks. SSFA's Branches, many of which lost staff to the war, were literally working day and night to cope with their commitments. Their problems were hardly eased when they found themselves bombarded by a growing series of circulars from Head Office which aimed to devise clear guidelines from the rapidly changing series of regulations sent it by the War Office. At the same time improved levels of payments were decided upon, 12/6 (63p) a week for wives and 2/- (10p) for each child.

In the early stages some deficiencies in the system occurred, although the delays were comparatively small. These arose for the most part where SSFA's network was incomplete, in large cities like Liverpool or Birmingham or in areas where military recruiting had been traditionally unpromising. New Local Committees were rapidly formed to fill these gaps. Despite the enormous task, the system soon shook down and the voluntary helpers performed their roles with dedication and rare efficiency.

Notwithstanding, the Government determined to assume official responsibility for all regular payments to servicemen by setting up a Select Committee on Naval and Military Pensions.[2] This resulted in the Naval and Military Pensions Act due to come into effect by 30 June, 1916. Austen Chamberlain, that long-time champion of Local Government agencies, was a leading member of the Committee. On the one hand, despite considerable scepticism, he was compelled to acknowledge SSFA's great work: "I cannot speak too highly in my admiration of the way in which the SSFA has attempted to tackle that enormous job. It has done far more than I ever thought it could have done". On the other hand, he did not believe the SSFA should have a monopoly, "[that] SSFA should be the sole pipe so to speak, leading from the Prince of Wales' Fund to the soldiers' and sailors' families . . . having what is practically a public fund administered by a society which is not in any way representative – a self-elected society."[3]

Yet the reason for SSFA's position was simple. It had taken on responsibility for relieving families of those soldiers who were away on active service long before any Government appeared willing to do so. Now the Government Ministry was more eager to take on the task for practical reasons – its earlier measures on old-age pensions had required it to set up a nationwide system of pension offices which could undertake the additional task of distributing allowances to soldiers' families.

It was perfectly understandable, and indeed encouraging, that the Government should, in principle, assume such responsibilities. The field of service pensions had long been a complicated and contradictory one, involving payment by a number of different bodies with different levels for each of the two services. On grounds of logic alone separation payments needed to be brought within the wider system and both the size and nature of the task of dispensing them during wartime had outgrown even a major pioneering body like SSFA.

More surprising compared with the continental countries was the fact that the Government took so long to assume this responsibility. That SSFA, admittedly with Royal support and guidance, had been given such wide powers at the beginning of the war was eloquent of the amateur and voluntary nature of the forces' welfare services in this country. That it coped so remarkably well with such a Herculean task was a tribute to its own thorough pre-planning, its sound organization and the dedication of its members.

Understandably after such remarkable efforts SSFA was none too pleased to be relieved of its responsibilities and to receive precious little credit for its vital contributions. This was the more marked when its experienced helpers found they were still needed to help man the newly appointed local committees. In some districts, despite the Government's decision to assume responsibility by the end of June, 1916, local officials were just not able to relieve SSFA workers until the end of the year. Many of these remarkable lady helpers were convinced that something valuable was going to be lost, that their caring and dedicated attitudes could never be assumed by local paid officials.[4] They were hardly redundant though. Relieved of the mammoth but largely repetitive task of providing separation allowances, SSFA was now able to resume its original role of making discretionary payments to families in need. It was also free to highlight the limitations of the national payment system, and, where they existed, the injustices it occasioned.

When a system conceived and pioneered by a voluntary body is institutionalised changes are inevitable. But important elements remained unaltered. Although the Select Committees would have dearly liked to make separation allowances variable according to locality and need, the precedent of paying standard allowances nationwide was too strong and SSFA's equitable measures here were retained. (These were based on the premise of a wife receiving her pre-war income less her husband's keep.) In this respect families of living British servicemen were treated quite as well as those on the continent, although the scale of widows' allowances generally condemned them to suffer material hardships in addition to their bereavements.

Unfortunately the same could not be said for the men themselves, particularly when they had been wounded. After the first months of the war it became only too apparent that Lord Roberts' seemingly alarmist predictions about vast numbers of maimed men were to be fully vindicated.

Just as SSFA was the pacesetter in assisting service families, so the Soldiers and Sailors Help Society led the way in its concern for the wounded. Like SSFA it fully expected to continue and expand the system established during the South African War. Then it had appealed for short-stay convalescent facilities and, from 1914 onwards, it was to do so again, on a much extended scale. In the first year of the war the public made more than 30,000 beds available. Its main crusading work, though, was among the severely wounded. Admittedly on a small scale only, it had already pioneered both training and sheltered employment for the severely disabled and had organized training for less badly injured men who could resume work under near normal conditions.

From experience the Society well appreciated the therapeutic and practical value of work. Through work men were able to feel they still had a purpose in life and often, through use, many came to recover a considerable measure of mobility in damaged limbs. If they were family men, wages were crucial to supplement the by no means generous disability payments, some of which were due to cease after 7 years. As its Controller, Major-General Sir Charles Crutchley, told the Select Committee on Pensions as early as 1915, "Many cases are coming in of men who have lost an arm, leg or eye in the war and unless these men can get employment the pension rate for partial disablement will hardly suffice." Among the disabled, some men suffering from neurasthenic problems were also taken on, individuals who suffered notorious difficulties with the Medical Boards and Labour Exchanges of the time.

Lord Roberts gave the main impetus to the Society's expansion of its workplaces through the £500,000 subscribed in his memory. A workshop for disabled men which opened at Fulham in March, 1915, was the first fruit, and others were projected nationwide. Further workshops were established in England at Colchester, Liverpool and Newcastle during 1916 and at Burnley and Lancaster in the following year. North of the border a workshop was set up in Edinburgh (a much smaller one had actually existed there since 1906) and during 1920 at Dundee and Inverness. These were subsequently joined by others at Bristol and, much later still, in 1950, by one at Belfast.

At Brookwood injured men were trained, as far as possible, for normal employment. It was the very seriously disabled, who would not otherwise get work, who were taken on by the Society's own workplaces. Their average disability was above 60%; 30% having lost an arm (or the use of an arm) and 40% a leg. The others were neurasthenic cases or men whose physical injuries had "affected their productive powers". By 1922 379 men were given sheltered employment, while over 2,000 in all had been found work.[5]

By any standard this was a remarkable effort. Unfortunately £500,000 didn't go very far where workshops were concerned. As a general rule these needed more mechanization than normal to compensate for their workers' diminished powers. Additional funds were difficult to raise at the end of the war, even for such a good cause. The appeal for the workshop at Inverness, for instance, was kept open by the local newspaper for over two years. Each week it conscientiously recorded local subscriptions, some for as little as 5/- (25p) each.

Although the numbers employed in the Memorial Workshops were to rise further, the scale of the problem far outdistanced any voluntary initiative made to solve it. In 1922 the number of disabled servicemen in receipt of pensions was over 934,000. In addition to this there were others whose pensions had ceased. That so many had survived wounds compared with previous wars was a tribute to medical science; nevertheless almost two-thirds of them had some permanent impairment. Taken from another point of view, 17% of the total British enlistments were to return as disabled.[6] The sum of continued human suffering can only be left to the imagination. Nearly every family could cite a death due to the war and whenever a group of young men came together after it they were likely to include some with missing limbs and other identifiable injuries. 30,000, for instance, had lost one eye (apart from the disfiguring wounds which often accompanied such an injury) and 2,000 returned completely blind. Over 43,000 had lost at least one limb. Of those with lesser wounds some would inevitably suffer physical or mental effects in later life. Many of the 'declared fit' would continue to suffer from the horrific experiences of war. Often they would require to undergo some form of catharsis, ideally in the stability of their previous environment with loved ones and friends, carrying out an occupation they enjoyed.

In 1922 the fledgling British Legion estimated that about 100,000 disabled had found no employment whatever and in the succeeding years of rapidly rising unemployment the total naturally rose even faster than that for healthy ex-servicemen.

During the 1920s the Roberts Memorial Workshops were not the only source of sheltered employment. There were other voluntary initiatives. In general they were quite small, although notable was a disabled village settlement at Enham (subsequently to be taken over by the British Legion) which employed 150 men, and the National Diamond Factories at Brighton, set up through the generosity of Sir Bernard Oppenheimer, initially employing 300. Others together employed another 203. To encourage such arrangements the Government paid an annual capitation grant of £25 per man! In round terms something like 1,000 severely disabled were found sheltered employment in Britain shortly after the war. Even with the further expansion of such places and the entry of the British Legion into this field, the numbers never much exceeded 2,000.

Once more the scale of the problem, this time far, far above any reasonable estimate at the beginning of the war, proved too much for voluntary action supported by derisory capitation grants. The Government itself entered the field, although it did so very late on in the war. And as a result the Society felt its efforts were insufficiently appreciated. All voluntary societies needed praise but Lloyd George was jealous of giving acknowledgement to anyone, especially those well-heeled members of the upper classes bent on good works for soldiers. Their very presence was an indictment of official shortcomings. The Help Society's Annual Report for 1917 put it uncompromisingly: "Though there has been little official recognition of the fact that the society's workers entirely saved the face of the government in dealing with (the) disabled men during the first two years of the war, there is ample evidence that the work has been appreciated by the men themselves and by the public generally."

A partial explanation for such inadequacies in sheltered employment lay in the fact that this form of provision did not represent official policy towards the disabled. Emphasis here was on training them as far as possible for normal jobs. This was in line with the most advanced medical thinking of the day, but, probably more important, it was far cheaper. By 1922 a Select Committee to Investigate the Training and Employment of Disabled Ex-Servicemen could record that 66,099 men had been trained, that 21,358 were under training and that 20,987 remained on the waiting list. However, by 1922 these central training facilities were already being closed down and the Committee criticized them strongly for being inadequate. A likely reason for their premature shutdown was anticipated opposition from the Unions against men achieving a relatively skilled level after a comparatively short but intensive training course. Mr Colin Cooke, a Canadian giving evidence before the Committee, said, "I do not think your Unions would let the seven months men come in [to a three-year trained trade] but our Unions will under special circumstances".[7]

The Committee also found the training system too centralized and rigid where injured men were concerned. During the long waiting periods between training many forgot what they had learnt. In the main their instructors were not ex-servicemen and some were said to lack understanding. Despite the formidable waiting lists for training the Committee noted that central grants for the purpose had been underspent by upwards of a third during both 1920–21 and 1921–22.

Apart from the inadequate training facilities which were rather insensitively and ineffectively conducted and a derisory capitation grant for those offering sheltered employment, the Government sponsored a further initiative for the wounded. This was the King's National Roll scheme, inaugurated by Royal Proclamation in 1919 and due to come into operation by October of that year. This weak measure did no more than 'encourage' firms to take on to their workforce a proportion of disabled employees in return for which in certain cases they 'might receive preferential Government contracts'. By 1922, 30,000 firms had joined, although only about a third of the local authorities had shown enough public spirit to do so. This initiative had many advantages for the government; it involved no expense other than keeping registers in the local Labour Exchanges; it put the onus on the patriotic spirit of employers and allowed Government to escape censure if Business would not accept its responsibilities.

By 1922, only three years after its implementation, the Select Committee found that the scheme was not flourishing and that traditional civilian attitudes to ex-servicemen, even after such a war, were re-asserting themselves. "The voluntary scheme is failing," it said. "It is necessary either to await a revival of trade or to reconstitute the voluntary scheme on another basis or *to adopt compulsion* . . . sentiment in favour of preferential treatment and generally sympathy towards the disabled serviceman is on the decline."[8] The proposal to make it compulsory was tempered with warnings about the possible dangers of industrial trouble, and, with the existing slackness of trade, interference in the market was felt to be dangerous. It might even prove disastrous. The Committee's main conclusions were undoubtedly critical. It estimated that special working arrangements were needed for 20–25,000 men. It acknowledged the efforts of voluntary institutions such as the Lord Roberts Workshops, Enham Village and St. Dunstan's. Yet, with the exception of St. Dunstan's, which dealt with the totally blind, it concluded that their efforts were inadequate and the funding insufficient.

Among its constructive proposals for the provision of special employment was encouragement by financial contributions which would lead to the expansion of the voluntary institutions, the conversion of certain Government factories into further sheltered workplaces, the organization of home industries working on co-operative lines and the canvassing of employers to earmark certain light jobs for disabled men. In respect of Government Training, the Committee argued that it should be made more flexible. Help should be given to candidates who were suffering from a range of disabilities to achieve a certain level of efficiency rather than lay down attendance for any set period.

As far as the King's Roll Scheme was concerned, it should be improved and decentralized. The machinery for administering it through the Labour Exchanges was seen as far too rigid (the Exchanges, for instance, always refused to recognize neurasthenic cases as being disabled) and above all it should be given legal status.

In short the Committee condemned roundly the Government's clumsy and limited arrangements for the disabled. It proposed a system which genuinely combined voluntary initiatives with enlightened Governmental action. "The principle of decentralization and devolution of authority and power should be adopted with a view to making the best use of local knowledge, local enthusiasm and local conditions." It said that, in view of the urgency, proposals should be carried into effect forthwith.

What the Committee's members did not doubt was that most disabled men wanted to work. They quoted one man employed at the new British Legion Poppy Factory who had lost both his legs. He propelled his wheelchair by hand 26 miles a day to and from work. As a demonstration of their practicality, they cited arrangements being made by one of the members, Major Cohen, who was himself disabled, to provide him with an auto wheelchair.

Unfortunately, in keeping with the historic British attitude to ex-servicemen, the Committee's humane and sensible recommendations were not to be implemented. While the individual organizations struggled to expand their facilities with funds garnered from increasingly reluctant contributors, central training continued to be reduced and the voluntary King's Roll Scheme was doomed to atrophy. For, by 1923 unemployment was rising faster in Britain than any other European country and the Government faced it with retrenchment, wage cutbacks, job sharing and other negative measures. During the same year an Interim Report on the King's Roll Scheme was produced and signed by its chairman, Field-Marshal Earl Haig, self-chosen leader of returning ex-servicemen. In face of the national situation, it acknowledged defeat, recommending decentralization of arrangements "without recourse to alternative methods of compulsion".[9] The Report raised the alternative of paying severely disabled men an improved pension at full subsistence level but then destroyed its case by doubting that, in the unlikely event of this being granted, it would be in the best interests of the men themselves. One is forced to conclude that it acquiesced in disabled British ex-servicemen remaining under-privileged not only in comparison with other European countries but also with those of the Empire, like Canada, Australia, New Zealand and South Africa. Foremost in the minds of Douglas Haig and other members of the Council was the strong fear that if firms were forced to employ disabled men they would shed healthy ex-servicemen to create the vacancies and there were already far too many fit men unemployed. It must be said that the Unions exercised a negative influence here. As early as 1915 Major-General Sir Charles Crutchley had observed that "Employers are very chary of taking on men with any disability or physical defect because of the chance of accidents (and the employers being sued by the Unions' legal representatives)."[10]

In national terms, while the near million disabled was a terrible statistic, of even more concern were the healthy men, almost 4 million strong, men who had shown such drive and such spirit in the fighting, whose contribution to the recovery of the country would be so vital. From early in the war the government had considered the nature of the problems arising from the release of such large numbers of men at its end. In January, 1915, a Cabinet paper had been prepared which proposed a month's demobilization leave and free travel home, surely the minimum possible assistance towards their re-integration with society, but more than had been given heretofore. When there seemed virtually no prospect of an early peace, the proposals were shelved and it was not until 1917 that a Committee of Cabinet Ministers – Lloyd George's so-called Ministry of Reconstruction – was formed to consider, among other things, the demobilization and resettlement of a whole generation. As the Prime Minister put it in his high-flown way, it was to mould "a better world out of the social and economic conditions which have come into being during the War".[11]

An elaborate and numerically impressive framework of commit-tees was set up between the War Office, the Ministries of Labour and Pensions and the Boards of Education and Agriculture. In the ideal situation men would first undertake training or conversion training, either immediately before their release or subsequently in Institutes of Higher Education, Workshops or Training Centres, after which they would be offered posts commensurate with their capabilities and aspirations. The reality fell far short of the rhetoric. Many of the proposals for training lacked any adequate structures and were largely unworkable. In employment terms, the main burden fell, as before, largely upon the long-standing voluntary agencies. This time, more than ever before, unemployment showed ominous signs of increasing to massive proportions.

With regard to in-service training, action came too late. It was not until April, 1919, that the Army assumed official responsibility for the educational needs of its troops, and only in August, 1919, that the Secretary of State for War and Air announced to the House of Commons that it had been decided that education was henceforth to be an integral part of Army training. The Report on Educational Training in the Army published in 1920 said that the classic situation of the past where a man of "say 25, improved physically, smartened and disciplined but with no special training to assist him find civil employment was unsatisfactory to the individual soldier, detrimental to recruiting for the Army and *wasteful of manpower to the industry of the nation*". It was, however, far easier to observe upon the situation than to change it.

Frantic efforts had been made to provide educational facilities for the mass armies prior to their demobilization. After the signing of the Armistice schools of military pursuits were converted into ones for skills leading to civilian employment. In 1919 the Army took over a University at Bonn and a number of schools at Cologne. But inevitably this took time. At the beginning of 1919 educational activity was at its highest; in January 195,000 books were sent out to France alone. Quite apart from the lack of time, other immense difficulties were experienced in setting up these new educational establishments. It was almost impossible to gather a permanent team of instructors, since teachers enjoyed priority of release and changed daily. Twin problems caused by changes in personnel and uncertainty as to the military future militated against both rapid and effective organization of education in Germany. In the end only limited results were achieved. A general and commercial college was founded to help any trade or profession to take up the threads of knowledge lost during the war, but its standards were basic. Halfway through the year a dairy farm was taken over and in July an Art Branch opened. A Technical College began offering a limited number of trades to some 300 students. The relatively straightforward training of bank clerks was instituted while all units received a standard set of educational books and technical apparatus.

Unquestionably more educational training had been conducted during the war than ever before, particularly for young recruits, while education of a more general nature had been provided through the YMCA Universities Committee. This had led to the recognition of education as an intrinsic element for all training. Yet at the end of the war time was not available to organize a comprehensive and integrated programme for men re-entering civilian life. While the war had lasted much longer than most had ever expected, when the end came it came quickly and caught people napping.

The significance of the arrangements made during 1919 lay more in the future than in what was achieved for those men who wanted nothing more than to return home. H.A.L. Fisher, speaking at the Imperial Education Conference of 11/12 June 1919, said enthusiastically and extravagantly that "the invention of education in the Army was an invention hardly second in importance to that of firearms". He alluded to the words of the Chief of the Imperial General Staff, Sir Henry Wilson, who had called it "one of those great steps forward in the social progress of the world for which the war had been responsible". The reality was that a smattering of knowledge – no more – had been given to a small proportion of those bored, restless masses. Even this was remarkable enough, given the difficulties experienced by Lord Gorell and his small staff in the, as yet unrecognized, educational branch of the War Office.

Back in civilian life all too many men found themselves unqualified in an increasingly unfavourable environment. Some had joined up fresh out of school. Others who lied about their age had left their workplaces without gaining any worthwhile experience. Many had broken their artisan or professional training cycle to volunteer. All had been away undergoing a most traumatic but hardly relevant experience for upwards of five years.

National training arrangements were partial casualties of the retrenchment and economies which quickly followed the end of the war. These were implemented across the board but no area required special treatment more than that of training young men whose careers had been interrupted by service to their nation. Partly due to Trade Union opposition, insufficient impetus came from the Government towards the provision of vocational training, particularly for skilled industrial work. In 1920, Lord Burnham, a former distinguished chairman of the Resettlement Committee under the Ministry of Labour, commented with sad candour on the limited amount of vocational training: "In this important matter I am afraid that the State has fallen far short of its duty".[12]

Even the training arrangements which were offered could not always be taken up due to the chaos which attended the demobilization scheme. With the best intentions, the Government was determined to avoid the indiscriminate demobilizations which had followed the Napoleonic and Boer Wars, hoping that by a deliberate and ordered timetable the worst problems of unemployment and dislocation, even with the vast numbers involved, might be prevented. In 1916 Edwin Montagu was appointed to chair a demobilization sub-committee which in August, 1917, came under the broad umbrella of the new Ministry of Reconstruction. Montagu's Committee, with representatives from both the services and the Ministry of Labour, drew up a carefully thought-out plan. Due to the fear of unemployment, it was decided that priority of release should be based not on length of service but on employability. Each serviceman was placed in one of five categories. The first two categories were small, embracing men needed to help everybody else demobilize and men vital to the industries of reconstruction. For the other three categories, involving the vast majority, Labour Exchanges were to be used to determine allocation. The third category consisted of those who had been offered jobs. Employers had to fill in special forms to confirm their willingness to employ them and the type of employment they offered. These 'slip men', as they came to be called, were released soon after the start of general demobilization. The fourth category was for men who, while not being offered definite jobs, were normally employed in industries concerned with reconstruction. All the other 'non slip-men' came into the fifth category and were to be released in the order of importance (as decided by the Labour Exchanges) of their normal civilian jobs.

On demobilization, in addition to their four weeks' paid leave and a railway warrant, ex-servicemen were entitled to unemployment benefits of 24/- a week for themselves and up to 6/- for each child. These were to last for a maximum of 20 weeks in their first year following demobilization.

While the scheme had admirable intentions, like so many central plans of the time, it was fatally flawed. Designed to avoid the misery that past ex-soldiers had experienced when unable to find work, it utterly failed in the crucial area of providing such employment. This was left entirely to individual employers. Because of this most men saw it as imposing unjustifiable and unfair delays on their job-seeking. Those last in were most likely to have retained contacts with their civilian employers and therefore were likely to be first out. Those who had joined up first were most likely to have lost all touch with their former employers and when they were eventually released on to a contracting job market they would find all the best potential vacancies had been filled.

Above all, the process, which started as the shared responsibility of no less than fourteen Government Departments, took an unconscionable length of time. The soldiers, especially those who found themselves going out to France again, lost patience and on 3 January, 1919, 10,000 men demonstrated at Folkestone and the next day a further 2,000 at Dover. On the 6th, 8,000 soldiers took part in a mass meeting at Brighton and that same day there were demonstrations in Whitehall itself.

As a result Winston Churchill, War Minister in the new Government after the 1918 election, announced changes which in effect discarded the whole elaborate, unfair and cumbersome process for something much closer to a "first in first out" system. Despite the immense differences in their temperaments, Churchill now came to see Douglas Haig on much more favourable terms than hitherto. He thought it surprising that the C-in-C's prescient warnings on demobilization had been utterly ignored and the

Army left to be convulsed by a complicated, artificial system open at every stage to suspicion of jobbery and humbug.[13] Under Churchill's new arrangements all but 900,000 men were to be released quickly, yet in February, 1920, 125,000 still awaited demobilization. During 1919, the year in which most returned, the employment situation was deteriorating. Prices rose sharply, especially in the case of rents, due to an extreme shortage of housing after the interruption of the normal annual building programmes. It was a year of serious strikes, led by the dockers and the miners, and industrial action even spread to the Metropolitan Police Federation.

For the first time among those looking for jobs there were large numbers of officers as well as soldiers. Edwin Montagu realized this and saw to it that his elaborate system of committees applied to both. For officers there were Appointments Departments linked to the Labour Exchanges' Professional and Business Registers, for soldiers the Labour Resettlement Committees and the Employment Exchange Registers. But it was one thing to set up committees to improve systems of registration and publicity, and quite another when it came to providing actual jobs. Shrewdly the Government incorporated on such committees people long dedicated to helping ex-servicemen find jobs. On all were representatives of the Territorial and Regimental Associations; affiliated were "ex-soldiers aid Associations and other voluntary organizations whose aim is to secure employment for and ameliorate the conditions of the ex-soldier".[14] Thus, very largely, the main onus lay on the same shoulders as before.

Labour Exchanges had the task of assisting everyone, civilians and ex-servicemen alike, but, while they set up Departments specifically to help the temporarily high numbers of discharged men, their normal role was to help civilian job-seekers. Among ex-servicemen their past reputation had not been particularly favourable and the word went round that things were still not all that different. As a result the majority flocked to the bodies trusted in the past, the voluntary employment organizations. As with other welfare societies these responded to the challenge, but the task of finding employment for such great numbers was far too great for them to handle, especially as the delays in demobilization meant that successive waves of men were joining a rapidly worsening job market. Under such conditions, and in the British tradition, organized labour turned its face against admitting into the ranks of skilled workers only partly qualified ex-servicemen. As the historian of the National Association has pointed out, "By adhering rigidly to their own regulations, these unions denied the opportunity of employment to those who had not been admitted to union membership before the war, or who were otherwise not qualified to earn the full trade union rate. Any dilution of labour by those whose skills were not considered to be up to the required standards was strongly resisted."[15]

Under the circumstances the voluntary organizations achieved wonders but received little or no governmental assistance. In fact, due to retrenchment, the most petty and ill-advised economies were exacted on them. In 1919 the National Association, for instance, had half its miserly central grant withdrawn at a time when it was struggling to reopen some of its forty-five branches closed during the war. At the 1921 Annual General Meeting Lord Salisbury referred to its achievements as "a record of good service conducted with insufficient means", but during 1919 its London Office had been choked by the number of applicants trying to register for employment. The majority were inevitably disappointed.

The financial constraints under which the National Association laboured and the unfavourable employment situation led to only 8,378 being placed during 1919/20.[16] This was far below the number achieved either at the end of the Boer War or during the annual placements in the immediate pre-war years.

The situation was the same with the other voluntary bodies. Despite the multitudes who besieged them, they were seriously hampered by previous staff losses and limited funding. The Corps of Commissionaires had less members at the end of 1922 than before the war and in 1919 the oldest voluntary body, the Army and Navy Pensioners' Employment Society, found the odds too great. It decided to close and transfer its Army work to the National Association.

By 1920 there were virtually no new posts to be found, despite widespread short-time working. In November, 1988, the author interviewed Victor Vercoe, an old contemptible of 93 in the Star and Garter Home. He had witnessed the very first engagement of the war, yet had been retained until 1920. When he was finally released there were no vacancies in his own trade of pharmacist and he went to the Corps of Commissionaires for work. The officer who interviewed him there advised him to return in about four or five months time. As he left their Head Office in Exchange Court and walked down the Strand he saw many men, including one of his officer friends who had the medal ribbons of MC and bar, standing in the gutter trying to sell matches or shoe laces. He was lucky enough to get a job with a London newspaper, due solely to his slight acquaintance with Lord Rothermere. After so many years he still spoke with anger of those many other brave friends in arms whom he felt were treated so shamefully.

In Britain at the end of the First World War it was the fate of a whole generation to suffer like their soldier forebears. As a generation they included men of greater ability than the typical soldiers of the past but there were so many of them and external factors exacerbated the problem, the size of which seemed beyond a Government still with collectivist ambitions but without the will and determination to establish more fruitful co-operation between voluntary and central organizations which could break the sad pattern of history. As in the past it could virtually ignore influence exerted by soldier MPs or through sporadic campaigning in the Press. Numerous official committees and carefully drafted, if sometimes misguided, regulations too easily met the expectations of such critics. These were, of course, quite inadequate without complementary financial commitments. No government could have prevented the increase in unemployment worldwide, but during the war it showed a reluctance to accept responsibility early enough or to co-operate wholeheartedly with those already in the field. As a result the voluntary bodies had to take on far greater responsibilities than they were ever designed or capable of assuming, particularly in the case of disabled and unemployed servicemen. The enthusiastic support which all such bodies received from members of the Royal Family was unparalleled in other countries and this doubtless played a part in allowing central Government either to assume its responsibilities dangerously late or to allocate inadequate resources towards the amelioration of such massive problems.

In other countries pressure groups on behalf of the forces were not so trammelled by historical precedents and the continental powers were traditionally far better disposed to the needs of their ex-land soldiers than the British.

Small wonder then that during the war men concerned with the difficulties already being experienced by the wounded and fearful of the age-old difficulties which were again likely to be suffered by British fighting men at its close were active. The result was the creation of new bodies on behalf of ex-servicemen who pledged themselves to compel British Governments to recognize their responsibilities and give these men a square deal afterwards. How they fared in the immediate aftermath of war has just been demonstrated; how they were to fare in the following years we must now see.

CHAPTER SEVEN

The Legion is Born

"The four million men who have
returned from our armies have not been
able to make their influence felt
sufficiently to find places for their
unemployed colleagues."

Earl Haig, Conference Dinner,
Leicester, 13/11/20.

THERE was a compelling reason why new organizations dedicated
to the cause of the ex-serviceman should arise during the First
World War. With the ascending scale of British and Empire participation it was inevitable that men who had never done so before
would become involved with the military, either directly or by
association through relatives or friends. No longer would the
affairs of ex-servicemen remain the province of those voluntary
associations established after previous conflicts. In the widest sense
the manhood of the nation shared the experience and paid a terrible
price for its patriotism. The nation severed its young men from
their communities and homeland, their jobs and professions, and
their loved ones. It brought them to see death and suffering in
every conceivable form, destroyed their innocence and, for many,
inflicted irredeemable physical or mental damage. Such injured
men were now too numerous to be cast off like so many earlier
soldiers. They were owed a debt which it was impossible to repay
fully but at least they had the right to expect there would be

equitable and thorough arrangements to help them resume their former existence.

Given past precedents there were, as we have seen, growing suspicions, almost amounting to convictions, that at the war's end difficulties over demobilization and obtaining civilian employment might occur in the pattern of the past although on a vastly increased scale. Yet if only all those who served together could unite within a body dedicated to achieving equitable treatment afterwards what Government would dare deny their just claims?

The first fruits of such thinking was a major new society formed to represent the interests of ex-servicemen called **The National Association of Discharged Sailors and Soldiers**. This was formed as a result of a meeting in Blackburn during September, 1916, when the costly Somme Offensive was grinding to a halt. It came about largely through disillusionment with the seemingly callous woundings and deaths of so many working men and through mistrust of their likely treatment afterwards. Affiliated to the Trade Union movement, it associated itself with the Labour Party. Its clear political relationship represented a novel development in ex-servicemen's organizations.

Such an initiative was bound to produce a counteraction from other men who feared their own political views were being neglected. The result was the **National Federation of Discharged and Demobilized Sailors and Soldiers**. Preliminary discussions had been held in late 1916 but it was not formed until April, 1917. The Federation was led by a Liberal MP, Mr J.M. Hogge, and was wedded to that party. It soon became more powerful than the Association and from the outset had a strong anti-officer bias, only admitting those officers commissioned from the ranks. Supported by the Liberals, it waged a vigorous political campaign, notably against the Military (Review of Exemptions) Act of 1917. Due to growing manpower shortages for the services, this laid down conditions whereby disabled men, or men who had previously been rejected, were required to have a medical re-examination to consider them again for 'further service in the Armed Forces'. In the event the 'combing process' was applied much too rigidly and loud protests from the Federation, among others, led to a Select Committee re-examining and revising the provisions of the Act and the recruiting system of the time. Led by a civilian politician rather than an ex-soldier, it was overtly political and even put up its own ex-service candidates for the General Election of 1918. All were defeated.

Partly as a counterbalance to the specific political initiatives of the Federation a third ex-service society was formed, **The Comrades of the Great War**. The initiator here was a Conservative MP, Lieutenant-Colonel Sir John Norton-Griffiths, who had served under Lord Roberts in the Boer War and in 1914 had raised the 2nd King Edward's Horse. He viewed with alarm and repugnance the activities of the first two organizations. To Norton-Griffiths a soldier should keep clear of politics, certainly clear of extreme political positions which were not of his persuasion. Lord Derby, the Secretary of State for War, was persuaded to send a 'private' letter to all Lords Lieutenant and Chairmen of the Territorial Force Associations enlisting their support for the new society, which he described as both non-political and democratic. One can imagine the reactions of the first two organizations to this semi-official approach. Many distinguished people, including Field-Marshal Lord French, the Duke of Westminster and the press barons, Lords Beaverbrook and Rothermere, attended the Comrades' inaugural meeting held at the Mansion House on 13 November, 1917. On this occasion the sums subscribed or pledged totalled £35,000. With such support the Comrades quickly became a powerful body which deliberately challenged the first two, particularly the Federation.

As if there were not enough, in the spring of 1919 these were joined by yet another body called the **National Union of Ex-Servicemen** or the NUX. Its timing was not irrelevant; by this time a number of serious industrial problems had arisen. The NUX was pledged to support organized labour, including ex-servicemen. It was aggressively left wing and some of its members floated bolshevik ideas.

The fish of different hues which circled each other in the eddying pool of ex-servicemen's affairs, a pool fed in its upper reaches by a turbulent stream of men discarded from the forces before it disgorged them into the rock-strewn rapids of civilian life, were joined by yet another. It was a larger, sleeker fish even than the Comrades, adept at self-protection, which aroused the envy and suspicion of the others. This was the **Officers' Association**, itself formed at the strong urging of the Commander-in-Chief, Field-Marshal Earl Haig, from eleven previous Officers' Help Societies. This, the most tangible demonstration so far of Haig's enthusiasm for his veterans, came after a succession of earlier initiatives on his part and was itself a halfway house towards his ultimate goal, one unified body representing all ex-servicemen regardless of previous rank.

Haig had long been conscious of the difficulties which many officers were experiencing on their return, particularly the large numbers who had been promoted from the ranks. For instance, on 20 February 1917, he had written to the Secretary of State for War demanding adequate pension schemes, medical benefits and or-ganized work plans for disabled officers.

"I strongly urge that there should be no dealing with this matter which if allowed to continue will constitute a scandal of the greatest magnitude".[1] His letter was disregarded and the demobilization scheme which he drew up in October of the same year was also ignored until unearthed by Winston Churchill in 1919.

The inaugural meeting of the Officers' Association was held on 30 January, 1920, also at the Mansion House. Apart from Douglas Haig, it was attended by the other two service chiefs, Admiral of the Fleet Earl Beatty and Air Marshal Sir Hugh Tren-chard. With such an august patronage it attracted public donations of some £637,000, and 18 months later, on 30 June, 1921, was granted a Royal Charter.

With five rival bodies one might justifiably conclude that unity in ex-servicemen's affairs would be well nigh impossible. For-tunately, in that particular British fashion, even as the rival bodies were being formed other men were frantically working behind the scenes to fashion a unified movement and significant developments had taken place.

Two men long associated with ex-servicemen's affairs were responsible for the first efforts in this field. They were W.G.

Clifford, the ex-gunner turned author, who had earlier founded *The Employment Gazette*, and Major Jellicourse, a veteran officer of the Royal Sussex Regiment. Whereas Clifford used his pen to considerable effect, it was Jellicourse who in the summer of 1918 brought the leaders of the rival bodies together under the chairmanship of General Smith-Dorrien with himself as Secretary. Unfortunately this attempt at unity failed, but it led to a second one which was sponsored by the three Service Departments, with Haig as the major influence behind the scenes. This called for a conference under Sir Ian Hamilton and representatives from all ranks of the three services and the Women's Auxiliary Forces attended. The bait to unity was custody of the massive profits from services' canteens during the war, but the Federation and the Association could not agree on common action. The money was then put in the hands of a distinguished figure, Lord Byng of Vimy, for distribution through the United Services Funds and under Byng's prompting some of it was used to build a considerable number of ex-servicemen's clubs all over the country.

Union seemed as far away as ever, but the current industrial unrest and the particular difficulties facing returning servicemen made further moves towards unity crucial. While Douglas Haig was ranging the country on behalf of the needy ex-officers and arguing for one Officers' Association he was, at the same time, working to bring the various ex-serviceman's organizations together. Simultaneously certain changes were occurring within the separate organizations themselves which made unity more likely. The Association largely sloughed off its Trade Union and Labour connection and, by late 1919, came much nearer to the Comrades in its general approach. In January of the same year Mr J.M. Hogge resigned the Presidency of the Federation and within months it amended its rules to admit all commissioned officers.

In any case its exertions, together with those of Douglas Haig, had already succeeded in getting the Government to improve the pension position for wounded men. With this success and the advantages it brought to many ex-servicemen, the Federation was becoming rather more wedded to the establishment than to its earlier *enfant terrible* stance.

While at first sight the formation of a separate Officers' Association might be viewed as yet another divisive force, its very success led in the other direction. It had come about through amalgamation and seemed all the stronger for that and its success in attracting substantial subscriptions had 'mopped up' the spare money which the Comrades had hoped to attract in order to broaden their own financial base. In a final attempt to confirm their position as the premier society, the Comrades now approached Douglas Haig to become their President. Although he was already their first Life Member, he refused. Haig urged on their spokesman, Colonel Crosfield, the need for a united ex-service organization for officers and men alike. He let it be known that this was the one and only organization he would be honoured to lead. Having united the different Help Societies into the Officers' Association, the next logical and necessary step was to unite all ex-servicemen's bodies into one great organization.

From now onwards Haig's great influence was crucial in the movement towards amalgamation. In the late 20th century after the inevitable denigration of him as commander and man, followed by the equally predictable reaction in his favour (led with particular distinction by John Terraine), it is difficult to appreciate fully the immense regard in which he was held by those he had led and the depth of his feelings for them. Conventional wisdom, perhaps too easily, sees his work for ex-soldiers arising largely from some sense of guilt. This is not borne out by his letters to his wife who herself saw his work for ex-servicemen as a perfectly logical progression from his responsibilites for them while serving. Notwithstanding, despite the many books subsequently written about him, he remains an enigmatic figure whose innermost feelings were always cloaked by habitual reserve and lack of ease in conversation.

Haig has attracted contradictory assessments even among his personal staff. John Charteris, who served so closely with him in India and during the war, emphasized the soldiers' regard for him as their leader. Acknowledging Haig's absence of small talk, he still maintained that, "if they did not love him, the respect in which the Army held Haig amounted almost to veneration."[2] More eulogistic still and far less reliable were the (ghosted) writings of his soldier servant for over 25 years, Sergeant Secrett. Secrett vouched for his chief's indifference to personal danger (a quality agreed upon by all), but his attempts to demonstrate Haig's sense of humour were laboured and unconvincing.[3] Perhaps they revealed more about the truth than the author intended. They showed Haig enjoying the irony of situations, if totally lacking the ability to make witticisms about them. Two more of his staff re-emphasize the markedly different reactions he invoked. Major Sir Desmond Morton, his ADC for the six months to April, 1918, wrote to Captain Basil Liddell Hart in scathing terms about Haig's separateness. "He was certainly tongue-tied in anything like public speaking. He was anyway a silent man but such silence was babbling compared with what he said when he gave an oral instruction instead of a written order. You had to learn a kind of verbal shorthand made up of a series of grunts and gestures."[4] Morton, doubtless chosen as ADC partly on the grounds of his own verbal facility and social graces, went on to become personal assistant to that master of language, Winston Churchill. He was plainly mystified and out of sympathy with a leader who had reached the pinnacle without oral skills or ease in human relationships. Harsh commentator that he subsequently became, he expressed no doubts, though, about Haig's capacity for physical, and moral, courage. An opposite approach was taken by another close colleague, Padre G.S. Duncan, who served Haig for well over three years of the war. In old age he produced a book, published in 1966, with the express purpose of contradicting writers who, while not knowing their subject personally, presented a portrait, as he saw it, which was "so distorted as to be essentially false" and because he believed the time would seem to have come "for a fresh appraisal of his greatness both as a man and a commander".[5] Duncan, a distinguished and analytic man who afterwards became Principal of St Mary's College in the University of St Andrews, had no reputation to make from his book. He felt that Haig, despite his non-volubility, had a quality of disarming sincerity. There were no doubts in his mind either about Haig's sense of purpose; to him it always ran true.

Wherever the truth lies about Haig's personal 'daimon', there was no denying his deep concern, not just for his 'gilded staff officers', but for all those who served him, though he was unable to express it in emotional terms. It had to be expressed in those regular and private letters to his wife, or revealed, on occasion, to his Padre.

Being strongly conservative, Haig feared new ideas and above all instability. He was by no means the first senior military commander to do so. To his thinking the Army approached the ideal state in so much as it represented a vast body of admirable men united together in a great, selfless, patriotic mission. After visiting the Somme battlefields he wrote to his wife, "I have not the time to put down all the thoughts which rush into my mind when I think of all those fine fellows who have given their lives for their country or have been maimed in service".[6] In a letter of March, 1917, he once more declared his "tremendous affection for those who are ready to give their lives for the Old Country at any moment . . . . I feel sad at times too at the thought of how much suffering is in store for many of these brave fellows before the war can end."[7]

By this time Haig's concern for his men embraced not just their present trials in battle (he was confident that despite all the sacrifices and possible reversals they would eventually be successful) but looked to the time when they would be no longer under his direction. The steadfastness and single-minded application he had shown during the war (a quality which enabled him to accept the terrible casualties sustained in some of his set battles) was transferred to the cause of his men after their service. This made him the deserved and unchallenged leader of the ex-servicemen's cause.

He was now a towering public figure, for, despite the shutters he put round his personal feelings at the end of the war, both his army and the British public at large showed their unquestioned pride in and affection for him. After Haig's death Ernest Raymond rather ingeniously attempted to explain why the soldiers should act like this by arguing "that the name of Haig will be one of the most picturesque names in our history, by reason of his very lack of picturesqueness . . . the huge temporary army of the 1914–1918 war . . . were simple direct people, a quiet obstinate crowd . . . and they knew, without knowing they knew, that they were commanded by a man after their own heart".[8]

Whatever the reasons, he was unquestionably popular. When, on 19 December, 1918, he came home to join his family for Christmas this seemingly undemonstrative man revealed himself very moved by the extent of his reception.

"I have taken part in many functions but never before have I seen such crowds, or such whole-hearted enthusiasm." After a reception with the King and Queen Haig returned to his home in Kingston Hill to find a crowd of 10,000 with torches and three bands, mostly workmen and women from the Sopwith Aeroplane works. He wrote that "such a spontaneous welcome . . . shows how the people of England realize what has been accomplished by the Army and myself."[9]

The euphoria continued during the Allies' great victory parade on 19 July, 1919. The papers reported that Haig received by far the loudest accolades of all. As the *Liverpool Echo* put it with unashamed emotion, "The wounded wave their crutches, legless men clap, armless men stamp and shout of one accord 'Good Old Duggie'. It is a delirious, unforgettable scene."[10] With more measured tones *The Times* endorsed the enthusiasm of the crowds towards their wartime Commander-in-Chief.

By now Haig the victor felt an indivisible bond for the men who had made it possible. Henceforth his life mission was to support and defend the brave men from that Army as they embarked on their most difficult campaign yet, re-entering the less ordered, often hostile and meaner-minded world of civilian life. On 19 November, 1918, he publicly rejected the Viscountcy offered him by Lloyd George because of the injustices suffered by disabled officers and men. Some have maintained that the real reason was because French, the leader he replaced in France, had already been made a Viscount. He was undoubtedly piqued on his own behalf but his concern for the disabled had already been shown on a number of previous occasions. For instance in a letter to his wife five months before, on 30 July, 1918, he had written about the State's duty to help disabled officers: "The voluntary funds should be in addition to state aid" (not instead of it). Over a month before his rejection of a title, on 4 October, 1918, he made his personal pledge to his wife that he would "give not only money, but *all the energy which I may have left after the war is over* to help disabled officers and men who have suffered in this war".[11] Lady Haig proposed their giving £5000 and he arranged for that sum to be transferred from his funds in France.[12]

He was equally faithful to the promise of giving his energy. After his death his wife wrote about his unstinting application. Shorn of his wartime staff, he admitted that he worked even harder for old soldiers than he had as C-in-C during the war. What is more, he endured a new cross which he hated, the endless speech-making to drum up support.

By rejecting a peerage he achieved his aim of compromising the Government, especially as Beatty (the First Sea Lord) had already accepted one. He remained impervious to the persuasions of Henry Wilson, Chief of the Imperial General Staff, who assured him that the disabled were well looked after by the service charities, and even the King who also intervened unsuccessfully on two occasions. It is impossible to visualize any other leader who would have been able to withstand such pressure.

When, in February, 1919, Haig's Private Secretary, Philip Sassoon, went to discuss the pensions and award question with the Minister, he was under the clearest instructions that no personal awards would be accepted until the Government accepted its responsibilities towards the disabled. Only at the beginning of March, 1919, when Haig was satisfied with the Government's new proposals (the former Pensions Minister had been sacked) did he accept an earldom and a grant of £100,000. In 1921, as a result of a subscription by his countrymen, he was also presented with Bemersyde, the ancestral home of the Haigs.

At a time of industrial unrest when severe difficulties were already being experienced by many ex-servicemen, Haig was criticized in some quarters for accepting the monetary award but he responded with succinct and, some might say, distinctly Scottish logic "that refusal to accept . . . won't benefit the ex-soldier. More important, the Government has promised to do its duty in the matter – indeed the whole country is now behind me in its determination to see that these gallant fellows and their dependants are properly treated".[13]

During the years 1919–1921 other awards were heaped upon the wartime leader and right up to his death in 1928 his diary was filled with functions at which he was principal speaker and guest. In the first three years after the war these tended to be freedoms of cities or corporations; later he acted as chief guest at the inaugural ceremonies for the major war memorials, while also attending more humble ones in his border homeland. On no occasion did he lose the opportunity to remind his listeners of their duty to returning servicemen.

It was only reasonable to expect that the ex-serviceman's organization created and headed by Douglas Haig should be both large and influential. Without his unyielding drive to unify service organizations they would probably never have become united. There were more reasons for the leaders of the existing organizations to agree on some loose grouping with common interests than to submerge their identities within a great new unified body. But to Haig the diverse elements within the ex-service organizations were anathema; unity was everything to him. He probably came to cherish it through his belief in the fundamental Scottish upper class virtues; hard work, a strong sense of purpose coupled with a common feeling of humanity with all men and, above all, deep loyalty to one's country and society. At the end of the war his quest for unity even extended to religion. Attending the General Assembly of the Church of Scotland in the summer of 1919 he made an appeal for unity among all the Protestant churches of the Empire. He argued not on doctrinal grounds but because an Imperial Church would surely help to bind all the Empire together. But this early ecumenicalist was still realist enough to acknowledge there would be difficulties in such amalgamation as far as the Roman Catholics were concerned!

The unity which evolved from the different ex-service organizations did not, of course, depend on Haig alone. Two other men, T.F. Lister and J.R. Griffin, President and General Secretary respectively of the Federation, did outstanding work in the difficult and protracted negotiations, and there were many others, like Colonels Crosfield and Heath, who were skilled and dedicated workers. But Haig was the supreme leader and his presence in setting the foundations was crucial. However, from the time of the industrial collapse at the end of 1920 actual starvation was increasingly significant in persuading ex-servicemen to sink their differences. Relief was desperately needed.[14] Without unity ex-servicemen could not benefit fully from the National Relief Fund and in December, 1920, representations from the four different organizations met to discuss joint arrangements for the receipt and distribution of such relief.

The detailed negotiations in the process of amalgamation are not our concern here.[15] The climax came on 14 May, 1921, when the Draft Constitution was approved. On the following day, in pouring rain, before the Cenotaph in Whitehall four men representing the four rival societies (the NUX had already gone its own way) went forward and each placed a laurel wreath at its base. Big Ben struck 9 am and when the notes died away four buglers of the Foot Guards sounded the 'Last Post'. On the Cenotaph was a wreath holding all four badges, symbol for the burial of disorder and the birth of that which Haig had long sought, unity. The road had not been an easy one and marks of the bitter and prolonged discussions were left on the unified body. (Probably little is worse than honest but material divergencies between like-minded men.) Its very title was a compromise for the Comrades nearly seceded over the issue. Compromises can, it is true, produce brilliant solutions but some criticized the name British Legion, as lacking the incisiveness of title given to veterans' organizations in other countries. Perhaps it is typically British, sonorous and dignified, with no immediate indication where its objectives or allegiances lie. For the very same reasons it is a title which can endure.

Unity came first in the coming together of the National Headquarters of the four bodies. This was no easy matter and in the *British Legion Journal* the General Secretary, Colonel Heath, described vividly the attitudes of the staffs from the original bodies "in their sects and sections—hackles up, suspicious, mistrusting, jealous, disliking each other with an almost brotherly hatred." The staffs of the National Executive Council were, if anything "worse—much worse—bristles vertical—claws out—swords drawn".[16]

At town and village level it was apparently even more difficult to achieve unity. Where a number of organizations existed either a merger was needed (no easy thing where proud independent local officials were concerned) or each one had to be given local autonomy as new branches of the Legion.

By 30 June, 1921, though, the Unity Relief Fund came under the British Legion, and the Officers' Association became the Officers' Benevolent Department of the Legion, subsequently reverting to its original title. Although, sadly, it was decided that women should not be eligible for ordinary membership, the National Executive Council set up a separate section for them, and, by May, 1922, there were 115 women's branches under their separate Royal Patron, HRH Princess Mary.

In the British fashion, by way of endless meetings both centrally and at branch level, the organization took hold and a new era thus opened for the ex-serviceman. During a war in which the nation's manhood had been mobilized on a scale undreamt of, the state had eventually been compelled to accept wider responsibilities for returning men. Now a new voluntary body had been formed, which, unlike its predecessors who were committed to helping special categories of ex-servicemen or to perform particular functions on their behalf, represented all. With the huge numbers of ex-servicemen, it had the potential to keep British Governments up to their commitments and to end the traditional neglect of such men when peacetime concerns became uppermost. There was no question of its aims being dismissed on the grounds of their superficiality, for among them was the hope that a brotherhood of ex-servicemen from within the Empire and beyond would constitute a powerful force towards continuing world peace.

CHAPTER EIGHT

Poppies and Privation

"There are many thousands of ex-servicemen still unemployed, there are many widows and children whose means are slender, there are tuberculous men who need special care and there are the disabled for whom the finding of employment is still a pressing need."

The Prince of Wales, Poppy Day, 1925.

BY mid-1924 unemployment was soaring and from its very birth the British Legion faced a massive crisis. The 250,000 unemployed ex-servicemen in 1920 had risen to over 600,000 out of a total approaching 2 million. As Graham Wootton expressed it:

"The land fit for heroes turned out to be a land in which heroes were selling bootlaces and matches in the streets, going with their families into the workhouse and tramping the heedless countryside in a vain search for work. . . . Tragedy became commonplace, deprivation and suffering entered innumerable homes."[1]

What could be done? The prime need was for selective reflation, together with especial and effective arrangements to help them find suitable jobs, and, when they wished it, the opportunity to acquire recognized civilian skills which the years away had denied them. But reflation was utterly at odds with contemporary economic doctrine and Lloyd George would not antagonize the powerful unions, already responsible for serious industrial unrest, by granting significant concessions in either the training or employment fields. At the top end certain universities offered shortened degree courses but the booklet on demobilization and employment issued at the point of release made no mention of other training concessions.[2] Ex-servicemen had to apply for places on technical and professional courses in the same way as everyone else, although doubtless the educational authorities would try to exercise some flexibility on their behalf. What was more, except for the disabled, the numbers who could qualify for grants while training were very restricted.

Could the British Legion induce the Government to amend its policy? This was hardly possible during its early months. How could it speak legitimately for those myriads of men who, on shedding their uniforms, were yet to join its ranks in any substantial numbers, men dispersed across the country re-establishing ties with their loved ones? In the initial stages most were able to find some sort of employment only to start losing their jobs when the economic downturn came to a far greater extent than 'normal' civilians. Apart from an understandable lack of 'know-how' about changed working conditions and an inevitable degree of restlessness, the hallowed principle of 'last in, first out' operated heavily against them.

The new pressure group was also constrained at the end of the First World War because no one could deny that the state had assumed more responsibility for its newly returned members than ever before. It was responsibility, though, largely of a negative kind, not by way of imaginative training nor employment arrangements but through the wholesale granting of unemployment relief. Granted for an initial 20-week period, such payments, along with their humiliating means tests, came to be extended indefinitely. The opportunity to work was what men needed most and although, mercifully, neither they nor the Legion realized it, a hard core of unemployed servicemen were to receive such unemployment benefits for fifteen interminable years until from 1935 onwards rearmament for the next conflict began to revitalize the job market. By then a proportion were virtually unemployable.

In the early stages, the Legion's main attention centred on the disabled where the most tragic cases were occurring. Although the state had assumed responsibility in the time-honoured fashion of granting pensions, these were pitched at a low level with many shortcomings in the arrangements and some cases of plain injustice. Douglas Haig had already drawn attention to a range of problems here which he viewed in the context of the state not fully accepting its liabilities. When receiving the freedom of the Skinners' Company he declared:

"Government had to be reminded of its responsibilities to provide more cash" (on a scale quite beyond the resources of any grouping of charitable organizations). Before the Legion's formation he had not been unsuccessful. "By badgering the state into facing up to its obligations for its fighting men an extra £104m (had been) allotted to the needs of those who fought for us and suffered in the fighting."[3]

From such reasoning one could be tempted to conclude that the Legion's essential role would be to act as an effective pressure group on behalf of the ex-service community and the only funds it required would be those to keep its administrative machinery in being.

The reality was far different. A major charity, when it identifies pressing cases, often the result of official delays and confusion, needs to be able to offer immediate assistance of its own. In the main such funds have to come from voluntary sources. Some money was made available, notably from the wartime profit of the Services Canteens (Byng's Millions) and the United Services Fund. But this was mostly for cases of distress through sickness (£2m was apportioned for such relief during the years 1919–1947). Another major source was the National Relief Fund which became the British Legion Relief Fund. Money was also being raised and spent by the long-established charities who gave grants, often of a modest nature, to individuals in distress. Special assistance came from newly established charities like St Dunstan's (1915), the Ex-Services Mental Welfare Society (1919), and the "Not Forgotten" Association (1920).

It soon became clear that, over and above such sources, the British Legion needed its own funds as befitted an organization of great potential, both to keep its structure viable and from which sums could be allocated to relieve distress, for instance, among its unemployed members and for other particular charitable objectives which captured its interest and compassion. As to its day-to-day running, the Legion was kept solvent chiefly from capital held by the Officers Association, although it anticipated that members' subscriptions, set at the very modest level of 2/6d (12½ pence), would soon grow large enough for the purpose.

Special efforts were urgently needed to built up its charitable funds. On the 7th Anniversary of the declaration of War an appeal was launched under Douglas Haig's signature. By this time the numbers of unemployed ex-servicemen alone had soared through the one million mark and distress was widespread. *The Times* endorsed the appeal and explained where the funds were needed. Apart from the vast numbers of men out of work who suffered privation, there were the widows and children of the dead.

"A large number of these persons require assistance to eke out the pensions and allowances they deserve from public funds. . . . There are wives of fallen officers, educated ladies whose husbands were in good positions struggling to keep themselves and bring up their children on what is after all a pittance. . . . There are ex-officers who threw up fine business and professional careers to serve their country when the call came. They returned to find their places occupied and their chances gone and are now seeking too often in vain to earn a bare livelihood. . . . There is an extensive clearance of men discharged from the Army who were given civil posts during or after the war."

The needs of ex-servicemen and their dependants who came from a full cross-section of the population were clearly different from those of an earlier generation of more humble fighting men with their wealthy gentlemen officers.

The *Times* article did not content itself with appealing for funds, it wondered whether more could be done to provide openings in the British Overseas States and went on to criticize the unhelpful attitude of the Trade Unions towards ex-servicemen and the fallacy of their proposals for such unreal bodies as national workshops.[4] Here were surely two issues that the British Legion, as a pressure group, could be expected to pursue. A creditable £10,400 was raised from the Appeal but much, much more was needed if the Legion was ever to gain the financial muscle required by a genuinely national organization.

Providentially, in the same month a form of appeal was suggested which was ultimately to bring almost unimaginable funds on a regular annual basis and, in the process, grant the Legion a special role and place in the nation's consciousness. Its origins were truly international. Among the Canadian contingent in France was a medical officer, Colonel John McCrae, of McGill University, who had previously served as a gunner during the Boer War. There in his crude first-aid post during a lull in the second battle of Ypres he wrote a poem which he called, "In Flanders Fields". It went as follows:

In Flanders fields the poppies blow
Between the crosses, row on row,
    That mark our place; and in the sky
    The larks, still bravely singing, fly
Scarce heard amid the guns below.

We are the Dead. Short days ago
We lived, felt dawn, saw sunset glow,
    Loved and were loved, and now we lie
        In Flanders fields.

Take up our quarrel with the foe:
To you from failing hands we throw
    The torch; be yours to hold it high.
    If ye break faith with us who die
We shall not sleep, though poppies grow
        In Flanders fields.

Colonel McCrae sent the poem anonymously to *Punch* and the juxtaposition of red poppies and their cross-like centres with the graves of men who had shed their blood and died for their country made a deep impression on many readers. Flowers had stirred the emotions of British poets and simple soldiers on a number of previous occasions. The roses plucked by British infantry at Minden over 150 years before as they went forward and, against all odds, inflicted a crushing defeat upon French cavalry are still commemorated each year by the successors of those who fought there. They place roses on their hats and bedeck their colours and drums, while after the Minden Dinner each officer eats a rose petal out of a silver finger bowl containing champagne. But the Flanders Poppy was to stir the conscience of whole nations over the sacrifices of their manhood. It was to become both the symbolic *raison d'être* and the financial life blood of the British Legion. Colonel McCrae himself died in France in January, 1918, which gave his poem added poignancy.

Among the readers of *Punch* was an American, Miss Moira Michael. Miss Michael persuaded YMCA representatives and then American ex-servicemen to adopt the poppy as a universal emblem of the dead from the Great War. Nine years later, in 1930, she wrote to Lady Haig explaining her original idea. As she put it, "In a high spiritual moment of my life . . . the memorial poppy inspiration came to me from reading the poem "In Flanders Fields" during the morning of Saturday before the Armistice in 1918."[5] During 1919 Miss Michael began her 'Memorial Poppy program' to raise funds. As the sales of poppies increased, she was helped by a Madame Guerin who arranged for French widows and children from the devastated areas of Flanders to make artificial poppies for her. In August, 1921, Madame Guerin arrived on the doorstep of the newly-founded Legion, showed them some of her artificial poppies and suggested they also adopt the idea as a way of raising money.

To the credit of the Legion's staff, particularly its General Secretary, the proposal was adopted (quickly endorsed by Haig himself) and the first hastily arranged Poppy Day was, like Moira Michael's initiative across the Atlantic, a great success. It confirmed the purpose of the Legion to remember their dead comrades in an inspired yet practical way, by urging public donations for the survivors who were suffering the traditional problems of returning men, exacerbated by the extreme economic problems of the time. The first Poppy Day's yield was £106,000, tenfold that of the recent *Times* appeal.

To prevent unauthorized versions the Legion poppy was registered and steps were taken to have quantities of them made in Britain. Again it was a rather involved but heart-warming story. In 1920 an ex-Sapper officer, Major George Howson, founded the Disabled Society with the primary aim of bringing about improvements in the quality of artificial limbs and other mobility aids for disabled servicemen. In this he was strongly supported by Sir Brunel Cohen, MP who had himself lost both legs and was to become the Legion's first Treasurer and its leading activist in the House of Commons. After learning about the process of making artificial flowers, Major Howson approached the Legion with a proposal that disabled ex-servicemen should be given the opportunity of manufacturing its poppies. This was agreed to and £2000 was made available from the Unity Relief Fund to establish a Poppy Factory. It began as a small workroom in East London just off the Old Kent Road which had been offered by a sympathetic collar manufacturer at a nominal rent. Five badly disabled ex-servicemen made up the original staff.

The demand for ever larger numbers of poppies each year seemed virtually insatiable; in 1930 about 30 million were produced, although the takings from annual 'Poppy Days' remained on a plateau during the worst years of the depression. In 1926 Poppy Day raised £272,426; by 1928 the sum was over half a million pounds and this level was maintained, at a time when the cost of living fell, until it rose to almost £600,000 in 1939. As the demand rose so did the employment opportunities for badly disabled men. By 1925 the factory had been moved to Richmond Hill where it employed about 190 men and this figure was to rise to almost 400 by the beginning of the Second World War. The numbers employed at Richmond far surpassed those in any single workplace established by the Lord Roberts Workshops. (In 1926 as a result of Lady Haig's prompting a second and separate Poppy Factory was opened in Edinburgh for disabled Scottish veterans which by 1928 employed 47 men.)

By such means the British Legion obtained the regular financial supplements it required for assisting needy cases over and beyond the state's provisions and for adopting major initiatives of its own for specially deserving sections of the ex-service community. At the same time it became a major employer of badly disabled servicemen and confirmed its position as the national body responsible for commemorating the nation's dead, a circumstance which gave great encouragement to the large numbers of Poppy Day collectors. Nearly 300,000 volunteers regularly came forward during the 1930s. From the beginning the burden of selling poppies fell largely on the Women's Branches both north and south of the border. (This daunting task of standing for long hours at windswept street corners during a dark November day continues to be shouldered with unquenchable enthusiasm and cheerful endurance by many who are now long in years.)

After such a cosmopolitan and rather hesitant beginning there seemed no end to the 'poppy story'. In 1922 nearly 23 million poppies were produced. They came to be *the* symbol of family commemoration throughout the country. Not only were they worn on coat lapels, fixed to the front of bicycles and motor vehicles but in some working class districts of both London and Edinburgh (and doubtless in other towns too) each year an additional poppy joined those already placed around the edge of photographs or around mirrors hanging above pictures of lost loved ones. In 1929 Major Howson had the idea of starting an Empire Field of Remembrance by planting poppies in the grass outside the national churches of Westminster Abbey and St Margaret's. This proved an immediate success and three years later poppies, attached to small wooden crosses, were planted also in Edinburgh and Cardiff.

In the euphoria of the poppy movement it is all too easy to forget that, although annual Poppy Days might give the Legion an inspired source of income through the nationwide contributions from ordinary people united in their homage to the dead, they alone did not make it a great organization. In the major role that Haig conceived, i.e. as a great and effective force both nationally and internationally, the size of its membership was crucial. In any case funds raised from the sale of poppies were never used for maintaining its administrative structure, which relied on the members' subscriptions.

During his address to the Federation at the Unity Conference of 1920, one of the arguments Haig used for the creation of a single body was that the 4 million returned men had not been able to make their influence felt. If they were ever to achieve this a significant proportion of that number would have to join the new Legion.

From the first the Legion's structure was clear. Its democratic nature was represented by a pyramid. At the base were the nationwide branches with their selected officers. Above them stood the National Executive Council, also the result of democratic voting. At the apex were the elected National Chairmen and President. During Annual Conferences motions originating from the Branches were voted upon and if carried by a majority vote (a $\frac{2}{3}$ majority was required for changes in the constitution) they were implemented. (In practice, over the years certain sifting processes have developed over proposed motions and the National Executive Council has ample time to consider them and, if necessary, to prepare its own counter-arguments.) Notwithstanding, no one, neither the President nor the Chairmen, can fail to carry out the terms of a motion supported by the specified majority of delegates at Annual Conference. No motion, however critical – or even outrageous – if supported and seconded by individual Branches can fail to be debated at Conference.

A sound bone structure was one thing, but to flourish it needed the flesh and blood participation from those millions who had served. Initially they failed to come forward. Surprisingly their reluctance did not become general knowledge. Haig's stature and the well-publicized unity campaign led the Press to credit the Legion with a membership proportionate with such high ambitions. At its foundation in May, 1921, *The Daily Telegraph* had put the Legion's strength at between 2–3 million and in June *The Times* mentioned 2 million. The reality was very different. At the end of 1921 affiliation fees had been received from some 18,000, rising to 43,000 or so three months later.[6] The papers could be excused their optimism (Legion officials would hardly be keen to correct them too vigorously) when they were told that by the end of March, 1922, there were 1728 Branches (including 10 overseas). Each Branch, though, had an average of just 25 members and many had considerably less.

Why, it might be asked, was membership so low when so many

ex-servicemen patently needed help? As ever the answer depended on no single cause. Certainly Haig's dream of 4 million men still united through the selfless suffering and comradeship of war acting as an irresistible force was hardly more substantial in the Britain of 1922 than Prospero's dream world of Shakespeare's *Tempest*. The unity of ex-servicemen had always been more evident on the continent and in the United States. After the Great War it was seen to remarkable effect in New Zealand. Yet it was utterly at variance with British military and political tradition. British servicemen had already demonstrated in the clearest way possible during the long chaotic period of demobilization their common heartfelt wish to get back home. This is evident from both the oral and written evidence in the Imperial War Museum. The exceptions, and they were few enough, came mostly from officers, some of whom were still star-struck with the dazzling responsibilities of having men's lives in their hands. In this context Captain (later Brigadier) A.E. Hodgkin wrote with the brash confidence of the young, "In spite of their glaring faults I have been very happy with [my special Company RE]. . . . If only they'd make the Army a well-priced profession nothing would induce me to leave it for the ramshackle business of civilian life".[7] Another officer, ambitious, newly-commissioned, Second Lieutenant Thorpe-Tracy, a former platoon sergeant, wanted to win his spurs on active service as an officer.[8] If soldiers were reluctant to go they almost invariably had special reasons. One who was in no hurry was a Wireless Telegraphist, B. Neyland. He wrote: "Infantrymen were very anxious to get home with their families. . . . But I must confess that we were having such a good time that I wasn't in any hurry to get demobbed." Sapper Neyland played his soccer and rugger matches in the assurance of a guaranteed position afterwards with the Post Office.[9]

For the vast majority their consuming wish was otherwise; the eager volunteers of 1914 had changed due to their sombre experiences, while conscripts, by definition, normally had no wish to retain their military connections any longer than necessary. The vast majority of men yearned to pick up the threads of their former lives, ridding themselves of military or para-military associations.

It was remarkable how quickly the one-time citizen soldier could revert after the war had been won into a sturdy civilian, independent, bloody-minded, his loyalty rooted in his family and home locality, harbouring suspicions about joining any nationwide organization, however admirable its declared objectives might be. This was especially so if such an organization smacked of an episode which was past. Harold Clegg, a Liverpool Rifleman, spoke about "men from one district being entirely different in outlook and speech from the men from another district, foreigners almost".[10]

After the war many men returned to their village and, with luck, to the same job. One such veteran was interviewed in 1989 when, in his 90s, he was still living in the village of his birth. In old age he greatly appreciated the assistance and comradeship which the British Legion brought him but immediately after the war he had wanted nothing of it.

Apart from their very insularity there were other reasons why British ex-servicemen 'dispersed' at the war's end. In an age of high unemployment they concentrated all their energies on getting or keeping their jobs. If unemployed, they had already approached other servicemen's organizations traditionally committed to the problems of job-finding and they might feel they could hardly spare even the modest membership fee of the Legion. In any event the Legion had already pledged itself to help all ex-servicemen whether they were official members or not. It was also, as yet, too early for many to develop the nostalgia and urge to recount past campaigns with old brothers in arms. For some, from the end of the war onwards the ex-serviceman's club came to represent a haven, but many clubs had been set up through arrangements with the United Services Fund. The majority of these would eventually come over to the British Legion but not for some years, and many men active in their Club's affairs never became active Branch members.

Both the President and Chairman were alarmed about the limited membership. Haig appealed to ex-servicemen, saying they could "no longer tolerate being the pawns in a three-cornered game of destruction, played between Government, employers and trade unions". They therefore must rally together to become a strong and powerful influence in the country. T.F. Lister warned prophetically that "just causes unaccompanied by the pressure of numerical strength pursue a slow and tortuous path".[11]

By early 1922 Haig, realizing the seriousness of the situation, undertook a drive for membership. In March the Press were invited to a special lunch at the Savoy and circulars signed by him were despatched to civic and clerical authorities all over the country. Both President and Chairman stumped the country and it was decided to award a cup to the branch responsible for bringing in most recruits.

Disappointing as the membership figures were, they did not stop Haig behaving like the leader of a major national organization. In Liverpool he emphasized "the importance of the British Legion not only to every ex-serviceman but to the General Public". It would press for something to be done for the half-million men eking out a miserable existence on the dole, for the unfit who needed representation about their pension rights (12,000 cases had been handled already) and the 35,000 ex-servicemen who had contracted TB as a result of the war. Because of its international contacts would-be emigrants could be assisted through the British Empire Services League.

At Birmingham he was even more confident and assertive in defining the Legion's great work, much of which depended on keeping the Government up to its responsibilities:

"The British Legion makes for industrial peace. [It] has three main spheres of work, combative, benevolent and social.

"Combative: One must be combative on behalf of the fit ex-serviceman who is still vainly seeking for work . . . but official bodies are often glib of promise and we must be active and vigilant to see that, other things being equal, the ex-serviceman really does get preference.

"Benevolent: Unless there is a great society whose business it is to watch over the interests of the disabled, the orphan and the widow, their interests will suffer at the hands of the state. . . . It is often thought the Anglo-Saxon temperament prefers a voluntary to a compulsory solution of its problems but *justice must override sentiment.*

"Social: These British Legion Clubs should be in most cases the solid background of our movement."[12]

He had great ambitions for them, even maintaining they could be a great advantage "in stimulating general education".

At the same time Haig lamented the present indolence of his wartime comrades, "The chief danger confronting us is that through the easy-going temperament of our race the ex-serviceman may not take sufficient interest in the one organization which can protect his legitimate interests until too late and consequently thousands of our comrades will not achieve the comfort and happiness which is their due after all that they have suffered."[13]

1922 culminated in a Great Autumn Rally and Sports Meeting at the Crystal Palace attended by the Legion's Patron, the Prince of Wales. On the day of the rally there were 1970 branches (by the end of the year 2089) and at the end of December membership reached about 116,000, still very small in terms of its national pretensions and aims but an increase of about 100,000 in the twelve months. At the same time the women's section had grown to 126 branches with a membership of about 6,500.

Despite its small membership, the Legion could cite the large numbers of ex-servicemen who, enthusiastic in their approval of its work, stood ready to join. With Haig at its head and Lister an outstanding Chairman, whose great powers were essential to cement its still fragile unity, it demanded regard from Governments of the day.

Regard was one thing, action another. Could a new pressure group far more ambitious than earlier organizations, headed by the country's supreme wartime leader, and purporting to represent all ex-servicemen, succeed where they had not? Could it change the course of British military history where the ex-serviceman had traditionally received less than justice on his return to civilian life?

Sadly, by the time it was established, three years after the war, the fleetingly brief span wherein great opportunities lay, had passed by. Towards the end of the war and after it Haig and others had orchestrated pressure on the area of greatest need, the disabled and their dependants. Improved pension arrangements were conceded. Special training was offered by the state for the unparalleled numbers of disabled men (however insensitively and rigidly applied it might have been). But their limited levels of skill and very physical deficiencies made them prime candidates for dismissal when the economic situation deteriorated. If the King's Roll Scheme had only been compulsory (like schemes adopted in other countries) the disabled would have been protected, but by the time the British Legion and its President became closely involved with the King's Roll Scheme they knew it was unrealistic to propose compulsion.

By this stage the greater, and traditional, problem was being revealed. Ex-servicemen not in receipt of disablement pensions were experiencing grave difficulties in their search for jobs or were losing those which they had obtained, often by heroic exertions. Due to the rushed and inadequate training arrangements offered them during their last months of service and the lack of preference granted by civilian institutes many still possessed only rudimentary skills and were obvious candidates for unemployment when more competitive conditions applied. Moreover, there was a problem here because guaranteed employment for the disabled would only have caused more fit men to be dismissed.

While the state could not be accused of ignoring its returning masses – in the context of improved social conditions generally it could hardly do so – its arrangements were hardly extensive nor particularly successful. The British citizen soldiers suffered like their red-coated ancestors of previous centuries. Their demobilization arrangements had been bungled. In-service training opportunities to acquire basic skills were hurriedly set up and superficial in content. If they wanted further training after demobilization they had to compete for places in the nation's Colleges or Institutes. Those seeking jobs got most assistance from the voluntary employment agencies established during the preceeding half-century, but these were overwhelmed by the numbers involved. Men wanting to take up landholdings found their opportunities to do so strictly limited. Employment opportunities for the disabled relied solely on the public spirit of private employers. The returning men found housing in short supply and only limited measures being taken to alleviate it. The central grant for local authorities to improve housing stock, which had seriously deteriorated during the war, was just £200,000 in 1921. Leeds' share, for instance, where there were at least 33,000 houses in atrocious condition was no more than £4000.[14] In these and other respects the ex-serviceman could conclude he had hardly received plain justice for hazarding his life for his country.

It was the British Legion's fate to witness growing problems for even larger numbers of men now becoming unemployed when all members of the nation were suffering from serious economic difficulties. The fact that they would not join the Legion limited the effectiveness of its efforts to support them in this grave situation. This did not prevent Haig, for one, from repeating energetically his accusations about the Government's failure to make national provision for his men.[15]

The tragedy of the British Legion's relatively late formation can be seen against arrangements made in other European countries and in the Empire. Among Empire nations New Zealand was outstanding. A paper circulated to ex-service delegates attending the Empire Conference of 1922 showed what could be done. The benefits negotiated for ex-servicemen were said to be "the outcome of persistent representations made to the Government by the New Zealand Returned Soldiers Association during the war". This had a wartime membership of 70,000 men when the Army which went on service overseas was just 100,000 strong. During the war 57% of these were either killed or wounded. As the paper proudly stated, "the problem of successful repatriation for those who returned has been solved by the co-operation of the Government and the Public. The former have introduced important repatriation legislation (on the determined prompting of the Returned Soldiers Association) and the latter has co-operated with the Government in giving preference to returning soldiers seeking employment."

The outcome contrasted with that in the mother country where lack of legislation betrayed the Government's fine promises and where the Trade Unions opposed any acceptance of part-trained men.

In New Zealand, an agricultural country, far more men could

return to the land. Through the Discharged Soldiers Settlement Act, passed as early as 1915, Crown Lands and freehold properties were made available and balloted for by returned soldiers. Advances of no less than £2500 were made to any soldier wishing to purchase a farm with a further £750 for stocking it and £1000 for building a house there. For those not wishing to purchase, rented properties were available with protection for returned soldiers against ejection. (Largely as a result of continued pressure by the RSA during the 1920s and 1930s the Government amended the value of land which soldiers bought at the inflated rates operating towards the end of the war and agreed many claims for mortgage relief.) Soldiers wanting to set up in business were offered loans of £300 with a further £75 for those about to be married.

For the disabled, pensions were more generous than those granted in the UK, up to £3.10.0d with a further £1 for wives and special hospitals run on enlightened lines were provided for all those who had contracted TB.

In the matter of training, comparisons with the UK were particularly striking. For the fit a subsidy of £3 a week was added to the wages of returning soldiers learning new trades, and all men who, because of their wounds, were unable to continue their pre-war occupations were offered training for appropriate trades. Education and tuition were provided free for all soldiers whose studies had been interrupted by their war service.

End of service gratuities were at the rate of 1/6d a day for every day spent overseas. Special concessions were made to those wounded or hospitalized and dependants of deceased men received a minimum of 2 years' gratuities. On average gratuities were three times higher than those for UK soldiers.* The Repatriation Department had its own efficient employment agency and placed 21,250 soldiers in suitable employment. With considerable pride it could say that during the previous 12 months (to 1922) the numbers awaiting employment had never, at any time, exceeded 150.[16]

* Returning British soldiers rarely received a gratuity greater than £25 and many had far less.

It is fruitless, but intriguing, to wonder how different the situation would have been in the home country if an organization like the Legion had been formed during the early days of the war and legislation had resulted from carefully drafted provisions rather than being the fruits of a chaotic group of committees within the Ministry of Reconstruction which worked to a very tight schedule.

From its foundation the Legion faced the problem of how best to make its voice heard with other competing groupings. The powerful unions were beyond its reach and the obvious avenue for influencing policy seemed to be through Parliament. Once more tradition played a major part. While the American Legion, for instance, could and did work through particular political groupings, its British counterpart, with the Prince of Wales as Patron and Douglas Haig as President, could not take the same path. Involvement in Party politics was anathema to Haig anyway. It went against his master principle of unity and he distrusted politicians as a race, while at no time could a future king be seen supporting any political party, even indirectly through an alignment with the British Legion. If effective moral pressure was to be exerted upon individual governments it could only come through a great national organization backed by strong public opinion. The British Legion had not yet reached this stage.

With the rejection of party affiliation, its Parliamentary influence depended largely upon those MPs, whatever their political colour, who favoured the cause of the ex-serviceman. In the past they had never constituted a powerful group, for MPs who embarrassed Governments by their outstanding knowledge and enthusiasm for military affairs had tended to be "captured" fairly quickly and offered Ministerial responsibilities. Haig tried to unify the "soldier MPs" by proposing a Parliamentary Section of the British Legion. This immediately produced an alarmist reaction from the left-wing *Review* which confirmed that, for some, the spectre of Cromwell still existed: "From the fact that it will be composed of members from every quarter of the House he [Haig] draws the comforting conclusion that the interests of the ex-servicemen are removed from the sphere of party politics. . . . Now that Lord Haig's intervention threatens to make it de rigueur for

139

the politician to represent its interests we can only hope that the
. . . sense of proportion of the British people will prevent it becoming a source of corruption in our politics."[17]

The Review's fears were groundless since the group of soldier MPs after the First World War was no more significant than in earlier times. For example, hopes might have been raised when, during May, 1922, Sir Brunel Cohen successfully moved the appointment of a Select Committee to examine and report on the employment of disabled men. Yet this represented no breakthrough. Such initiatives had occurred in the previous century, and the findings of Committee and Commissions were all too likely to be ignored. The Legion, in the person of J.R. Griffin, its able Assistant Secretary, spoke before the Committee, but its recommendations when they came remained at variance with the practice of most other countries. It proposed giving the voluntary system a further trial, with a 'tightening up' of the administrative arrangements.

The problem of exerting Parliamentary influence was also hampered by unexpected changes of Government. With the collapse of Lloyd George's Coalition in October, 1922, the Legion attempted to gain influence by submitting a questionnaire to all candidates so, as it phrased it, "Branches could be made aware where their interests stood in relation to ex-servicemen's concerns". It was not a success. A high proportion of the new MPs declared themselves greatly in favour of the Legion programme but they were hardly prepared to defy the Government's whips for it. Haig's own strong Conservative allegiance persuaded him not to hound the new Ministry too hard for, as he wrote to Colonel Crosfield:

"I think it will do the Legion no good to attack the Government publicly at the present moment. . . . Personally I don't think it possible for the country to get a better Government than it has for the time being. I certainly don't want to strengthen Lloyd George's hands and restore a coalition of rascals. . . . I am in friendly correspondence with the PM regarding a decoration for Lister *and believe we can get more from friendly discussion than by open attack in the Press.*"[18]

During 1923 the Legion had to content itself with inaugurating a campaign against unemployment, the centrepiece of which was a proposed work loan of some £200 million to provide employment in public works, and Haig for one was not convinced that such a definite amount should have been specified at all.[19]

This attempt to exert pressure was broken by a further General Election in late 1923 which resulted in a setback for the Conservatives and the country's first Labour Government. In September, 1924, the Legion initiated a National Work Drive with the aim of finding work for as many of the 800,000 unemployed ex-servicemen as possible. Haig inaugurated it with a broadcast from 2LO, but once again the change of government meant the work of lobbying ministers had to begin all over again. In November the Conservatives returned. Since its formation the Legion had witnessed political as well as economic instability. Already three General Elections and four changes of Administration had taken place. Perhaps, it was hoped, with a Government likely to complete a full term, one which already knew about the Legion's main objectives, more significant progress might be reached. It was not to be. The King's speech contained nothing about the special employment claims of ex-servicemen, even with over 800,000 of them unemployed. J.R. Griffin thought even these figures understated the problem. He estimated that 88% of the total unemployed were ex-servicemen and he feared greatly for the physical and mental effects of prolonged unemployment on them, saying, "Despair is rapidly making many of our men unemployable."[20]

In short, though much that was positive had been achieved, the Legion's main aim to alleviate the widespread unemployment experienced by the typical ex-serviceman, who was young, semi- or unskilled, and whose life struggle so far had taken place in the demi-world of the trenches, Gallipoli beachheads or harsh prisoner-of-war camps, where conditions were beyond the imagination of his civilian contemporaries, had failed. Given the circumstances described it is hard to see that it could ever have succeeded.

Under the circumstances one might have expected its position to be diminished. Just as the New Zealand Returned Soldiers Association lost membership once its main objectives had been achieved, many might have turned from the Legion in despair at its unsuccessful attempts. This was not the British way in ex-servicemen's affairs. All the major voluntary organizations on behalf of ex-servicemen had the common feature of being long-standing through thick and thin times. From the rebuffs of its main campaign the British Legion turned to other ways of helping the ex-servicemen which were more easily achieved. From initial frustration it was to become a major and growing force. There was to be no shortage of long-term initiatives in both the national and international field. Some of the latter were idealistically inspired and, after Haig's death, to prove monumentally wrong. Nationally it was to get its fingers into many pies in an effort to ameliorate the tragedy of unemployment and, as the years passed, so it gained in stature and dignity, with great rallies fronted by ranks of waving standards and its immensely impressive Remembrance ceremonies. What was more, after their initial family building the men began to yearn for the comradeship of those terrible years. By instinct their first loyalty would be to their own Ship, Regiment or Flight, but in the clubs of the British Legion and at Remembrance Day ceremonies they could forget the monotony and dullness of contemporary living conditions and recapture the excitement, sacrifices and selfless heroism of the past.

Those men of the First World War are now almost all gone from Legion Clubs and from life but from the written and oral records held in the Imperial War Museum and by interviewing others yet surviving the author has gathered a series of vignettes from that group who were quite different from others before them, although sharing the sufferings which were the common lot of earlier ex-soldiers and which are by no means absent among contemporary ex-servicemen.

The conclusions, tentative as they must be, were that in the main they did not query the reasons for their going to war. They accepted that Britian was right and that the war had to be won. They were remarkably uncritical both about the conduct of the war and their difficulties on returning to civilian life. Some felt the betrayal of promises about a land fit for heroes but most were stoical and uncomplaining. The majority showed relatively little interest in public and world affairs, lacking the broader critical awareness of their successors in the Second World War. As young men, they preceded the revolution in communications, when men's senses came to be assailed through mass-circulation newspapers, endless commentaries transmitted on radio's sound waves about matters both great and peripheral and the unique visual and aural impact of talking movies (whose double-feature programmes included news features).

While as sensitive as any generation, to the young men of the Great War conformity was the norm. Most left school on their 13th birthday so their schooling had been limited. Learning was often by rote and enforced through strict discipline (under the system of payment by results a teacher's efficiency relied upon the evidence of written and oral learning demonstrated during their annual inspections).

They came from communities which were both clearly stratified and regional in nature. Most servicemen had travelled very little before enlisting and often never far from their home localities. Although religious observances were to weaken during and after the war the soldiers of 1914 were widely influenced by the codes of Christian and patriotic duty expounded during their weekly church attendances or earlier at Sunday School. The church was often the centre of their social and recreational activities and many of these prior to 1914 had military connotations, like the Church Army and the Boys' Brigade. Many churches also ran their own Scout Groups.

Strong patriotic influences worked on them, specifically through such youth organizations and the new Territorial units, especially active in the rural areas. The newspapers played their part, conscious as they were of the Empire's relatively increased vulnerability and the likelihood of a great conflict to come. So too did the songs and sketches in the Music Halls, unfailingly chauvinistic during the early years of the twentieth century.

Societal pressures to conform continued during the war. A noted example was the white feather campaign implemented with great but unselective enthusiasm by young ladies who were largely unaware of the horrors across the channel. Thomas Painting was awarded the Military Medal for being one of the first prisoners of war to escape from Germany into Denmark. He returned to Britain suffering from both frostbite and malnutrition. On his discharge from hospital in Newcastle he was allowed to go into town immediately prior to entraining for his Depot in Winchester. There he was straightaway given a white feather by a zealous young lady.[21]

It is typical that he should recount this incident without rancour or emotion. His generation was slow to anger and because of it was more difficult to mobilize on its own behalf after the war.

The statistics of the million disabled have frequently been quoted but many others who were nominally fit suffered physical and mental effects from their service. While some were bitter and vociferous in their misfortune the vast majority were stoical and uncomplaining. Many had injuries which shocked those with whom they came into contact. John Joseph Pickard, a private with the Northumberland Fusiliers, who served on the Western Front from 1916–18, was wounded in the face and received early plastic surgery which was only partially successful.[22] In his home locality of North London the author recalls an ex-serviceman, 'Mac' Standen, who first drove for a firm that specialized in weddings, then for the local undertakers, Blake and Horlock (the wedding firm suggested he move to the undertakers). He too had sustained serious facial injuries. Part of his jaw was shot away and as a result the right side of his mouth twisted downwards, his right eye had a permanently shocked, demoniacal expression and his speech was slurred and harsh. As he sat in his cab during funerals on cold days his puckered skin would take on a blueish tinge and large tears from his right eye would form and roll down his grooved cheek. For almost forty years of his working life he had to witness the shocked expressions and whispered asides of adults at his frightening appearance and the unrestrained and raucous shouts of taunting children. His normal reward from people already affected by the emotional nature of such occasions was in stiff measures of alcohol. When he had the chance he usually poured most of these away into conveniently placed aspidistra pots. On no day could he forget the effects of the war but he continued with seeming passivity and outstanding fortitude to carry out his duties.

One man who was unquestionably disabled was Henry Taylor

of the Lincolns. While serving in France he was wounded twice in the legs. On the second occasion all the others in his small group were killed. Alone he gazed at his badly shattered leg and, by using his bootlace, prevented himself from bleeding to death.[23] On his admittance to hospital, it was amputated. As he wrote imperturbably, "I served 2 years 261 days in the Army. It was a period of great experience. I spent some very happy days and some not so good. I shall always remember the happy times but prefer to forget the others."

The better-educated and more worldly-wise soldiers were usually much more critical, but they were the exception. Harold Clegg of the Liverpool Rifles was undoubtedly well-educated and eloquent.[24] He had previously been a cashier with the White Star Line Shipping Company in Liverpool and had become a victim of mustard gas, largely because an NCO who was both ignorant and a martinet had forbidden his platoon to move from the hollows where the gas lay. Initially blind and unable to speak due to burned vocal cords, he lay in Winchester Military Hospital. There among the beautiful countryside he wrote in the manner of Siegfried Sassoon:

"The woods, the birds and the sound of church bells ringing on a Sunday made it hard to realize that the world had gone mad; it seemed a long way off from the artillery fire; the men with their heads and legs shot off; the men with their intestines hanging out of their stomachs; the men blown to pieces of flesh by whizzing bangs . . . the men going mad with shell shock, the groans of the wounded and the glassy eyes of the dead."

Clegg was eighteen years old when he enlisted, with a fine physique; after being discharged as medically unfit it was five years before he fully recovered. As he said, "In the early days of May, 1919, I returned home; the war of nations was finished; the battle for existence had begun." Clegg got his old job back but his peace of mind as well as his health had been lost. He felt betrayed but his cry was a cry of pain and regret rather than one for action:

"During our absence the old order had changed; the genteel of 1914 were gone, blatant riches reigned in their stead; money was the power in the land; money that had been reaped from the bodies of the dead. This was Victory. The War to end War."

For every Clegg there were scores who, although not impressed with the arrangements made for their return to civilian life – the poor-quality suit (they couldn't even keep their old greatcoats) one month's paid leave in which to find a job and a small gratuity – took their sacrifices for granted.

A Cockney soldier, Walley Claydon, who served with the Middlesex Regiment and was wounded on the Western Front, remarked of his traumatic experiences, "Poor old Tommy had to take the can back every time". But there was no anger over his treatment at the end of his service. He just reported how he had been demobbed at Crystal Palace where he handed his overcoat in.[25]

There was Wally Clarke who volunteered for the infantry, "because going into the Army was an honour and fighting for your King and Country". Wally had also been gassed. Temporarily blind, he was vomiting continuously for three days until he regained consciousness.[26] Horace Manton served both in the Dardanelles and the Western Front. He was twice hospitalized. When asked as an old man whether or not he regretted volunteering he replied, "Didn't regret volunteering . . . I went up . . . I thought I would fight for me country and just went in. No, I never had any regrets for it myself. I was just glad to get on with it. I volunteered. I took it. I've got to get over it."[27]

James Tolley who was in Mesopotamia for 3 years, when asked years later whether his service was worth it, replied "Necessary evil. I expect I would have done it again," and when asked the same question William Dawson with the Sussex Yeomanry on the Western Front replied, with the touching pride such men seemed to have, "I am glad I experienced it to know what I went through for other people."[28]

In many respects those who suffered most were those made prisoners of war. While they escaped the risk of continuing combat they faced other problems – humiliation, boredom and impotence while in the hands of their captors.

Some, like Thomas Painting, felt that it was a disgrace to be taken prisoner. As he said, "It broke my heart. I thought I was a better man than Jerry, you know, man for man. But there it is. It broke my heart."[29] All prisoners during 1914–18 suffered from problems of bad diet and discomfort, some more than others. In an extreme case, Sergeant T. Simpson of the Lancashires had the misfortune to spend over $2\frac{1}{2}$ years in captivity under the Bulgarians. His introduction was a stockinged march (his guards stole his boots) of 100 miles in five days. The prisoners were without food for the first three days and then given one black loaf a day. He was made to work on a railway where for over three months he had no proper wash, no medical assistance and was frequently beaten. The British soldiers' conditions improved dramatically after the intercession of the American Consul (America was not at war with Bulgaria at this time), but other nationalities continued to be treated abominably. With the improved conditions, some of the British then seemed to give up: when they were hospitalized a number went mad and others died.[30]

Due to poor food over a long period many prisoners of war suffered physical problems later, while others developed phobias as a result of the brutal punishments allotted them. Corporal 'Nutty' Edmed, a captive in Germany who lit a fire to make porridge against orders, was awarded ten days' detention which he spent in complete darkness on bread and water. For the rest of his life he couldn't stand being shut up.[31]

The reactions of many released prisoners were more self-critical than deprecating of the authorities, either during their incarceration or afterwards. Thomas Painting, after venturing into Liverpool from hospital and being given his white feather, was then refused any payment for his journey to Winchester. Arriving at Waterloo late at night he found there was no train to Winchester until the following morning and so he spent his first night out of hospital in the Salvation Army Dosshouse in Waterloo Road. He related this in a dry, matter-of-fact, non-recriminatory way.

Nutty Edmed, on being asked what effects his captivity had on him – he was 15 on joining up and $19\frac{1}{2}$ when discharged – said, "I think sometimes I might have made more of my life if there had been no war . . . always thought I was capable of learning, doing more."

Due to the particular environmental factors which operated upon the young generation of 1914 and to the immemorial reactions of British ex-soldiers they were not easy to band together into a formidable pressure group. In the main they were hardly eloquent. In fact, like their leader, they found it immensely difficult to communicate verbally with civilians about their terrible experiences. Victor Fagence, a machine gunner in France said, "In common with most of the men returning from the front, we didn't talk about it much then. Very peculiar. I probably answered questions."[32] Charles Quinnell, MM, who lost a leg in France was even more forthright: "One thing I really noticed was that after being with the young fellows in the Army we were a race apart from civilians. You couldn't talk to civilians about war, they hadn't got the slightest conception of what conditions were and so forth. So after a time you didn't talk about it."[33]

They had pride in their endurance and sufferings (however pointless they were later to feel the war had been). Like other soldiers before them they knew they had stood up. They, unlike the eloquent Clegg, contented themselves with being wryly observant of post-war difficulties. Anger was to come in the next few years at the humiliations suffered by some of their mates, but then it was too late. "Bloody terrible, no one could get a job."[34] In the main they never saw the British Legion as some great military Trade Union which could force Governments to give them special help. They had been given the initial privilege and subsequent curse of the British fighting man, and, although service charities might help, they each had to endure their fate.

CHAPTER 9

Honour the Dead, Serve the Living

"Ex-servicemen never became a separate,
let alone a violent political group as they
did in some countries. Their
organization, the British Legion, over
which Haig presided, brought all ranks
together on a more or less democratic
basis. It voiced their grievances when the
need arose and sometimes exerted
discreet pressure on parliamentary
candidates. Its usual activities were
benevolent and social. The war was, of
course, not forgotten. There were new
memorials in every town and village; the
grave of the unknown soldier in
Westminster Abbey; and the Cenotaph."

A.J.P.Taylor,
English History 1914–45

A.J.P. TAYLOR'S dessicated, admirably cogent, but con-
descending summary of the British Legion's mission – without a
mention of the work done by other service charities – fails utterly
to acknowledge the ambitious plans or the ferment of activity in
ex-servicemen's affairs during the 1920s and throughout the next
decade. This paralleled the struggles and rebuffs experienced by
many of the returning masses. Only when the many attempts to
change things were frustrated, and frustrated they undoubtedly

were, did the Legion come to spend the greater part of its resources on benevolent and social work.

Haig and his colleagues were in no doubt from the outset that they had a fight on their hands to redress serious injustices. This was the combative role of the organization which he outlined at its founding. In his case there was never such "calm of mind, all passion spent" as was inferred by Taylor. After the early, at the time almost single-handed, crusade by a major public figure on behalf of the disabled, Haig ceaselessly addressed the issue of the ex-servicemen who remained unemployed in far greater numbers than civilians. This continued until his death. It should not be forgotten, either, that the Legion's first Chairman, T.F. Lister, and its Assistant Secretary, J.R. Griffin, had been doughty fighters when leading the Federation and certainly had not lost their taste for a struggle, while Brunel Cohen's advocacy both in the House of Commons and elsewhere was fearless, and Colonel Crosfield, for many years Haig's right arm and subsequently the Legion's second Chairman, was even more ambitious in the international sphere than Haig himself.

To some extent the number of different ideas flying about and the task of building up a nationwide organization led to some dissipation of effort. Haig's ability to sustain pressure in Britain was inevitably affected by his attendance at allied ceremonies in Europe and when establishing his British Empire Services League, whose biennial conferences required him to travel for weeks at a time on journeys to, for example, South Africa and Canada. But they had positive results. His visit to Canada, for instance, caused the coming together of all their ex-servicemen organizations into the Canadian Legion. He plainly considered the trips worthwhile for he envisaged a powerful connection between the League's higher aims of achieving greater Empire unity and helping to maintain world peace, with easing unemployment among British ex-servicemen at home.

His belief here was that, whether a man was born in Britain or in one of the Dominions or Colonies, he should be able to move anywhere in 'this great empire of ours' and be welcomed as a friend or brother. In the post-war world, though, the movement would be mostly one way – from the home country to the Empire beyond. Sadly his dream that significant numbers of jobless – along with their families – would be offered a new chance in the Empire was never realized. The Dominions suffered serious economic problems of their own and were hardly likely to welcome indigent ex-servicemen. Men who emigrated with their families to Canada under Legion sponsorship soon became disillusioned with the serious problems which faced them there.

Haig was an early Keynesian in some of his economic ideas. The cutbacks and layoffs in the UK sickened him; instinctively he believed in greater productivity coupled with the preferential sale of manufactured products within the great market of the Empire. This would surely help to create more jobs for all, including his veterans. When opening *The Times* War Memorial he gave it as his opinion that "(the Buy British campaign) would bring back in redoubled measure the once envied prosperity of all Empires". At the international and strategic level Haig's vision for the Services' League was to help unite the Empire with that other Anglo-Saxon giant, the United States, in common principles of service and comradeship.

Other idealistic notions on behalf of the ex-service community came from overseas. FIDAC (Federation Interalliée des Anciens Combattants) was established in Paris by Monsieur Charles Bertrand in November, 1920. As one of its founding members, it was inevitable the Legion should become involved. Like the British Empire Services League, FIDAC's principal object was to maintain peace by developing the spirit of comradeship forged during the war. From the start it strongly supported the League of Nations and set itself up as a channel of communications for allied ex-servicemen through which they could consider a range of issues, particularly ones associated with commemorating their lost comrades. Unlike the BESL though, concerned as it was with the member nations of a great Empire, FIDAC's members were from countries (some with traditional antagonisms) which had been thrown together by the exigencies of war. Eventually it looked towards making contact with all ex-service countries. In fact its aspirations flew far ahead of reality. How could agreement be reached when, in the early stages, only the United States and Britain had a single unified body representing their ex-servicemen? Belgium had five, France ten and Poland no less than twenty-seven. And the French and German ex-servicemen's associations were far from the stage when they could begin to work together. Many of the Legion's leaders were to become strongly attracted by FIDAC and its associated ideas, including that of rebuilding bridges with ex-enemy veterans' associations. This particular 'Foreign Policy' was to take it into very dangerous international waters just prior to the Second World War.

Instinctively Haig, by favouring his own Empire initiative, had somewhat less enthusiasm for FIDAC and continental involvement than some of his colleagues. In a letter to Colonel Crosfield in September, 1921, for instance, he showed reluctance to divert resources from assisting the needy unemployed in the UK to entertaining French visitors:

"I agree generally with your views to improve our relations with France but at the same time I am strongly of the opinion that our main energies should be devoted to making the relations between ex-servicemen of the British Empire and their comrades in the USA much closer and friendly. . . . *The maintenance of peace rests with the English-speaking people in the coming century.* . . . All my energies are required to get funds for old comrades . . . so it would be foolish on my part to try and support you in this."[1]

Haig did not lose his head either about the role of his own BESL and the Legion in maintaining world peace. His mien contrasted with that of Brunel Cohen, who, when speaking at Ottawa, referred emotionally to the British Legion as one of the component parts among the English-speaking peoples, saying that the latter were strong enough and good enough to impose peace upon the rest of the world. "And not only would the English-speaking peoples impose peace—they could also enforce it." He said he regarded the passing of and debating upon the BESL resolutions at Ottawa as being vital to the future peace of the world.[2] Such language had a hollow ring about it with the traditional cutbacks in the UK's Armed Forces and their virtual disbandment in other Empire countries. In contrast Haig questioned the same conference in the fashion of Margaret Thatcher addressing the Western Alliance in the late 1980s: "What is the practical requisite for the attainment of the ideal of peace? There can be but one answer to that question and it is as old as Christianity—'a strong man keepeth his goods in peace'. We ex-servicemen stand for the adequate defence of the Empire. We have seen what unpreparedness for war has cost this generation."

Yet in the field of home affairs Haig was to place even greater credence on the pivotal role of the Legion than Brunel Cohen had done in the Empire beyond. Its arch-conservative leader saw the Legion as a rock of stability in a society unbalanced both from the effects of war and from the impact of revolutionary ideas. He was not alone in his fear of revolution but it was a remarkable claim, nonetheless.

Initially there was understandable pre-occupation with consolidating and extending the organization itself. Branches were required in all localities and good leadership necessary at every level. For example, it was only after many prolonged difficulties and much concern on the part of the President that the women's section acquired Lady Edward Spencer Churchill as its Chairman with Miss Niven Gerds as organizing Secretary; through their combined efforts and initiative 270 branches with an active membership of 15,700 had been established by 1925.

While a nationwide structure was necessary, the good image of the Legion required Branches to conform to the high standards set out in its Charter. At Haig's personal insistence the sharp-minded J.R. Griffin inspected them all during 1924 and unsatisfactory ones were pruned out.[3] Although this was to impose a temporary check on the organization's growth, it was considered crucial with regard to what was even more important, its reputation. In any case, the overall pattern was of a Legion steadily extending its strength and national coverage, even if its manpower remained far too low. In this respect it enjoyed a boost during 1925 when both Southern and Northern Ireland agreed to become areas of the parent body. In terms of numbers this was not that noteworthy. Southern Ireland had 127 branches with 2840 members, while Northern Ireland had 61 Branches and 560 members; but in symbolic terms the union of all Ireland with the British Headquarters was important. Now only Scotland stood aloof, although while Haig was National President little danger existed of any significant divergence in policy on either side of the border. At Whitsun in 1925 the organization, which had developed genuinely national proportions and stood to represent all ex-servicemen, received its due acclamation in the form of a Royal Charter.

Despite its leader's single-mindedness on unemployment and because of its very lack of success in this area, such a body could reasonably be expected to pursue a number of major objectives simultaneously. No one, least of all Haig himself, would have argued that concern for the disabled was other than fundamental to the Legion. Even more than the able-bodied, the success of their job-hunting was subject to external economic factors. While employers were strongly encouraged by the Government to employ a proportion of such men under the King's Roll Scheme, it remained voluntary. As a result it was taken up unevenly across the country and inevitably lost momentum as memories of the war receded. In the case of the badly disabled the Lord Roberts' Workshops and the British Legion could provide some limited opportunities for sheltered employment but it was a capital-intensive process. If nothing else, men who were seriously disabled had their modest Government pensions, although the payment system was rigidly administered with some 'genuine cases' losing out. At the Legion's headquarters a separate department was formed to continue the work started by Haig on pressing for improved terms of pension eligibility. While it endeavoured to keep successive Ministries up to their pension commitments, it pressed at the same time for improved arrangements generally and made representations over individual cases of hardship or difficulty with the Government department concerned.

From the beginning particular disquiet was voiced over the system of awards made to those who, while not seriously disabled, were undoubtedly hampered in their job-hunting, i.e. those with a 20% disability or below. These were subject to the 7-year rule by which ex-servicemen (or their dependants) had to claim pensions for any injuries aggravated by war service within 7 years from the date of discharge. Following the disappointing outcome of Brunel Cohen's work in the Commons for a Select Committee, during 1925 a great National Petition was organized for abolishing the 7-year time-limit. Its effect was somewhat weakened when, after talking of millions of signatures, the final total delivered was for 825,000. This antique (and somewhat ineffective) form of political pressure evoked no overt Government response, although, to the surprise of many, pension rates were held to the levels agreed at the end of the war – contrary to persistent rumours that they would be reduced as the cost of living fell. Despite such hard-won concessions, it was not until the Second World War that most of the Legion's requests in the pensions field succeeded. This represented a particular triumph for the devoted work of A.G. Webb, its enthusiastic and long-serving head of the Headquarters' Pensions Department. Apart from general agitation, large numbers of individual cases were brought before Appeals Tribunals throughout the inter-war years. Between 1921 and 1941 there were 65,651 of which 52% resulted in revisions being made in the men's favour.

The Legion's other initiatives were not always so uncontroversial. Due to the poor results achieved by Government Employment Exchanges and limitations in the arrangements of the voluntary bodies pledged to help ex-servicemen, it decided to become involved directly in employment finding. The Officers' Branch had always been active in this respect, but in July, 1921, a London Employment Bureau was established with complementary Bureaux throughout the country. In its first year the London Bureau found work for 439 men and a further 2000 openings were obtained by the area branches, but, while admirable, such figures hardly started to dent the problem. The importance of its employment-finding services increased during the late 1920s and early 1930s, but in themselves they were never large nor successful enough to reduce significantly the huge total of the unemployed.

In addition to finding jobs, the Legion also came to undertake or sponsor specialist employment schemes. By granting loans for promising individual or joint business ventures, initiative could be developed and hope restored. Monies for the purpose came partly from outside sources, notably the National Relief Fund, and as loans were repaid the process could be repeated and further ventures sponsored. Up to March, 1922, 950 individuals were advanced nearly £19,000 in interest-free loans to set themselves up in such occupations as hairdressers, painters, builders, newsagents, electricians, smallholders and blacksmiths.[4] This was a small number but the effect on those concerned was understandably dramatic.

Pre-eminent among the Legion's joint ventures, of course, was its sponsorship of and then subsequent involvement with the Poppy Factory. Other schemes followed. Among them was a loan made in 1923 to a chairmaking factory at Warminster, in Wiltshire, which came to employ sixty ex-servicemen. At about the same time £350 was loaned for a herring-curing scheme. In 1924 two very considerable loans of £12,000 and £10,000 respectively were advanced for ship-breaking enterprises. In the first instance most of the loan was repaid during the following year and, in the second, about half had been repaid over the same period. A number of grants were made to the King's Roll Clerks' Association Ltd, founded during 1925 to help unskilled ex-servicemen with at least a 50% disability who were trained in office skills and a proportion of whom were subsequently able to obtain further employment.

In April, 1927, the Legion was itself offered, and accepted, a fully equipped factory manufacturing Welsh tweeds, at Crickhowell, in Breconshire. Since 1919 this had employed eight disabled ex-servicemen, but now the Legion formed a small company and advanced £500 for working capital. Sixty-four years later it continues to flourish, still producing good quality cloth and employing twenty-eight disabled and ten other men.

In November of the same year two more joint employment schemes were undertaken, one of which was to prove of major importance and an outstanding investment. A grant of £250 (quickly repaid) was made to help ex-service fishermen at Youghal, Southern Ireland, to buy salmon-fishing equipment. During the same month a grant of £2000 was made payable at the rate of £500 a year to the Legion's Metropolitan Area in order to inaugurate the British Legion Taxi-Drivers Training School. No fewer than 862 ex-service drivers were trained during the inter-war period, and, although numbers declined in the years leading up to the Second World War, after it there was another surge and up to 1987, 5360 men had received their licences there.

By such initiatives the British Legion was not only actively helping ex-servicemen through its range of benevolent measures, it was developing into a major organization. Its senior officials were now on the Management Committees of three sizeable industrial ventures, the Poppy Factory, the Cambrian Factory and the Taxi-Drivers Training School.

In 1924 came its largest commitment yet. This related to that special category of men, 55,000 in all, who had contracted TB as a result of their wartime service. At the end of the war an Inter-departmental Committee on Sanatoria for Soldiers had been set up by the Ministries of Health and Pensions under Sir Montague Barlow. This proposed that £1m should be allocated for Village Settlements where such men could be treated and when fit enough trained for subsequent employment.[5] In such settlements accommodation would be available for them and their families so that careful monitoring of their health could be made during their early recovery years. The model for Barlow's recommendations was the Village Settlement and Training Colony at Papworth, in Cambridgeshire, which had been established earlier as a voluntary venture. Its Medical Director, Dr Varrier Jones, reported on Papworth to the Barlow Committee. He cited its thirty-eight patients who were mostly soldiers but said it could house up to 350 men providing a state subsidy was available. Unlike other countries, notably New Zealand and Australia, adequate Government funding for such settlements was not forthcoming. Papworth, and the five other schemes examined by the Committee, were never fully developed. The Legion adopted the cause but the economic background was stark and in 1924 it had to be content with the promise of a supplementary grant of just £20,000. Previously, this central assistance had been limited to an annual capitation grant of £25 per man. Government inaction was not without its results. Neglect and the passing of time had already combined to reduce the problem; by May, 1924, 18,000 of the servicemen suffering from tuberculosis were dead.

It was largely as a result of continued prevarication and cheese-paring by the Government that the Legion came to be offered, free of charge, the Village Settlement of Preston Hall near Maidstone. This was a going concern, the responsibility of a charity (Industrial Settlements Ltd) which ran into financial difficulties and was forced to mortgage its assets to the Government. On behalf of the Legion, Colonel Crosfield investigated its possible viability and recommended acceptance. (Dr Varrier Jones was persuaded to help and his proposals for the initial reorganization were adopted.) Crosfield wrote enthusiastically to Haig about it, but one gains the impression from a decidedly one-sided correspondence that his chief needed convincing that actual involvement in such a daunting, if potentially exciting venture, however admirable in itself, was in fact a central concern of the Legion. It concerned one group only, however sad their condition, and might prove ruinously expensive.

However, Crosfield's vision and faith were to be rewarded by the resounding and continuing success of Preston Hall. But Haig's gaze was ever on the fundamental dilemma—the main body of men who were still unemployed; men and their families who, when starving, were in no state to concentrate on the arduous process of employment-finding or able to present themselves favourably to would-be employers. Above all he believed that continual pressure must be put on the Government for it to come up with some major initiative to create new jobs. Failing this, much time and the bulk of one's resources must be devoted to those applying for immediate short-term help. In his study at Bemersyde Haig himself often worked far into the night responding in longhand to the regular requests from distressed individuals which were addressed to him personally. Reading through such heart-rending cases, he had strong fears that, as the organization grew and diversified, it might be in danger of losing its human face. He wrote on this to Crosfield: "As charitable organizations develop and their machinery becomes more systematized, so do they act 'according to Regulations'. . . . We must guard against this and I think occasionally change the subordinates who interview the needy ones."[6]

Although this deeply human side of Haig's character was not generally appreciated, it is remarkable how many servicemen plucked up the courage to contact him personally. In fact the word must have surely passed round that the erstwhile remote Commander-in-Chief would not only respond to their letters but do so in a positive way.

Apart from the need for employment (after, in many cases, some opportunity for training), there remained another question of basic importance for returning men, especially the disabled—whether they would be able to find a roof to put over their heads or whether the 'homes for heroes' declaration by Lloyd George would prove to be another hollow promise. The short answer was that it did. During the war the maintenance, repair and building of houses had virtually ceased. Between 1911 and 1918 the increase in the number of households needing separate dwellings amounted to 848,000, with only 238,000 units being added to the stock.[7] The Government planned to meet the massive shortfall by granting a central subsidy to local authorities to erect houses for renting. This became law in July, 1919, but it was cancelled exactly two years later due to the collapse of the post-war boom. With this went all commitment to build houses fit for heroes. Even during the two-year period the number of buildings was far lower than anticipated and their unit costs higher. One reason for the poor figures was union resistance to increasing the supply of skilled workers in case this would weaken their bargaining position at a time of slump. In fact, by 1923 there was a greater shortage of houses than at the end of the war! Reliance was now placed on the private sector. While eventually it responded in a quite dramatic way to the pent-up demand, the process took about a decade to gain momentum. This was far too long for the returning masses, most of whom had never yet occupied separate accommodation. They were offered neither direct concessions nor other assistance to obtain their own houses, as in other countries within the Empire and beyond. In their desperation many opted for the older and often insanitary accommodation built during the previous century or for temporary dwellings.

During SSAFA's Annual Meeting of 1925, for instance, a case was cited of a man, his wife and eight children, who lived in a caravan "because they cannot get a house to live in". A grant of £3 was made by another service charity to help them clothe the children, but, to prevent its use for other purposes, the payment was made in the form of flannelette from which the overburdened wife had to make up the family's clothes.[8]

During the middle 1930s houses were being erected at the rate of 350,000 a year and they included a good proportion built for letting. "New semi-detached houses with bathrooms and garage could be bought for as little as £450. Mortgages were available on easy terms, with an average interest rate of around $4\frac{1}{2}\%$ and repayments which come well within the range of most of the middle classes and a significant portion of the better off working classes".[9] After a decade of prolonged unemployment, for many ex-servicemen such outlays would still be beyond their means.

The British Legion felt it had a bounden duty to help in this area too, but, due to the high cost of any housing project, its ability was strictly limited. Assistance was therefore confined to the most unfortunate. In 1926 the Prince of Wales laid the foundation stone of purpose-built flats for the disabled Poppy Factory workers near their place of employment. During the following year it made plans to buy small properties for men on low incomes which could be let at nominal rents. After Haig's death a new opportunity arose. The Prince of Wales inaugurated a National Fund which became the Haig Homes Trust Fund, also with low-paid ex-servicemen in mind. By 1955 the Legion had acquired 156 small dwellings accommodating 560 people at rents of no more than 4/6d (22½p) a week. After the Second World War the Legion collected money to maintain the Haig Memorial Homes but its main contribution to housing was to come in 1964 when it established the Royal British Legion Housing Association, a major independent charity and Friendly Society which obtained capital either through Government Funding, from local authorities or by raising a proportion on the open market. In the early years after the First World War the British Legion was in no position to give significant help towards housing the great numbers in need.

The final great theme of the Legion's work during its relatively early years was in the provision of social activities. For the most part this meant its clubs, that 'solid background' of the movement.

To the serious-minded Haig the clubs' role would include the stimulation of general education but their chief function in the period following the war was a cathartic one. Many found during the first months – for some it stretched into years – that experiences in the trenches had drained them of ordinary civilian emotions. Like Charles Quinnell and Victor Fagence they could not talk about the war, even to their loved ones, but within the clubs they would find their tongues loosened and their hearts uplifted as they renewed comradely associations and developed new friendships among men of like spirits.

The number of clubs grew past the 1000 mark (including affiliated ones) before the end of the inter-war period and, like the growing number of other responsibilities, they required both local and central supervision. While providing recreation, their work did not by any means stop there, since they endeavoured at the same time to keep the Legion's ideals of 'service not self' alive. Little that occurred in their local communities escaped the notice of some club member or other and the names of their mates who might be suffering misfortune could be passed on to the welfare committees of their associated Branches. Often they were fertile recruiting grounds for men who would subsequently graduate to Branch and ceremonial responsibilities.

At the very least the clubs helped to relieve the gnawing boredom and humiliation of unemployment and, through regional and national contests, men reawakened their competitive urges and recovered their confidence. A less agreeable feature of some clubs lay in their deliberate exclusivity and a certain contemptuousness for much of the outside world. To this day some remain defiant male preserves, harking back incessantly to the 'great days' and even greater deeds of the past.

By the late 1920s the British Legion and its leaders found themselves heavily involved with a wide range of initiatives both domestic and international. With energy and dedication, the organization pressurized Governments to step up their help for veterans. Invariably it did so by using traditional and 'civilized' approaches and did not question the fundamental economic and political systems of the day. For instance, in its pamphlet publicizing, among other things, a series of recitals which the eminent conductor Paderewski was undertaking to assist Legion funds, the preamble asserted it was "not by any one's fault but by the merciless operation of the law of supply and demand [that] about 750,000 ex-servicemen are out of work."[10]

Such pressure had its limitations, as A.J.P. Taylor rightly observed. In response to repeated requests, the Government agreed in 1925 to set up training facilities for the hard core of unskilled ex-service unemployed, but the results proved to be bitterly disappointing. In the following year the number of places offered, at one location only, Wallsend, near Newcastle, was a minuscule 420. Equally serious, the Trade Unions were unwilling to recognize such six-month-trained men – derisively termed dilutees – as legitimate tradesmen.

Months and years after their return ex-servicemen found themselves, like latter day Robinson Crusoes, marooned by their lack of skills; not only were they surrounded by the high seas of official indifference but before they could reach the open water they faced the thunderous and unforgiving breakers of organized labour. There were virtually no materials, in the form of training opportunities or civilian contacts, for building rafts to reach the mainland where jobs could be found, although never in abundant supply. Official training was almost non-existent and democratically-inspired movements for training adults, like the Workers Educational Association, with its insistence on liberal education, was completely irrelevant for ex-servicemen. There were plenty of courses about the Soviet system of five-year economic plans (for a society which nominally had full employment) but none for free men to acquire the skills to survive in their own chaotic capitalist system.[11] Happily, after the Second World War the WEA courses were somewhat different but this was of no help to inter-war veterans. Too often what many came to require was short-term aid to keep body and soul together.

By late 1927, shortly before Haig's death, virtually all the major domestic initiatives for which the Legion has since become justly famed had been adopted. In the following seventy years or so some were to be expanded almost beyond recognition, but the elements were in place and the nature of the organization distinct. It was the only membership body for all British veterans. Initially pledged to assist those from the First World War, it would (not without a certain reluctance on the part of some) embrace the generation who came to it after the Second World War and beyond.

By November, 1927, even its ceremonial for the Remembrance Pageant had taken on contemporary features, though not, it must be said, at Haig's instigation. In that year the Cenotaph contingent was increased to 2000, including women, and in the evening the *Daily Express*, in conjunction with the Legion, promoted a great ex-service reunion at the Albert Hall. The main feature, as Colonel Crosfield explained to Haig, was to be communal singing, the songs being the old wartime ones. He mentioned too that the Prince of Wales had agreed to attend and say a few words on the subject of ex-servicemen's employment. Haig did not attend. Apart from personal antipathy for such occasions, perhaps he felt it pointless to mouth anodyne words on the continuing tragedy of unemployment without being able to offer relief. He certainly was not impressed with the theatrical elements proposed by the newspaper, including a torchlight procession to the Cenotaph.[12] (A few years later it was a method used to great effect by the growing Nazi Party.) His dislike of such gatherings prevented him from anticipating the later pattern of the Remembrance Festival when it took on the character both of an emotional, fiercely patriotic reunion and a religious ceremony, but the torchlight procession was never repeated. Doubtless he would have approved of the religious element, although his personal preference would surely have been for ceremonies taking place in local churches throughout the country, or like those he attended during the war in the modest wooden chapel near his French Headquarters. He could not have foreseen that due to the miracle of television a Festival of Remembrance could be transferred from the magnificence of the Albert Hall into private homes countrywide, be they Bemersyde or a modest cottage, nor that by the combination of skilled camera work and a sensitive commentary, an intimacy of experience could be attained which in some respects exceeded that of the actual spectators in London.

It was not disinclination but unexpected death which prevented him from accompanying the delegates and pilgrim Legionaries paying homage to the allied dead in Europe during the following year. The great climax of the rituals during 1928 was the ceremonial parade at Ypres on 8 August, with its Service of Remembrance and March Past.

Douglas Haig died on 29 January, 1928. No book concerned with the interests of the British ex-soldier can neglect a summation of his work, short as it must be here. Without doubt, by reason of his supreme position in the war and the personal fervour he gave to their cause afterwards, he is the most notable champion British ex-servicemen have ever had. In this respect Graham Wootton's treatment of him seems less than generous or fair. Wootton's statement that the Legion has "no founder, only founders" verges on the absurd. Other remarkable men certainly did and will continue to play major parts in its work and development but it owed its foundation to him. There was no reason for thinking, as Wootton does, that without him a united ex-service organization must have emerged. This history of British ex-servicemen's affairs gives a contrary picture, of different and separate organizations from which it is reasonable to assume that without Haig such a unified ex-service organization would never have developed.

For better or worse, the body he created opened its arms to all ex-servicemen, eschewing political affiliations and (formally at least) its members' past military ranks. In a troubled post-war society it stood for the social cement between the extremes of potentially rapacious employers and angry men with Bolshevik ideas. It was the agency through which citizens could honour their dead guardians and through which living ex-servicemen, particularly if they had been injured, stood a chance of obtaining a true measure of justice from Governments. At the international level it was the only means of uniting ex-service organizations within the Empire and with those of the United States – all this was Haig.

So too were the qualities of leadership associated with a great commander, industry coupled with selflessness in the decision to proselytise the country (and the Empire) on the Legion's behalf, the eye for significant detail demonstrated through his correspondence with Crosfield, the ability to spot opportunity in the quick support he gave to Poppy Day collections, the sure knowledge of the harm that defunct branches might do to the organization, the humanity and generosity in helping individuals whose wants must not be denied by adherence to regulations, which, however carefully drafted they might be, were proving too strict.

If Haig is to be credited with the formation and early development of the Legion, he must equally be open to criticisms about the limitations of its early achievements. Why, one might ask, was the vision so far from being fulfilled? Why, after British ex-servicemen had achieved a great membership organization of their own, should they remain disadvantaged? Was it due to the powerful drag of tradition or could it be that Haig's aims for it were too grandiloquent? Certainly nothing less than full justice for his men would satisfy him. But, equally important, his new body came late on the scene; being formed after the war, the Legion had no opportunity of influencing the traditional, ramshackle and inadequate plans already drawn up for returning men. By the time it was established the economic climate had taken a turn for the worse and, while major concessions still might have been won if large numbers of men had joined quickly, for reasons already discussed they were reluctant to do so on the scale required.

With the physical and moral backing of most ex-servicemen Haig might have been able to demand changes to past patterns in such key areas as training and employment. Yet nothing could have stopped large numbers of veterans suffering unemployment at times of economic downturn, although, in plain justice, the numbers of fit ex-servicemen unemployed ought not to have been greater than the national average. For the disabled, special – and effective – arrangements were necessary. With only small numbers at his back, his only chance, if indeed chance it was, to achieve these things was by engaging in political infighting. This he was unwilling to do and probably incapable of doing. During the war his gaze had never been diverted from the Western Front where he was sure it would either be won or lost. After the war he similarly eschewed indirect approaches through political sleight of hand. It was contrary to the basic precepts of his organization and would certainly have lost him his Royal Sponsorship. It was not Haig's way. Both during and after the war his aims were consistent and his concentration absolute, but whereas in the earlier years of the war serving armies had to pay a terrible price before the final breakout during 1918, the continuing difficulties experienced by Haig's veterans after 1918 became part of the cost from which a future generation demobilized in 1945 would gain some benefit. This time he himself would not see the fulfilment of his aims. Haig's natural unwillingness to indulge in knockabout tactics and to attempt short cuts, enshrined in the Legion's Charter, rightly earned him the faintly dismissive remarks of A.J.P. Taylor about discreet pressure. An organization with such high ideals was perforce required to confine itself to dignified means in achieving them.

Haig died in the year preceding the Wall Street crash and therefore missed both the darkest hour of the modern capitalist system and the sharp recovery from 1933 onwards, with its vast growth in consumer industries based largely on credit. He missed, too, the depressingly familiar problems which so many of his veterans would continue to suffer. For those in work during the 1930s the drop in the cost of living by over 50% between 1920 and 1938 meant a substantial improvement in living standards. In 1937–8 the average family income was more than double that of 1913–14. Families were smaller, they were housed better ($2\frac{1}{2}$ million houses were built in these years) people ate better, had more leisure, wore better clothes and enjoyed many more domestic conveniences, notably through the development of electric power.

The picture was marred by the 11% who still lived in poverty, i.e. the old, the sick, the widowed, the low-paid and the unemployed. As yet most of the Great War veterans were not old, although some had aged prematurely, but ex-servicemen and their dependants made up a disproportionate share of the other categories. While many returned and successfully picked up the threads of their former lives, larger numbers than in any past conflict had either been injured, had lost resilience, had no qualifications or just could not adjust to civilian life. And as a result of the

$\frac{3}{4}$ million dead, unequalled numbers of widow and their dependants were in need too.

While the working population as a whole was improving its standard of living, not without grave periods of crisis and uncertainty, the unfortunates of the war steadily lost ground and sadly many were to lose hope too. In 1925 the average income for those on the dole was 18/2d (91p), compared with a building labourer's 65/2d (£3.26p) and a bricklayer's 79/2d (£3.96p).

With the fragile state of the economy, successive British Governments were not prepared to venture central funds on ex-servicemen beyond pension and unemployment payments, which, even when set at humiliatingly low levels, involved massive payouts. With such adverse conditions, the Forces' charities were compelled to use most of their resources plugging the dam of human misery by small grants either of money or clothing, or more frequently through vouchers which could be exchanged for necessities.

Year by year the figures spoke for themselves. In 1921/2 the Legion (through the Unity Relief Fund) distributed £321,000 in benevolence. Over 4500 applications were made from a single Northern town and those in need were in a pitiful state. *The Journal* at this time gave a number of examples including one man who was "unemployed, with wife and seven children, home sold up and clothes pawned; no food in the house". In the later 1920s the number of grants made to individuals ran at some 400,000 a year. In 1928, whereas £300,000 was spent on such benevolence, only £10,000 was allocated to the Legion's Village and Disabled Men's Industries. In the early 1930s the Legion's expenditure remained around £300,000 and in 1934 400,000 men were again assisted. The total of spending on benevolence did not significantly drop until 1939 when it was less than £220,000 – still many times in excess of any other commitment.

Despite the large sums spent, shortfalls still occurred in the funds needed to reduce hardship. In 1932 Colonel Crosfield thanked the better off areas of the Legion for their sense of comradeship in surrendering the bulk of their money to the distressed areas—"otherwise it would be impossible to cope with the terrible distress which still existed." In the next year Major Brunel Cohen deeply regretted the curtailment of grants to certain committees in the distressed areas.

The same pattern applied with the other two major charities. The Lord Roberts' Workshops were carefully sustained through the economic gyrations of the time, rendered more serious by the severe handicaps of their workforce. As extra funds were gathered, their capacity was gradually extended, with the last major factory being opened in Belfast just after the Second World War. Yet simultaneously their other wing, the Soldiers' and Sailors' and Airmens' Help Society (SSAHS) was heavily involved with its traditional and equally large task of helping the near-destitute with money grants and clothing. SSAFA, the Association for families, continued its great work of supplying district nurses and providing accommodation for the needy widows of officers. By 1938 sixty nurses operated worldwide in support of families in garrison locations. But its chief requirement was granting relief to families of ex-servicemen in desperate financial need. New bodies like the Royal Naval Benevolent Trust and the RAF Benevolent Fund also joined the movement by relieving needy members from their two services.

Despite the emergence of a great membership body of veterans, expansion in the work carried out by the Lord Roberts' Workshops and the Families Association and the establishment of new charities like St Dustan's and the British Limbless Ex-Servicemen's Association (BLESMA) for groups with special needs, it seemed that in Britain nothing could release the large hard core of long-term unemployed from their suffering. In this the situation was fully in accordance with the British tradition towards its veterans.

In contrast, Governments in other countries, both within the Empire and beyond, tended to approach such questions with more urgency and determination, although their philosophies on how best to assist veterans differed widely. Apart from the enlightened arrangements already seen in New Zealand,[13] in Australia the Returned Services League succeeded in obtaining preferential employment rights for both fit and disabled men and a greater incidence of vocational training took place there than in Britain.

27,685 men (both disabled and fit) participated and War Service Homes were offered them (admittedly at the high cost level operating just after the war). These were taken up by 35,954 men. The whole approach of the Australian League, while non-political in the party sense, was more muscular than in Britain. Each state Branch had its Employment Bureau, and in addition to placing advertisements in the local newspapers it directly canvassed major employers and 'jogged their elbows' into finding posts for maimed and other returned men.

On the continent, France, with a long appreciation of its land forces, started from the presumption that any disease, wound or disability contracted by a soldier or sailor while in the Army or Navy, or during a period of six months after discharge, was due to service and *entitled* the man to a pension.[14] As in most other continental countries, ex-servicemen had absolute preference for public appointments. A proportion of these were suitable for disabled men (doorman, lift attendant, etc). Such preferences applied in Belgium and Germany but in the latter country a further scheme required all sizeable employers to take on a proportion of men with over 50% disablement.

Of all the continental states Italian ex-servicemen were probably best off, due in no small measure to the influence of Mussolini. By law disabled men had to be employed. In 1924 Colonel Crosfield reported that no more than 10,000 disabled were out of work and these were unemployable due to the seriousness of their wounds. For these pensions were granted on a good scale.[15]

For tangible results the American Legion's employment campaign, set for just one day, 20 March, 1923, was unrivalled. It was said, surely with no exaggeration, that its 11,000 Branches worked unremittingly and the women's branches "enrolled themselves with irresistible enthusiasm in the good cause". Their success was phenomenal. In Detroit the Ford Motor Company alone increased its work force by 20%, jobs being given *exclusively to ex-servicemen.* In a period of three weeks following 'Legion Employment Day' no less than 500,000 unemployed were back at work. As a marvelling Colonel Crosfield remarked, "If the Legion had done nothing else but that it would have justified its existence ten times over".[16]

In Britain no comparable preferences were given by industry for its ex-servicemen. Britain did not share the strong continental traditions of cossetting their land armies nor the fierce determination of some Empire nations to assist their returning men. Notwithstanding, there is an impression (latched on to by A.J.P. Taylor) that, working in the sombre climate of the inter-war years, the Legion did not always press home its improvement campaigns to their fullest extent, even by the strict rules it set itself. This becomes rather more apparent during the 1930s when justifications for such lack of success were put forward. Writing about the 1929 Remembrance Ceremonies at the Albert Hall, Colonel Graham Seton Hutchinson referred to some men in that great congress who has risen to high position and esteem among their fellows. "And there were others, shattered in limb, disillusioned in mind, disappointed, shabby, who had fallen by the wayside . . . men ill-equipped to run in a commercial race whose Master of Ceremonies is Moloch." Such a sad – and suspect – rationalization where so many citizen soldiers were concerned hardly helped the individuals. What many needed was medical treatment at the least and better opportunities before being written off. More serious, it conveniently absolved the nation from its disregard for its returning men.

In July, 1933, the Legion held a Great Rally at Brighton where over 30,000 men and their families took part. As the Lord Mayor of Brighton so rightly said when he addressed them, "The Legion was giving a helping hand to its less fortunate comrades", but the Rev Canon Meyrick who conducted the service, after referring to past memories, ended with a somehow upbeat but limitlessly vague exhortation, "Your power is great, and that power must be used unselfishly urging those present to keep together, keep moving and keep looking upwards". To some the high ideals of Douglas Haig obviously presented a God-sent opportunity for indulging in nothing better than sonorous claptrap.

In fact, during 1933 the organization gave clear indications of being a mature body rather unwilling to rock the domestic boat too much when negotiating with Government. Over the years, through working closely with both the permanent officials and the Ministries concerned, the Legion's leaders, whose fair mindedness sometimes bordered on the naive, had inevitably forged personal relationships with them. Sir Brunel Cohen said that, even in disagreement, "the Legion's representatives before the Ministry had always come away feeling that broadly speaking the Ministry was out to help the ex-servicemen". Unwittingly or not, it was a damning remark. Such sentiments were confirmed at the 1933 Annual Conference when the Duke of Windsor, in support of the platform, delivered a script which must have been prepared by the Legion itself and which included the extraordinary and utterly untrue words:

"I do not hesitate to say that the ex-service men of this country have more reason to thank successive Governments than those of any other country that fought in the Great War."

The situation was such that it is difficult to see how large-scale ex-service unemployment could have been avoided. There was a limit to the early sense of outrage and to the number of initiatives one's representatives could devise to put before stone-walling, if essentially friendly, politicians. For more than twelve years the Legion had wrestled with the problem of finding work for some and even longer with the task of helping to ease the suffering of those who remained out of work. But in the early 1930s unemployment was the lot of large numbers of civilians and in 1932 Sir Brunel Cohen argued that possibly no more than half the unemployed were ex-servicemen. In reality, the proportion of ex-servicemen unemployed was likely to be much higher than that of civilians. And within that group there were many who would be much less likely to be re-employed than ordinary civilians. Some indication that new ideas were running out came when the Legion's Parliamentary representative on the National Executive Council, Mr Smedley Crooke, proposed a "share-out-the-work" scheme. This required employers to take on 20% or so more workers, with the equivalent percentage of those already employed dropping out for one week in six to make way for the new men. How he reasonably expected such a scheme to gain the ready acceptance of those in employment is hard to imagine. In 1935, twelve years after the Legion's original National Employment

Week, it launched another, almost as a last throw, but its benefits were unclear. It certainly did not meet with dramatic success. Then, at long last, help came through improving economic conditions and the start of rearmament. The National Chairman, Major Francis Fetherston-Godley, wrote in the Legion *Journal*, "A golden opportunity for Great Britain to redeem that wartime promise, sunshine for heroes, is provided by plans for national rearmament". The irony of such words would hardly have been lost on many readers.

The sad part was that the half-million ageing ex-servicemen who were workless throughout most of the inter-war period had been passed by. They were shouldered aside by a new generation, younger, more skilled and energetic, with no ghosts from the past. The hard core still needed benevolence, despite all the Legion's initiatives and the better employment climate nationally. For these prematurely aged, burnt-out men the Legion and its brother organizations in the Empire requested financial help. They recommended that it should be given without the humiliating and often protracted system of investigation traditionally required for would-be pensioners. The British Government's response, through a Prime Minister more firm in his attitude to shabby veterans than towards fascist adventurers in their glittering uniforms, came with a flat rejection of special assistance.

For special and enduring reasons, British ex-servicemen from the Great War neither enjoyed the particular advantages of veterans on the continent, particularly those in the Fascist States, nor found their main representative body, the British Legion, willing to pursue the rough wooing tactics adopted by such as the Australian Returned Services League. Positive gains were made, however. Joint exertions by British ex-service organizations prevailed upon the state to close some of the gaps in its arrangements for the broken and the bereaved, they sponsored a wide range of limited but pioneering schemes of their own and through subsistence payments they helped sustain a proportion of men who were either suffering serious temporary difficulties or who proved incapable of coping with the harsh problems associated with civilian life between the wars.

CHAPTER TEN

A Vain Search for Peace

"At the present time hundreds of
thousands of workers were employed on
the Siegfried Line, the sole purpose of
which was defensive. This supported the
view that Germany had no intention of
attacking France."

Sir Neville Henderson
at Cabinet Meeting, 17 September, 1938.

"The decision to dispense with
plebiscites relieved us of the
responsibility for sending out the British
Legion to police the plebiscite areas."

Statement at Cabinet Meeting,
19 October, 1938

A<small>NY</small> account of British veterans' affairs between the wars would
be incomplete without reference to the international initiatives
which were pursued by the leading ex-servicemen's body after
Haig's death. Under the immediate successors to Haig and Crosfield, there was no indication of what was to come. That eminent
sailor, Earl Jellicoe (Haig had favoured him as a likely successor),
assumed the senior appointment as National President, while an
outstanding soldier of the Territorial Army, Colonel (later Lt-
General Sir) John Brown, took over the Chairmanship. Jellicoe's
reign was to be quite short; due to failing health he stood down in

173

1932 and John Brown completed his own arduous four-year term just two years later. The second President followed his great predecessor in viewing the scourge of unemployment as the greatest issue of his time.[1] He too stumped the country indefatigably, trying to lift the morale of men, particularly those in the regions devastated by unemployment. Employers were urged to contact the Legion when they needed more staff and he led deputations to the Ministries of Employment and Health on behalf of his followers. But John Brown's period of office was overshadowed by domestic problems within the organization. At the time of his election a Committee under Viscount Bridgeman reported upon the Legion's general finance and administration which had earlier been the subject of a major attack by the *Sunday Express*. The Legion had requested the investigation and was given a generally clean bill of health, although the Committee recommended some changes, including the appointment of a professional editor of its *Journal*. The end result of this was a serious divergence of opinion between the Legion's Executive Committee and the *Journal's* editor over how vigorously one should campaign for improvements in ex-service pensions. The editor advocated far more robust tractics and used the *Journal* to support his unilateral ideas. A full-scale crisis developed, which was followed eagerly by the national press and the editor was finally dismissed. This caused the 1934 Annual Conference to be particularly lively, for, among other things, it was told that John Brown was initiating libel proceedings against a daily newspaper for comments against him of a personal and damaging nature. He was subsequently to receive a settlement out of court which he had paid into Legion Funds.

This excitement apart, and its chief significance rested on whether the Legion was really exerting its authority as effectively as it could, under Jellicoe and Brown things proceeded along the course mapped out in 1921. The central aim, a domestic one, continued to be re-employment of World War veterans. Even with an organization stronger than ever before (its membership now exceeded 342,000), there were no obvious signs of a breakthrough, for in fact unemployment now ran at a far higher level than even in the mid 1920s, reaching 2.7 million in 1931. In the aftermath of the Wall Street crash this was a most unsatisfactory but hardly a surprising position for both long-suffering veterans and their leaders. The Bridgeman Committee had already voiced the hope that new initiatives might be found and under its third President and fourth Chairman the Legion set about a re-appraisal of both the organization itself and its main aims.

The two men who followed Earl Jellicoe and John Brown, Major-General Sir Frederick Maurice and Major (later Brigadier) Sir Francis Fetherston-Godley, certainly did not feel themselves trammelled by past tradition. Maurice was both an idealist and man of action, an outstanding staff officer during the First World War until his military career was ended by a letter he felt compelled to write to the London newspapers. In this he accused Lloyd George of deceiving Parliament about the strength of the British Army on the Western Front. Such a man would hardly hesitate to move the Legion towards new policies if he considered they might offer more chance of success. After leaving the Army he became a prominent academic and was Principal of Queen Mary College, London, from 1933 to 1944. Concurrently with his other responsibilities — he also wrote a number of historical studies on war – he had already proved himself an indefatigable worker for ex-servicemen. A founder member of the Officers' Association, he became the Legion's Treasurer in 1930 and continued as its President for fifteen years from 1932 to 1947. It was unthinkable that such a man would exert anything less than a major influence on policy.

Fetherston-Godley, a career soldier, and a junior officer in the First World War, was described by Graham Wootton as an "exceptionally vigorous man who passionately sought action". He held no strong allegiance to earlier policies and determined to seek a 'cause' beyond the endless domestic issues, a proportion of which he considered were stalemated if not moribund. Surely, he argued, there were other initiatives beyond those "sentimental influences which, while a source of strength in the past, were diminishing in value".[2]

Any reappraisal had, of course, to start at the Legion's Charter, which was already virtually sacrosanct, describing as it did a democratic non-sectarian, non-political body pledged to safeguard the interests of both those from the Armed Forces and the dependants of the fallen. Little debate was required either about such laudable aims as the need to inculcate a sense of loyalty both to the Crown and the Nation or to promote unity amongst all classes. Loyalty to Crown and Country was the essence of the Legion's being: during Annual Conferences men who had hazarded their very lives broke into frenzied applause at the very sight of their Patron, the Prince of Wales. Fortunately Haig's worst fears about a breakdown in the nation's social fabric had proved groundless. There seemed little prospect either of exciting developments on the home front with the continuing unwillingness of Governments to intervene in the employment field or to grant major concessions to suffering veterans.

With the Legion's International aspirations things seemed very different. Here its Charter spoke of "securing peace and goodwill on earth". It was in the search for that glittering but so elusive goal of world peace that the new leaders came to invest much of their time and on which to place so many of their hopes. Earlier initiatives in this field had proved disappointing.

Haig's British Empire Services League had not produced the material results he had hoped for, either through increased inter-Dominion trade or significant emigration of ex-servicemen from Britain to the Commonwealth. And FIDAC's early aims to admit former enemy ex-service organizations had failed, largely through implacable French opposition.

From his accession as President in 1932 Maurice began to pursue a policy of rapprochement with ex-enemy servicemen, particularly those of Germany, and from 1934 onwards this began to assume ever greater importance. It was entirely consistent with his earlier activities; as early as 1921, along with Crosfield and others, he had represented the Legion on FIDAC and he was assistant rapporteur to the FIDAC Peace Committee of 1924. In his judgement the Treaty of Locarno in 1925 and Germany's subsequent admission to the League of Nations seemed to offer new international opportunities in this quarter.

One can fully understand the attraction of 'foreign policy' over domestic issues at this time. At home it seemed that whatever skills and energies the leaders displayed, adverse political and economic factors predominated. Much of the most important work, aimed at preserving morale by helping men who, during the long calvary of joblessness, had begun to doubt themselves, was being performed at Branch level. Decisions about the allocation and distribution of short-term aid were the business of innumerable local committees. At the least it must have been disturbing for their national leaders to meet those who carried about them an aura of resignation and hopelessness. Many of these men, who while still unquestionably patriotic and loyal had, due to their sufferings, become bitter and awkward and therefore increasingly difficult to help. Some would patently never fully recover: they had missed the boat and had joined past ranks of neglected British veterans. If a future war could be prevented the lines of shabby, dead-eyed men would not, at least, be joined by their sons or nephews.

Before turning to the remarkable story of the Legion's international undertakings during the 1930s, it would be wrong to leave the impression that veterans in other Western countries were not suffering problems of a similar nature, despite the greater assistance they had received initially, or that some other veterans' associations were not also looking for ways of avoiding future conflicts.

Within the Empire, employment preference in the Australian Public Service had been strongly attacked by the Scullin Labour Government of 1927 and, although successfully fought off by the Returned Services League, it could not prevent cuts to pensions of around 20%. Not only were pensioners receiving reduced payments, but, with the depression, the light jobs they needed to supplement their pensions were often lost too. The League was compelled to set up an informal network to help the many men who were forced to "go on the tracks" as tramps and such assistance literally saved their lives. Men were given "a meal, a bed and a few bob to tide them over". In 1931 the Newcastle sub-branch established a camp for up to forty-five destitute diggers. The men contributed their 'susso', or unemployment relief, and in return received far more than their money's worth in food and clothing.[3] Many of these were, in fact, ex-imperial soldiers, men who had emigrated from the United Kingdom and had not been able to establish themselves successfully. The ex-imperials also found themselves with inferior benefits than the Australians. At this time an Australian soldier who was totally incapacitated received a war pension of £8 a fortnight for life, an ex-imperial similarly incapacitated received exactly half.

In the United States provisions for its veterans were traditionally more lavish than in Britain, although as individuals they suffered the problems common to all their kind. The American Stock Market crash of 1929 which launched the great depression hit veterans hardest of all. Just as in Britain, those in work lost their jobs to a greater degree than civilians: the burning question was whether anything could be done for them over and above other unemployed Americans. Much of the debate centred on the idea of a 'bonus', something never considered for British veterans. Although all had received 60 dollars mustering-out pay (certainly no less than British servicemen at demobilization) they recalled that, while they were given a dollar a day 'for being shot at', equivalent civilians engaged on war work earned infinitely more. Jack Dempsey, the former prizefighter, for instance, earned a bonus of 14 dollars a day for working in a shipyard.[4] After some initial reluctance the American Legion came to support the 'bonus' concept and its support strengthened as its investigations confirmed that members had also lost out in the short boom years immediately after the war. A 'bonus' bill was passed by Congress in 1924, but there was a snag in that its benefits were not actually to be paid until 1945 on the principle that by this time men would be past their prime and probably in need of some insurance. The delay would also avoid bringing about a deficit that it was anticipated 'would be a disaster to the nation's finances'. In 1929 the bill was extended to allow veterans to take out immediate loans (with interest liabilities) on 50% of the face value of their bonus.

To the surprise of the veterans' bodies and Congress alike, this was not considered good enough by either starving men or their families and under the leadership of an ex-sergeant of the Idaho National Guard, Walter W. Waters, a group decided to journey the 3000 miles from Oregon to Washington in order to buttonhole their Congressmen on the steps of the Capitol for payment, not loans. Between 25 to 40,000 veterans hopped freight cars and hitched lifts until they arrived in Washington, where the police chief Pelham Glassford, an ex-veteran himself, helped them set up a shanty town of sorts on Anacostia Plain, an isolated part of South-East Washington. They remained there from 29 May until 28 July, 1932, venturing out to march down Pennsylvania Avenue and picket the Capitol in favour of a new bill. Some of course lost hope and returned home, but significant numbers held on. On the 28th attempts were made by the police to evict them from a partially demolished building. In clashes with the police two were shot and killed. Reports abounded about the movement being Communist-inspired (these proved utterly unfounded) and the remarkable decision was made to have Federal Troops called to remove them. Responsibility fell upon General Douglas Mac-Arthur, then Army Chief of Staff. He was aided by a reluctant Major, Dwight D. Eisenhower, and the cavalry was led by Major George S. Patton. MacArthur first advanced on the veterans who were near the Capitol. He was preceded by tear gas and his men had their bayonets fixed. After the veterans were dispersed MacArthur went on to the camp at Anacostia. As he approached the veterans, they met him singing "My Country, 'tis of Thee", but the camp was soon burning anyway (Eisenhower said the veterans fired their own huts) and the men were forced to straggle homewards.

It all backfired on President Hoover whose growing unpopularity was not aided by MacArthur's bludgeon tactics. But despite public sympathy the veterans suffered too. Hoover's successor, Franklin D. Roosevelt, in his Economy Act of 1933, pruned many of their existing privileges by up to 25 per cent, including allowances for service disabilities. Notwithstanding, in the next year Congress was to pass a motion for the veterans' cash bonus–over Roosevelt's veto.[5]

The difficulties experienced by their veterans in the 1930s no doubt added to the other reasons which the American Legion had for advocating non-participation by American troops in the coming European War. It is, of course, to be noticed that the British

Legion, too, energetically sought ways of preventing such a war happening.

The catalyst which helped to spur the British Legion's leaders on this road was surely the endorsement by their Patron, the Duke of Windsor, of a resolution drawn up by Major Fetherston-Godley for consulting the ex-service organizations of Germany. During the 1935 Annual Conference the Duke declared, to hearty cheers, that "There could be no more suitable body or organization to stretch forth the hand of friendship to the Germans than the men who had fought them and now forgotten all about it".[6] It earned him a rebuke from his father, the King, and disapproval in Government circles where some considered the Legion had a "blinkered view of Germany and especially of German designs".[7]

In fact the Legion had already made contact with the Germans. In the previous year, at the invitation of German ex-servicemen, John Brown had visited Munich, but, following the Prince of Wales's speech, the German Foreign Minister Von Ribbentrop made a statement that "British ex-servicemen will certainly be heartily welcomed by German ex-servicemen and by the German people in general." After this the pace of exchanges quickened.

In July, 1935, a Legion delegation went to Berlin. They were received by Hitler at the Chancellery where conversations took place between Major Fetherston-Godley, Colonel Crosfield and the German leader. They came away much impressed by the man who had so rapidly set Germany on her feet, a man who had restored order and national pride, and, equally important, had got Germany working again. They were of course by no means the only British leaders to be affected by the charisma of the German leader. According to his Private Secretary, A.T. Sylvester, Lloyd George had also been captivated by Hitler's powerful personality.

A crowd of thousands, who, no doubt, had been carefully assembled by the Nazi Party, welcomed the delegation. They were flattered that people had waited hours in the boiling sun to catch sight of them. The new mood in Germany at this time impressed everyone and the Legion's leaders, eager to be impressed, were certainly no exception. The delegates returned firmly believing that Germany was pacific and that visits by German ex-servicemen should be accepted. They had even been allowed to visit a concentration camp. Hardly surprisingly, on his return Major Fetherston-Godley faced criticism from the Legion's Polack Branch in Bristol. Here a Captain Roskin remarked that he would have been glad if the Legion delegates had shaken hands not only with Generals but also with Jewish prisoners in concentration camps. He was told, "We did do so", and was passed the name of the camp visited. In fact it was Dachau, where the Nazis had pulled the wool over the delegates' eyes by replacing most of the real prisoners with healthy SS men.

Soon afterwards Sir Brunel Cohen and Colonel Ashwanden visited Czechoslovakia and Austria, where they were treated with the utmost hospitality and friendship and were clearly captivated. Brunel Cohen came to the somewhat naive conclusion that the Hungarian ex-service organization was not a political one and not very different from the Legion "except that its members were always dressed in uniform".[8]

Late in 1935 German ex-servicemen paid a visit to the British Legion's Brighton Branch where they paid homage by raising Nazi salutes over their dead comrades lying in Brighton cemetery. At this period praise of Germanic virtues started appearing in the Legion's *Journal*. In an article on patriotism, Lt-Col Graham Seton Hutchinson quoted General von Seeckt (the man who in secret had prepared the German Army for its subsequent massive expansion) as saying, "The soldier, having experience of war, fears it far more than the doctrinaire who, being ignorant of war, talks only of peace."

In January, 1936, there took place the return visit of German ex-servicemen agreed upon in Berlin, but it was cut short by the death of the King.

From now on, though, there seemed no end to the enthusiasm for an increasing interchange of visits. The April number of the Legion's *Journal* justified such movements with the words, "Ex-servicemen's organizations thread Europe like the meshes of a net. They are composed of men of mature age, great numbers of whom are leaders in their communities. Get them all together under one banner of comradeship and they will constitute the most powerful organization for moulding public opinion that the world has ever known."[9]

For innocence and unreality the article had few contenders. In June a House Party for Great War Adversaries was held by the Earl of Harrowby (Patron of the North Staffordshire formation of the Legion) who entertained representatives from the different nations, including Germany, Austria, Hungary and Bulgaria. The new King Edward sent them a message of best wishes.

Representatives from both wartime allies and adversaries attended the Annual Conference of 1936 and the Legion's President, Sir Frederick Maurice, proudly and formally justified the Legion's policy, "This platform demonstrates that we are doing our best to carry out the object set forth in our Charter to promote peace and goodwill amongst ourselves and with all nations." The King, wearing his Legion badge, received the foreign ex-service delegates at Buckingham Palace. In the Autumn he was to receive the Duke of Saxe-Coburg-Gotha who brought over another delegation of German ex-servicemen.

During the next year's Annual Conference, just $2\frac{1}{2}$ years before the outbreak of the Second World War, the President referred in glowing terms to the Permanent International Committee of fifteen ex-allied and ex-enemy nations which had grown out of a FIDAC resolution of 1935 put forward by the Legion. Colonel Crosfield was its Secretary. He said that he had been assured on the highest authority that the Legion's work in promoting a bond of comradeship and service with other countries had been one of the most effective means of improving international relations.[10] The Committee's Delegates, including Colonel Crosfield, had been received first by Goering in the Hall of Honour at the Imperial Air Ministry in Berlin and then by Hitler himself at Berghof in Berchtesgaden. Hitler, at his most cordial, thanked the delegates for visiting him in that remote part of the country and went on to tell them that the gigantic effort which the German people was making at the moment was only possible because absolute peace was reigning in Germany. The German people had not the slightest rancour about the war. Nothing remained but a great respect for their former enemies who had undergone the same troubles and the same dangers as the German people.[11]

Immediately after the Annual Conference a Delegation consisting of Major Fetherston-Godley, Colonel Crosfield, Colonel Ashwanden and others visited Italy to be welcomed by Mussolini with these grandiloquent words:

"The new Italy which has greeted you is largely a creation of veterans who have brought into civil life that spirit of boundless devotion to the country which has been, and is, the real and everlasting foundation of every state and every civilization in history."

While it was undoubtedly true that Italian veterans were well-favoured, the Legion's leaders must surely have harboured some qualms about the spectacle of veterans as Fascist nation-builders.

The international exchanges continued through October when, during a visit from the American Legion to London, their National Commander, Mr Daniel Doherty, emphasized the importance of the ex-service movement in a troubled world. In March, 1938, Major (now Sir James) Fetherston-Godley speaking at the Annual Conference of the Legion's Midlands Area declared, "There are 18 million reasons why the situation is not so dangerous as it was in 1914, the 18 million servicemen who have shown that they want no more war." In the same month Germany invaded Austria.

With rapid German rearmament and Hitler's expansionist ventures, the process of rapprochement could hardly go on much longer, but, if anything, the pace of activity accelerated. On 22 September 800 German ex-servicemen arrived as guests one week after Mr Chamberlain had flown to meet Hitler at Berchtesgaden to try and avert war. On the very day they arrived he flew off again to meet Hitler at Godesberg. The Germans' programme was revised and reduced in length, although they toured the Poppy Factory and Preston Hall Village and marched with British Legionaries in a parade at the Royal Hospital, Chelsea. They were actually taken round the House of Commons by Sir John Smedley Crooke but the main ceremony at the Cenotaph was wisely abandoned. Before they went, however, they rose early one morning and, shoulder to shoulder with Legion leaders, placed a wreath on it.

The euphoric bubble had to burst, but not before a last remarkable incident. This occurred in late September when the Legion's President made a proposal to the Foreign Secretary, Lord Halifax, for a mixed force of German and British ex-servicemen to act as a screen in Sudeten German territories before the advance of German troops.[12] They were to supervise a plebiscite for the Sudetenland. The numbers considered were for a contingent of 5000 men to be followed by a further 5000. With the approval of the British Government, Sir Frederick flew to Berlin on 22 September and saw Hitler alone on the next day. On 7 October 1200 fully-equipped Legionaries were assembled, sworn in and briefed at Olympia. The next day they marched through London wearing civilian suits, peaked caps and carrying walking sticks, preceded by the band of the Welsh Guards. They embarked in two troopships but sailed no further than Southend where they dropped anchor; in the interim the plebiscite had been abandoned, the ships returned and the contingent was disbanded. No plebiscite would now stop Hitler recovering the Sudetenland and much more besides.

It was not quite the end of the story of the Legion's international initiatives. On 11 February, 1939, Sir Frederick spoke at Brecon of his hopes that old contacts, i.e. with German ex-servicemen, would be resumed. But it was not to be. After the Germans had occupied Czechoslovakia, a strong party of legionaries led by the President and Chairman went rather belatedly to France to rebuild bridges there. Hopes for lasting peace through an international brotherhood of veterans were dead, although Sir Frederick still refused to accept the inevitable. Three days before the outbreak of war he broadcast on behalf of the Legion to the soldiers of the German Army and appealed to them not to bring about another fight by joining in the attack on Poland.

The Legion's international crusade can now be seen for what it was – unreal, credulous and with absolutely no chance of success. Yet one should not forget that all the main actors had been through the agony of the Great War. They had experienced the bitter loss of relatives and friends and seen the consequences of war on those who returned. They had seen the turmoil caused in Europe and could not accept that another even more terrible conflict was inevitable. Whereas the Foreign Office viewed their initiatives with some reservations, they were in fact not out of step with contemporary thought. The Cabinet meetings of this era reflect both the deep apprehension about the possibility of another war and the Prime Minister's belief, up to the very brink of war, that some accommodation was possible with Germany. The Legion's leaders, while clearly ingenuous, were not markedly out of kilter. It was another veteran, Winston Churchill, whose pugnacity and courage shone like a beacon through others' swirling doubts, who was.

None of this international activity in itself helped the Legion's rank and file achieve their humble and vital goal of worthwhile employment. Their state only improved when, from 1936 onwards, preparations for the next war, through rearmament, revived the economy.

After the outbreak of war the Legion rapidly transferred its attention to how best it could support the nation in the conflict. Proposals were made to the Government about using it as a Home Defence Force. These were quickly rejected. By 1940 it was firmly back on track. The new National Chairman,* Colonel Ashwanden, re-emphasized its main aims and activities which were every bit as relevant to this second generation of men involved in world war as to those of 20 years before. These were to include further efforts to improve pension arrangements, necessary proposals for sound demobilization procedures and a host of other matters concerned with the successful return of men at the war's end, among which were emigration and land settlement.

For the first time in British military history at the start of a major conflict there existed a great membership organization dedicated to helping servicemen after their release. Equally important, the War Cabinet was to be led by a man who could remember well the shortcomings in the arrangements for the men who returned in 1918.

---

* Major Fetherston-Godley had left for active service at the beginning of the war.

Was a new era about to open for British ex-servicemen? Before such a question could be answered a war of unrivalled proportions was to be fought, at the end of which a further 300,000 poppies would join those released during the British Legion's Festivals of Remembrance, and during which a combination of new weapons and man's continuing inhumanity to man, particularly in prisoner-of-war camps in the Far East, would rend apart both the minds and bodies of many who took part – and survived.

CHAPTER ELEVEN

Unfinished Business: The Second Great Call to Arms

> "I shall come limping back to you
> On a couple of sticks when this war is
> through,
> . . I won't complain and you won't
> complain
> If I come limping home again."
>
> *John Sibley, Burma, 1942*

TWENTY-ONE years after their demobilization from the Great War some of the ageing unemployables were at last being offered jobs. In the capital these were often humble posts in the London clubs and hotels, taking messages or helping in the kitchens. The reason, of course, was that once more war and its munitions industries were taking off the able-bodied young. This time it would be different in that from the very beginning of the war all men in the age groups 18 to 41 were to be conscripted and from 1942 all men and women between 18 and 60 obliged to carry out some form of National Service. White feathers were now redundant.

The burden of service fell more evenly from the outset and, although during the Second World War, mankind's greatest cataclysm so far, more than 50 million people were killed, the reaper's scythe fell more lightly upon Britain's young. This time the services' toll of killed and missing was over 271,000, not much above a third of those killed during the earlier war, and under

300,000 wounded. On the debit side there were over 172,000 prisoners of war who suffered unspeakable horrors, particularly under the Japanese. (In addition and unlike the Great War there were over 60,000 civilian casualties, far less than anticipated.)

Through luck and deliberate policy-making – the luck came with Hitler's decision to invade the Soviet Union and the policy with Churchill's determination to ally with anyone (not excluding a communist devil) who would fight against Hitler – Britain reverted to the traditional alliance policy whereby other nations were sought to take the predominant part of the land fighting. During the Second World War, for instance the Soviet Union suffered over 13 million military dead and 5 million wounded while the United States' Forces had over 292,000 fatalities and more than 670,000 wounded.[1]

In the simplest terms many more men would return than from the First World War and the proportion of those badly wounded would be less than 20%, which would have the most important consequences for their successful integration into civilian society afterwards.

The generation of 1939 went to war in a somewhat different frame of mind from their forebears. Despite the infamous motion of the Oxford Union in February, 1933, that 'this House will not fight for King and Country', a motion in favour of pacifism rather than national disloyalty, there was still idealism enough – but the young entered the forces without the same innocence or ardour as their parents. In many cases the sufferings and waste of war had been all too apparent in their environment. Everywhere there were memorials bearing hideously long lists of the dead; virtually every family would still mourn someone, notably at the Remembrance Day Services when, during the 2-minute silence, the whole country would hold its breath and remember the loss and the pain rather than the glory of war; with factory machinery and vehicles stopped, the commonest sounds would be the half-muffled sobs of women.

The sombre and complex aspects of war had been illustrated by contemporary films and writings. At this time the movies were, of course, the most popular form of mass entertainment. Lewis

Milestone's film of Remarque's book *All Quiet on the Western Front* (1930), the most notable of all war films up to this time, was about the brutality of warfare with the hero in his despair shouting, "When it comes to dying for your country it's better not to die at all." In the same year James Whale completed a faithful film adaptation of R.C. Sheriff's *Journey's End*, a study of disillusionment among upper-class young officers in the trenches. Two years later Frank Borzage produced *A Farewell to Arms*, Ernest Hemingway's tragic love story of an American officer (Gary Cooper) who fell in love with an English nurse and even deserted to look for her. Some less remarkable but more patriotic films were produced between the wars like *Cavalcade* and *Farewell Again*, but more still were concerned with spying and espionage. One of the earliest and best of this genre was Victor Saville's *I was a Spy* (1933) where the character who evoked most audience sympathy was the German Camp Commandant.

Books on the war like Edmund Blunden's *Undertones of War* (1928) or Robert Graves' *Goodbye to All That* (1929) were essentially a means of writing out the traumas of wartime by remembering the 'truth' about it; these had their humorous incidents but more often they dwelt on the waste and subsequent bitterness. More didactic and cruder in approach was Richard Aldington's *Death of a Hero*, but its overplayed message was clear enough: that war was pointless and those who took part in it were robbed of life and all its possibilities.

For many, including growing numbers of students and 6th form pupils (traditional officer fodder), T.S. Eliot's *The Waste Land*, abstruse and difficult as it was, evolved haunting images of the past war. Its incoherence echoed the readers' own confused reactions, its myths of ritual sacrifice, of regeneration, of fertility and waste, above all the sense of greyness and disillusion caught the predominant sentiment of the time.

As a result of the past war many young people had known hardships. If their mothers had been widowed and were without independent means, both they and their families would have suffered privation. Some children would have sacrificed further education to help supplement the family budget because pension rates, especially for those who had known better times, were humiliatingly low. If women were to find employment, and in the difficult employment market between the wars most women earned hardly more than half the average man's wage, their pensions were diminished accordingly. With the population imbalance caused by the war most women lost utterly the chance to remarry and a proportion of the young people available for call up in 1939 had never known a household with two parents. They were left in no doubt that the Great War was to blame.

Among the men who did return there were the remarkably high numbers carrying permanent injuries or those, in their eagerness to enlist, who had neglected educational and skill-training. In those cases it was likely that the whole family would suffer the continual penury which accompanied the curse of prolonged unemployment.

The 'rewards' for many ex-servicemen were all too painfully obvious to the potential conscripts of 1939. Septuagenarian book-seller Stanley Webb, who joined the RAF, remembered well when, as a child of 7, walking to school in the respectable London Borough of Twickenham, he was forever being approached by ex-soldiers begging for a penny. His abiding impression of other such men is of them standing in the gutter, some selling shoelaces or matches, others as buskers, often missing an arm or leg, wearing their medals and carrying cardboard placards of their past campaigns.

Above all a great universal sense of loss was occasioned by the war. Those who had lived through the Great War needed no reminding, but it was customary at most secondary schools for a member of staff who had served in France to lead the annual commemoration ceremonies – often with unashamed emotion. The continued sense of bereavement was hardly surprising with $\frac{3}{4}$ million dead from the British Isles alone, when $1\frac{1}{2}$ million more were rendered serious casualties and when ten years after the war there were almost $2\frac{1}{2}$ million men in receipt of a pension for war dis-abilities – almost 40% of all those who served. Over 30% of all men who in 1914 were between 20 and 24 and over 28% of those aged 16 to 19 had been killed. The story by no means ended there. During the first two years of the war a higher proportion of non-manual workers joined up, for example over 40% came from the professions compared with 25% of miners. Widows of these professional men would tend to be more eloquent in their descriptions of the war's costs. Of those who went, the middle-class officer casualties were higher than those for all ranks, 15.7% compared with 12.8%, and the percentage of casualties from the Universities was higher than either. Ten years after the end of the war casualties were still occurring: over 6000 new issues of artificial limbs were made during 1928 as a result of unhealed or deteriorating wounds.

Figures can, of course, be manipulated. Some have pointed out that with the cessation of emigration during the war (before 1914 it ran at 300,000 a year) the population in 1918 was actually higher than it might have been if the war had never occurred. Such facts, however, in no way lessened the sense of society's loss, the mourning for those who had suffered untimely death and those whom young people could see were so evidently injured and diminished in strength.

At times of national remembrance it was certain that some newspaper or magazine articles would recall those young men of rare promise whose very initiative and drive had carried them to the cannons' mouths and to swift death. The object and result was to emphasize the sense of loss. Doubtless if they had lived many would have been seduced by the world's luxuries and disappointed the high hopes placed on them, but some would surely have helped to rescue the world from the apparent banality and the moral poverty of the inter-war years when an older generation retained the reins of power beyond all expectations, even its own. In some cases this retention was seen as a hollow and half-hearted act. With the loss of their sons many older men no longer displayed that same zest in planning for the future. Attendant on the general sense of loss was a strong feeling among many, not just the ageing, that the reserves of national and moral fibre must have been depleted.

In 1939 the blitheness of Rupert Brooke's generation was entirely gone, partly because the introduction of conscription meant that volunteers only pre-empted the general call to arms.

Due to the nature of the war heroic actions were in short supply during its early stages. Whereas in 1914 the British Expeditionary Force confronted an immensely stronger foe from the very start, during the phoney war period the BEF was not engaged at all. Instead of that outburst of patriotic enthusiasm during 1914 the early months of the Second World War were marked by puzzlement, feelings of frustration and even disbelief over Hitler's intentions. When the panzers started rolling westwards, quickly destroying the myth of the Maginot Line's invulnerability, the BEF, while keeping its cohesion in a most admirable way, was soon bundled out of Europe. The sufferings of the trenches were not for these soldiers. The saviours of the homeland during August and September, 1940, flew from home bases.

When the Germans turned to their bombing offensive of cities there was absolutely no discrimination between combatant and non-combatant. The great military camps were usually in rural areas and so, in the main, it was the latter who had to take it. After Dunkirk the bulk of Britain's land forces were at home. The Western offensive to regain Europe through Normandy was four years away and although, to be sure, there was much hard fighting before Rommel was defeated in North Africa in December, 1942, and during the invasion of Italy, many of the best teeth-arm troops were brought back to Britain in order to work up for the Normandy invasion.

In short there was never the same irredeemable gulf between the battlefront and civilian life, something of great significance both to civilians and their fighting men. The one theatre of operations which was as apart as those of the First World War was in the Far East where men of Slim's 14th Army felt themselves virtually on another planet, forgotten and unappreciated until the European War had been concluded. It is not insignificant that in the late 1980s the most jealously guarded and probably the most active association among old soldiers of the Second World War is that of the Burma Star.

The British conscripts who served during 1939–45, particularly those of the land and air formations, differed from their forbears of only 21 years both in their attitudes to and their experience of warfare. Capable as they were of performing remarkable acts of bravery and sacrifice, it is still doubtful whether they would have endured so uncomplainingly the conditions of trench warfare, or so obediently moved forward on repeated occasions into that mael-strom of shells and enfiladed machine guns so characteristic of the Western Front during 1914–18. Being more discerning, it was only to be expected that they would also expect better arrangements at the end of the war, which for some lasted the full six and a half years. Because of these circumstances there appeared to be a greater chance than ever before that returning British servicemen would at last receive adequate assistance to reassimilate them-selves within the greater civilian community.

Compared with the previous war, immeasurably better arrange-ments were made for men to use their spare time constructively whilst serving. Educational training, which in many instances helped awaken the interests and ambitions of men to their future occupations, was conducted on a wide scale, virtually throughout the conflict. In much the largest of the military arms, the Army, a Corps dedicated to in-service education had been established since 1920, largely as a result of the need for vocational training at the end of the Great War. At the beginning of the Second World War it was scheduled to assume cipher duties, but from 1940 onwards the Army Educational Corps regained its central role and expanded continuously during the war period.

It could hardly be otherwise in the face of an irresistible demand for some form of educational provision during the phoney war period, when, after the evacuation of the BEF to Britain, literally tens of thousands of serving men and women occupied camps over the length and breadth of the country. Engaged in training for a land battle which no one thought could happen in the near future, many became bored and restless.

The Army's interest in education as a means of combating such threats to morale was demonstrated in a Report made during September, 1940, by General Sir Robert Haining called "Educa-tion in the War Time Army". This proposed a voluntary scheme, taken in out of duty hours, which concerned itself with three areas of learning activity, viz, the humanities (lectures or work on such subjects as history, geography or economics), vocational training and hobby interests. Where no relevant vocational courses were organized, correspondence courses were offered. In the Army

117,000 students enrolled for such courses and from all three services the total number studying by correspondence was 220,000. Hobbies and handicrafts were by far the most popular activities but, to the authorities' amazement, the desire for serious music also seemed unquenchable.

The fact that the voluntary scheme was not reaching 80% of the Army led the authorities to consider bringing back education into the training activities conducted during working time. Accordingly, in September, 1941, the Adjutant General, Sir Ronald Adam, proposed a weekly discussion of Current Affairs to be conducted by Regimental Officers using bulletins supplied by an Army Bureau of Current Affairs (ABCA). Sir Ronald plainly had in mind the need to create a climate whereby Cromwell's famous dictum about the citizen soldier "who must know what he fights for, and loves what he knows" would become a reality within the mass citizen army of the 1940s. In September, 1942, in addition to the ABCA scheme, it was decided that at least 3 hours of working time each week should be devoted to education, one hour to a military subject, one to a subject of the soldier's choice and the third to instruction in citizenship. In the United Kingdom the actual instruction was to be constructed by civilians, Army educational staff or suitably qualified regimental personnel, for whom in the case of citizenship written booklets were supplied, entitled *The British Way and Purpose* (BWP). Educational training became accepted as a valuable adjunct to morale and motivation for the citizen soldier. It was carried out in the battle theatres as well as the base areas and its newfound importance in such places as hospitals and especially in prisoner-of-war camps is hard to exaggerate.

In a conscript army men naturally looked forward with longing to life after the war, and education was a popular experience, particularly if it involved talking about the nature of their home society and Britain's future role in the world, or, when there was sufficient regularity, it could help them obtain qualifications which could be of assistance towards their future careers. For the most part such continuity of study as to enable men to take worthwhile civilian qualifications was hardly possible, the major exception being in prisoner-of-war camps in Europe. It was in the period between the end of hostilities and demobilization that a golden opportunity for vocational training beckoned and careful and thoroughgoing arrangements were therefore made for training during the pre-release interval.

In October, 1944, the Army Scheme (Release Period) was published. From the first it was aware of its own limitations, emphasizing that retraining for the professions and for industry was primarily the task of the civilian educational authorities and the Ministry of Labour. The stated aim of the Release Scheme was to give men and women some preliminary training in vocational areas to 'tune up their old skills', although general subjects were also to be offered. Subjects were grouped into six broad categories, Technology, General Science, Home and Health, Man and Society, Commerce and the Professions, Art and Music. In all 130 subjects were offered upon which 4 to 6 hours a week were to be spent, apart from ABCA and BWP sessions. At the apex of the scheme were residential 'Formation Colleges' both at home and overseas. Their role was to provide Further Education mainly in technical subjects and to train Regimental Instructors to conduct the main scheme. No examinations would be taken except for "the Forces Preliminary Examination". This was for those who were seeking a qualification to assist entry to the Universities or the professions. The scheme was no small undertaking; $1\frac{1}{2}$ million men were expected to participate for whom 2,600,000 books were required.

Despite all the careful planning even the modest aims set for it were to be frustrated. Everything worked on the assumption that after the German defeat there would be at least a year before Japan surrendered. The scheme was therefore scheduled to start on the 1st of July, some two months after VE Day. The rapid succession of VJ Day totally undermined the plans made. As after the First World War, demobilization took away the very instructors necessary for its success. Under the circumstances it was impossible to keep either a class together or an instructor available for any length of time.

In addition to the 'flavour' of education provided for many by the pre-release scheme, the Army's Educational Corps and its colleagues in the other two services found themselves with another major responsibility, the dissemination of the necessary information needed to help men on their release, like the Ministry of Labour booklets, *Release and Resettlement: an explanation of your position and rights* and *For your Guidance*, a booklet produced for each service. These publications were directly related to the arrangements for demobilization. Here plans were made relatively early in the war. For fit men true resettlement could only start at the end of hostilities. With the disabled it was different. They began to return from 1940 onwards and measures to help them overcome their disabilities, and incidentally to help them make a better contribution to the national war effort, were quickly taken. By the autumn of 1941 an interim scheme to train and resettle the disabled came into operation. A milestone in helping them over employment came with the setting up of an inter-departmental Committee under George Tomlinson (Parliamentary Secretary to the Minister of Labour). This was required to make proposals both for immediate effect and to prepare a comprehensive scheme which would come into force immediately after the war. Apart from George Tomlinson's own deep and genuine sympathy with the handicapped, its findings demonstrated that much had plainly been learnt from the sufferings of those disabled during the previous war. As the Report put it:

"Successful rehabilitation of a person disabled by injury or sickness is not solely a medical problem . . . when restoration in the medical sense has been achieved the services of the social and industrial expert are required."[2]

The Committee made recommendations for a reconditioning and vocational training service under the Ministry of Labour. For those unfit for immediate training or employment, rehabilitation facilities were to be provided either at special centres or at those already provided by voluntary institutions. When men were able to enter training, regardless of the level, maintenance payments were to be available for both the trainees themselves and their dependants.

The Report concluded that the King's Roll Scheme had not been a success (hardly a difficult decision under the circumstances) and recommended that legislation be introduced for employers to take on a prescribed quota of disabled. Certain occupations should be scheduled for disabled people only (lift attendants, car park attendants, etc) and a register for the disabled should be created. For those incapable of working under normal conditions the voluntary bodies would continue to receive grants but in addition a system of special centres under Government auspices, both for training and employment, should be set up. (St Dunstan's, for instance, was recognized as the body responsible for all vocational training and assistance in employment-finding for those blinded in war.) It was recognized that in some cases people would be incapable of doing anything other than working from their homes, conducting small businesses or making up products for large industrial organizations. Most importantly, the Committee recommended that as a valuable social service the whole cost of the scheme be met from central funds. The Disabled Persons (Employment) Bill introduced by Tomlinson himself received Parliamentary approval on the 1st of March, 1944; by June, 1945, the full scheme came into force.

By this measure the state finally assumed full responsibility for those maimed by war. Pioneering work by the dedicated voluntary organizations now became standard practice. Appropriate facilities to prepare trainees for normal employment, for so long the province of the Lord Roberts' Workshops, rather than the larger but more inflexible arrangements offered by the state after the First World War, were now to be offered by the Ministry of Labour within centres at Egham, Leatherhead and Exeter. Employment opportunities for the severely disabled in sheltered workplaces, already offered by the Lord Roberts' Workshops and The British Legion, were now to be supplemented by a public corporation, expressly formed for the purpose, called REMPLOY. (Set up in 1946, REMPLOY presently employs some 9000 disabled people in 94 production units throughout the UK and in addition operates a small number of homework units linked to factories for disabled people who are housebound.[3])

Those disabled during the Second World War had immeasurably better opportunities. In any case they were far fewer in number and, through improvements in medical treatment, better training and changing attitudes generally, a higher proportion than ever before were able to obtain normal employment. The opportunity to do so was made possible by the quota of disabled in relation to their total work force imposed on all major employers. For those who experienced increasing physical problems there were now vacancies with REMPLOY.

By the end of 1948 there were on the disabled register over 913,000, of whom over 70,000 were unemployed. Nothing could compensate such men for the cruel diminishment of their lives —the frustrations of relative inactivity, constantly attendant pain and personal humiliations—but since 1946, after centuries of efforts on their behalf, they were at last granted the opportunity of retaining the dignity and self-respect which came from worth-while employment. Less happily, as yet the wise legislation out-stripped the facilities for implementing it. In 1945 28,000 disabled still awaited training or placing in employment, but the commit-ment was there and REMPLOY made strenuous efforts to develop its facilities. By the end of 1948 forty-six factories had been opened.[4]

Arrangements to help the fit men and women coming out of the forces were also considered quite early in the war. In November, 1942, a Committee headed by the Paymaster General, Sir William Jowitt, presented its Report. To avoid the serious problems which arose at the end of the earlier war, it recommended that the timing of demobilization should depend upon a combination of age and length of service (although immediate release would still be given to the relatively few special priority cases). The oldest or longest-serving were therefore to be released first. The whole process was complicated by the likely event of the war ending in two stages, and the White Paper was not issued until September, 1944. Despite the war with Japan ending just three months after Germany's sur-render, the scheme of reallocating manpower was not modified and it worked effectively. Class A, much the largest class, was released relatively quickly. From September, 1945, through to September, 1946, virtually 3 million men were released at the rate of some 225,000 a month. Unlike the previous war, considerable thought was given to the changeover from war to peacetime production, in order to avoid a similar short boom followed by a depression with widespread and persistent unemployment. In any event the gross number rejoining civilian life was that much fewer due to the retention of conscription for all men when they became 18. Their length of service was first set at a maximum of eighteen months, then, with continuing military commitments on a large scale, extended to two years.

Despite the careful planning, no one could have described the arrangements for the returning men and women as lavish. This could be justified by the severe economic strains brought about by the immense cost of the war, but a more likely cause was the traditional British attitude to veterans, whether they came from great or lesser wars. Each was granted two months' leave on full pay, during which they were to re-establish themselves; one was considered as leave, the other for training. All received a modest gratuity and civilian clothes as in the previous war. Yet this time the demobilization process itself was seen to be fair. And infinitely more important than the size of the gratuity or the quality of the 'demob suit', as a result of sound planning and even more because of the immense economic opportunities which beckoned world-wide, unemployment – that greatest of all stigmas for returning servicemen – had been removed. The industrial capacity of Britain's main commercial competitors, save of course the United States, had been gravely weakened by the conflict.

The Committee considered possible training arrangements according to need. Under the conditions of full employment it was assumed that those who had established themselves in professions or trades before the war would be able to find comparable employment after, at most, a short refresher course. Those who had been called up before they had started or, if started, completed their training needed special training arrangements. Men and women with the necessary educational qualifications who proposed to study at a University or for one of the professions were allotted grants towards their fees and maintenance. For those wanting to enter business, three-month courses were to be set up in technical and commercial colleges with equivalent maintenance grants. (These turned out to be limited in number.) For the men and women who wished to learn a skilled trade or occupation and who displayed the necessary aptitude, arrangements were to be made in

Government Training Centres, Training Colleges or in some instances Employers' Establishments. By the end of 1944 schemes for just nineteen such occupations had been arranged.

The fourth main provision was the so-called 'interrupted apprenticeship scheme' whereby the unexpired portion of the apprenticeship was reduced by not more than a third when a man had worked at his trade while undertaking his duties in the Forces. The apprenticeship could be completed either by a full-time or a sandwich course and the same eligibility for fees and maintenance applied.[5]

In practice it did not turn out nearly so well as the sonorous words of the Report suggested. The Universities were flooded with applications and responded admirably. Flexibility was exercised by reducing the length of courses for 'mature' service students by up to a year. Discretion was also exercised, for instance, over the academic qualifications held by men who had volunteered, thereby interrupting their studies. Despite such constructive devices, in 1948 over a third of eligible students could not be accommodated, and unable to wait for a later academic year many took up employment which was hardly proportionate with their ability. The three months' Business Training Course, whilst admirable in principle, was heavily oversubscribed. Only about 50% of the suitable applicants were accepted in 1948. This also applied to apprenticeship schemes. The 'interrupted apprenticeship scheme' was far less generous than it sounded. A man might have practised his trade for the whole duration of the war and attended a clutch of in-service trade courses, yet his apprenticeship could not be shortened by more than a third. The arrangements for Cromwell's Army were far more generous. But then the Trade Guilds, powerful as they undoubtedly were, exerted far less industrial muscle than the British Trade Unions of the 1940s.

The process of demobilization in 1948 was considered to be generally fair. Its conditions were due to lessons learnt from the previous war and were the result of the advice given by the voluntary service organizations, particularly the British Legion. This had established a strong Planning Committee on Demobilization and Resettlement with T.F. Lister as Chairman and J.R. Griffin as

Secretary. The Committee submitted documents to the Government planning bodies, which undoubtedly played a part in their deliberations.

Voluntary bodies were also active in the welfare of the disabled. An Interdepartmental Committee sitting at the end of the war to consider the assessment of disablement due to specified injuries accepted both written and oral evidence from BLESMA and St Dunstan's and written evidence from the British Legion and British Legion (Scotland).[6] Their continued battle for the disabled represented a sacred trust for, while this category now had immeasurably better prospects over training and employment, British Governments seemed as hard-hearted as ever when deciding on the extent of disabilities and the appropriate pension awards. This continued parsimony was illustrated right through the Second World War by the intensity of the struggle between the ex-service bodies and the Ministry of Pensions over awards. The organizations primarily involved were the British Legion and BLESMA which, although still a relatively small body, was most active in seeking improvements for its disabled members.

To the dismay of those representing ex-servicemen, the Royal Warrant of 1939 had set the rates of pensions for war wounded at a far lower level than during the previous war. The 100% pension was reduced from 40/- (200p) to 32/6 (162p) and, whereas a 1914–18 man was receiving 20/- (100p) per week for a leg amputation below the knee, identical Dunkirk casualties were awarded 9/9 (48p) per week.[7] In 1942 the rates were still lower than for the 1914–18 war. As a result of constant pressure a breakthrough occurred in 1943 when the onus of proof was removed from the claimant, who henceforth received the benefit of any reasonable doubt. It was now up to the Ministry to satisfy an independently constituted tribunal that the disablement had not been affected by the conditions of Service. During the same year an unemployability Supplement was introduced for men whose severe disabilities rendered them unable to work. The rate of allowance was 10/- (50p) but it was very difficult to obtain. Pension rates were also now raised to the level of the First World War.

At the conclusion of the Second World War, as in the past, all those who returned had much catching up to do. In a financial sense alone their service handicapped them, for soldiers' pay was just a fraction of that received by civilians. Civilians who found themselves directed to essential industries worked long hours to achieve wartime production targets, but they were properly rewarded for their exertions. All were drawn in. In June, 1935, there had been over a million male unemployed; by June, 1942, this had dropped to 61,000, or to all practical purposes to nil unemployment.[8] By D-Day all available men and women were involved in the war effort. Rates of pay had increased markedly: in October, 1938, the average pay for men of 21 or over was 69/- (345p), by July, 1945, it had risen to 121/4d (607p).[9] In comparison, at the beginning of the war a soldier's pay was 14/- (70p), of which about a quarter usually went in compulsory stoppages. By 1945 172,000 of those serving in the Forces were aged 44 or over and this category, which was most likely to have served in both wars, had not only faced extreme physical dangers but also suffered great economic disadvantages on each occasion.

But at least during the second conflict, with the exceptions of those who had served in the Far East or had been prisoners of war, most had not lost touch completely with society at home, although they still faced many problems on their release.

It would be presumptuous to attempt to single out or to encapsulate the suffering of Second World War veterans. They are still too close to us. Anyone of middle years, though, can think of many who in some ways represent that generation who spent up to six wartime years in the Forces. Perhaps we can fittingly conclude this chapter by referring to five such men.

Willie (Dos) MacKenzie died about three years ago. Like most spirited young men in the Highlands he was a territorial soldier. From his small township twenty-five men joined the Seaforth Highlanders. In January, 1940, Willie and the rest went with the Regiment to France and during the withdrawal to the channel ports all were captured. There followed a six-week march to their prison camp of Stalag 9c on which a number died from exhaustion. Happily Willie and his great friend Hector MacLeod were young and strong. They had the durability of countrymen, making soup out of nettles picked on the march, and they 'captured' a duck—both would have been shot if they had been caught—which they cooked and ate in a field the same night. On arrival all were drafted to the stone quarries where they laboured for $3\frac{1}{2}$ years. The work was extremely hard, their accommodation primitive and the food poor. Willie had his right hand crushed during a blasting operation, but after much pain its function was restored by a skilled German surgeon. Towards the end of the war the prisoners were moved into a salt mine and finally had to march west away from the advancing Red Armies. Willie was repatriated in June, 1946, and to ordinary observers seemed to bear no mark of his ordeal. He returned to a grocery business and in later years his bacon counter was renowned as a place where lively conversation and good jokes were taken along with one's purchases. It seemed that after that long interlude on the flat German plains each day spent in the Highlands among his own people was a rare pleasure, especially if he could enjoy an hour's fishing after work. Only two of the twenty-five survived, including Willie's friend Hector MacLeod. It is likely their hard physical experiences took a toll in later life and 'Heccy' believes that a sense of grievance and bitterness diminished some. To Willie this was a condition which was entirely absent.

During a fortnight's interlude in 1953, between the end of National Service and the resumption of full-time education, the author travelled around Southern England with a sales 'rep', Fred Eggleton, an ex-trooper of the Normandy campaign. Fading memories are of tobacco smoke, innumerable saloon bars and endless talk of the war. On the whole Fred maintained he enjoyed his war, especially the exciting advance through France in August, 1944, when girls plied the tank crews with wine and flowers. Again and again, though, he dwelt on the desperate attempts to break out around Caen (Operation Goodwood), the brewing-up of so many tanks and the loss of his friends. Nine years afterwards the smell of roast meat tended to nauseate him and he seemed to live on a diet of sandwiches liberally washed down with bitter beer. Fred hated being alone and his movements were jerky, his nerves tightly strung. Without doubt in the late 1980s he would have been classified as a victim of post-traumatic stress. When we met again some few years later, he had obviously aged. Since then all contact has been lost.

Sapper 'Bert' Cronan came from a regular soldier's family. His father had many traits of the archetypal old soldier, a love of drink and restless irresponsibility. When he deserted his wife and six children, Bert, the youngest, had to enter an orphanage. From the age of 14 he had a number of jobs until becoming a joiner's mate with British Transport. Conscripted in 1940, he joined 105 Corps (Bridge) RE and with this formation he went through the North African campaign and was with the Allied forces who fought their way up the spine of Italy. A genuinely modest man, he maintains it was not a particularly dangerous experience for him, although he admits to the loss of many good friends there. Bert, like many other Irishmen, has a love of good music and a facility for language. (At the end of the war he volunteered for a course at Bologna University to learn Italian and still loves to recall the rich cadences of that language.) When asked about his experiences, he shrugs his shoulders, never seeing himself as a "warring sort of person". In 1940 the ex-orphan boy had recently married and there was an infant son. After his boyhood experiences through six long years away from his own family were a great sacrifice, for, as he says, "It was something you can never make up".

The fourth veteran of the Second World War came to my acquaintance through his book *18 Platoon*. Sydney Jary was commissioned in the Hampshire Regt but was made a platoon commander with the Somerset Light Infantry during their service in North-West Europe from July, 1944, to May, 1945. Young as he was he undoubtedly deserves the title of veteran, surviving ten months of continuous action, and being awarded the MC, although he was not 21 until May, 1945, when his shooting war had ended. Now a publisher, he declares that he started up his own company to avoid the undefined, insincere and often brutal relationships found in business life compared with the special community of those in war.

Towards the end of his book Jary faces up to the most insistent question put to all battlefield veterans, namely whether they suffered emotionally or nervously from their experiences. His own answer was that he had not, but he acknowledged that his experiences had had a profound effect upon him.

"Obviously I have been deeply influenced, particularly by my soldiers who produced a metamorphosis in my attitudes, which, I like to think, has been wholly good for me. I now value all life, human and animal, very greatly. Hunting revolts me. ... An infantry soldier requires patience and sufferance. Both, I hope, have stayed with me. Perhaps, on occasions, I have shown too much to certain people. As a result they have considered me ineffectual and lacking in the sort of aggressive drive which is often mistakenly considered a prerequisite for achievement."[10]

Like others Jary found the unquestioned loyalty of the active soldier absent in civilian life. There was, too, the dissonance; he has, for instance, been angered by the insensitivity and lack of perception shown by some clergy at subsequent Remembrance Day Services.

Like all veterans, his experiences have marked him, in his case not by frayed nerves nor emotional instability, but because during that experience of conflict he experienced a level of comradeship and selflessness among his platoon members which has put him permanently out of sympathy with many of the compromises and selfish customs inseparable from civilian life.

Not all those who warrant being termed veterans of the Second World War necessarily saw shots fired in anger. Their years of service away from normal civilian pursuits still represented a unique experience. In many cases the fact they did not man the firing line was no fault of their own.

Such a man was David Harland. A bank cashier of 29, he volunteered early in 1940 despite a congenital abdominal weakness which he concealed from the doctors. He was provisionally accepted for RAF aircrew training but after inexplicable delays in being called (he later learnt that it was due to enemy action which had destroyed some of the RAF records at Uxbridge) he presented himself at an Army Recruiting Office and was accepted for the Provost Branch. Unfortunately, during the three-day selection tests for Officer Training (WOSB) his cover was blown! His abdominal weakness reasserted itself, an operation was necessary and he was medically downgraded. Notwithstanding he became a Provost Staff Sergeant (QM Branch) and served right through the war in the UK and India.

Now 79, he is still ramrod straight, manifestly fit and an enthusiastic churchwarden of his Aldershot Garrison Church. When asked about the effects of his service, he makes no simple response. He acknowledges it hardly made him more patriotic; he could not have lived with himself if he hadn't volunteered. It did not enhance his faith either, for he had always been a great believer. What he does admit to, though, is a far greater feeling for people. The experience of meeting so many different men while in the forces, often under circumstances of mutual discomfort and frustration, has led him both to a fuller appreciation of individuals, whatever their credentials or appearance, and the wish actively to communicate with and assist them. Like Sydney Jary, he also seems to have rethought his priorities and found that the orthodox ambitions of many civilians no longer have the same attraction for him.

As a group, unlike many from the Great War, they soon took up the threads of civilian life and in the main appeared to slough off their former military connections. Apart from those who were disabled, the physical effects – which often became manifest long afterwards – varied widely, although a high proportion in their later years would find themselves suffering from "Gunners' Ear", the damage to eardrums caused by exploding armaments or long days on the firing ranges without the benefit of ear protectors.

For most, their personal and social sacrifices were immense, something they share with their brother veterans down the centuries. Like them, they look back on the discomfort, danger and occasional moments of elation shared with wartime comrades in arms, a proportion of whom were left behind on the battlefield.

Due to their experiences, they realize, often half apologetically, that their values cannot concur with those of men who did not serve.

CHAPTER TWELVE

Post 1945: From Conscription to the All-Regular Forces Again

"And life is coloured and warmth and light
And a striving evermore for these
And he is dead who will not fight
And who dies fighting has increase"

Julian Grenfell
Into Battle

As in past centuries the experiences of ex-servicemen since 1945 have to be seen against the major influences on British society at the time, resulting from both national and international factors. During the last forty-five years there have been sharply different levels of threat perception, from the Cold War period which culminated in the Cuban Missile crisis of 1962 to the current rapprochement of the super-powers. Within British society massive changes have occurred due to the provisions of the 'Welfare State'. The austerity years of the early post-war period have given way to the greater freedoms offered by growing affluence and the taste for more hedonistic pursuits. Throughout, there have been periodic checks and setbacks to national plans caused by recurring economic weaknesses. All have had their effect on both the nation's military arm and its veterans. In this respect it can be argued that the first thirty-five years of the post-war period exhibited a pattern in veterans' affairs quite different from that of the present decade.

Immediately after the Second World War the relationship between the nation and its veterans differed fundamentally from that at any time since the founding of a standing army. While it had always been customary for men to return home in large numbers at the end of great wars, all comparisons paled before the figures involved in 1919 and 1945. At the end of the Boer War the total numbers of Imperial troops were just $\frac{1}{3}$ million, of whom 100,000 became casualties (21,000 dead). When the Armistice occurred in 1918 the Army's strength exceeded 5 million and over 1,600,000 had already returned home as casualties. During the final stages of the Second World War, in June, 1945, the total British Armed forces exceeded $4\frac{1}{4}$ million and most of the 700,000 casualties had already come back to Britain.

While the numbers of fighting troops involved in the Second World War were slightly lower than in the previous conflict (though still vast), it was the rapid sequence of two such immense conflicts which was so significant. In 1946 the vast majority of the male population were veterans of 20th century wars. Military service had become a universal experience. These men were to be joined from late 1948 to 1962, not only by ex-regulars as their careers expired, but by annual outflows of some 160,000 young men on completion of their National Service. Initially required to serve 18 months (later extended to two years), many National Servicemen, because of their very time with the colours and the proportion spent either on active service or anti-terrorist activities, had every right to be considered full veterans. In some cases their claims might even be stronger than those of some wartime soldiers who had witnessed the war's last stages or had spent it on Home Service only, although the ex-service organizations were slow to recognize National Servicemen as veterans.

National Service, with its large annual outflows, lasted for so long because, uncharacteristically in British military experience, the ending of the Second World War did not signal an end to international tension, with its continuing needs for high numbers of military personnel. The Cold War caused the creation of the two greatest military alliances ever and in the United Kingdom's case her Western alliance commitments were supplemented first by responsibilities to defend, and then, with changing policy, to cover her withdrawal from, the Empire. In the early 1950s these commitments were powerful contributory factors towards Britain's siege economy. Fully 10% of its Gross National Product had to be allocated to Defence. At no other point in our history were so many men serving during peacetime nor were there so many veterans —three generations who had experienced the rigours of serving their country at times of national threat. By 1962 over a quarter of the population had served and their dependants virtually trebled the numbers who might have to be helped.

In the previous chapter mention has already been made of the main arrangements for those returning after 1945: the more efficient system of demobilization itself; for the first time sound and workable plans to help the disabled; the attempts made to help personnel prepare themselves for civilian life through training given before release (an initiative thwarted by the unexpected swiftness of VJ Day) and the general arrangements for healthy men and women on leaving the Forces. While undoubtedly better than any previously, by no stretch of the imagination were they generous or even comparable with those offered by the United States or the Dominions. The whole system was redeemed by the more favourable employment opportunities which were available.

Why, one might well ask, should British veterans, members of a greater national brotherhood than ever before, continue to be treated with bare justice compared with other countries? This question becomes all the more important when it is discovered that the system which operated in 1945 influenced fundamentally the subsequent resettlement arrangements through the later 20th century.

One of the reasons surely lay in the very numbers. From central Government's point of view, the scale of demobilization, together with the immense economic burdens of the war, operated against granting more lavish arrangements. Current political ideas, too, were against advantages being given to any one group. Among the population at large their emotions in 1945 were probably more of gratitude than of strong sympathy for the vast numbers of returning veterans. At the end of the Boer War they had come back marching behind their bands through streets laced with bunting and lined with applauding spectators. In 1945 there were just too many of them for such pomp. Anyway men were now demobilized by category rather than by complete units. This war, because of its universal nature and because it was the third in under fifty years, was no longer novel and was far less alluring to the general public.

Popular sympathy was surely affected by Britain's geographic position as a front-line country during the Second World War, open both to the threat of invasion and prolonged aerial bombardment. In such circumstances the whole population needed to be mobilized. Everyone had to make sacrifices and the country's labour force was directed on grounds of national efficiency. How many 'Bevin Boys', for instance, would have opted to work in the mines? Many might have preferred the armed forces and would not have been slow to say it. At home the population had to undergo the endless and enervating routines of war, the long working hours, broken nights in damp air-raid shelters, food rationing, endless other restrictions and always the interminable queueing. The required dress of female munitions workers, with their turbanned hair, long smocks and clogs hardly compared favourably with their sisters in smart military uniforms. There could be no swaggering for them. Some of the soldiers' letters home (determinedly cheerful as they were) painted a picture of adventure and excitement calculated to raise the envy of anyone in 'blacked out', austerity Britain.

Civilians knew they were also open to dangers, with everyone a potential victim of bombing and later of the V1 and V2 raids. It was only to be expected that such people, exhausted by the many demands on them and chaffing against controls, should be less generous towards returning men than their counterparts in countries like the United States or Canada whose home populations had no direct experience of war. Undoubtedly there was strong and general approval of the better arrangements made for the disabled, those who needed treatment, special training and preferential employment rights. And, of course, it was well understood that some, while not obviously disabled, would never be the same again. No doubt many prisoners of war had suffered terribly but so had

Mrs Jones: after being blown out of her bed that time; her nerves would never be the same and weren't they always hearing about it? But an equally understanding attitude was barely extended to healthy personnel and some of the skilled unions were far from sympathetic. Were ex-servicemen not receiving help? Were they not already filling all the training establishments, the Universities, Colleges and apprentice schemes? The high sensitivity of the Government to Trade Union interests was commented on in the British Legion *Journal* for July, 1946, where profound dissatisfaction was expressed over the slow progress in granting training places. The chairman of the Legion's Employment Committee said the Government was only prepared to "endeavour to arrange training . . . when the tradesmen concerned were *willing* to accept trainees".

The arguments for giving ex-servicemen preferences over job-finding lost much of their bite at a time of full employment. Ex-servicemen seemed to have little excuse if they did not find something. And, sadly, probably for the first time the resettlement of servicemen moved into the political arena.

Colonel George Wigg, MP, in the British Legion *Journal* of March, 1946, wrote that "British Legion policy of preference in employment for ex-Servicemen and women is, in my view, short-sighted but I can well understand the advocacy of such a policy by those who remember only too well what happened after the last war. . . . Now with a Labour Government pledged to a full-employment policy there are more jobs than men . . . a square deal not only for the ex-serviceman and woman but for the whole community."

This article was answered comprehensively by Captain Quintin Hogg, MP, writing in the May Issue. He started by answering citizens who, during the war, maintained, "We are *all* in the front line now". "If the saying means that there has been in the main any comparable degree of sacrifice or hardship between those who worked in civvy street and those who underwent the rigours of life in the field, or the prolonged heartache of separation from their families, I must say I have yet to hear more pernicious and dangerous rubbish. . . . The point is that real equality of opportunity between one who has spent the last six years in the service and one who has not, is only pious humbug unless some degree of preference in the early stage is given to the ex-service man and woman."

George Wigg's article illustrated the additional problem faced by British ex-servicemen in 1945 compared with returning men in other countries—national hopes for the projected Welfare State. This package of economic policies sought the quintuple aims of full employment, social security (sufficient income at times of misfortune), adequate medical services for all, good housing for everyone and the right to a decent education.

If *all* the population came to enjoy these services there would be absolutely no need for veterans to have special medical facilities of their own, like those of their American counterparts or those offered in such places as the British Legion Village at Maidstone or through SSAFA's maternity facilities at Devonport. If the local authorities were able to offer sufficient houses for everyone, including veterans (at reasonable rents), there would be no need for measures like the guaranteed house purchase loan system which was part of the 1944 GI's Bill of Rights.

Self-evidently the massive jigsaw of legislation which together would bring about the Welfare State could not produce dramatic results overnight and so, in the pattern of the past, those who suffered the greatest housing problems immediately after the war were the returning men and women. In 1946, at its National Conference, the British Legion urged the Government to accelerate its housing programme and in June, 1948, Mr T.F. Lister moved a resolution drawing attention to the "thousands of ex-servicemen [who] were having to live under intolerable conditions". One national delegate, Mrs Carlisle, cited "thousands of ex-Service men and women having to live in tin huts", while others re-emphasized the shortages and pointed out that some training courses for building trainees had actually been stopped by the unions for fear of a possible economic rundown.

It was the same story with ex-servicemen needing general retraining. The 1944 Education Act applied in the main to schoolchildren rather than those who required further education and, with the exception of university education where new opportunities opened up (just too late for the bulk of the returning men), the number of vacancies remained limited. In 1947 the Legion's President, Sir Ian Fraser, deplored the numbers still awaiting vocational training schemes.

Apart from its influence on restricting official resettlement arrangements, the concept of the Welfare State offered a challenge to the very existence of the veterans' voluntary bodies by envisaging a new group of professional workers providing community care. Henceforth local authorities would be required to provide domiciliary and residential facilities for the handicapped, the elderly and the homeless. For this they needed a new army of trained social workers. Once again years were to pass before such people became available in sufficient numbers (some would say in excessive numbers), but the implications for the ex-service charities were clear enough. Within a relatively short time many of their responsibilities would diminish and disappear. Hardly surprisingly, they became uneasy about the possible submerging of veterans' special concerns within a system organized essentially for civilians, and began to ask whether the roles which they had formerly carried out could ever become the province of others, even if they were trained public servants.

Unquestionably a number of powerful influences were at work in Britain during the immediate post-war years to prevent ex-servicemen receiving any concessions measurably greater than those granted to the population at large. For quite understandable reasons improved arrangements would never be forthcoming for National Service veterans either, some 1,100,000 of whom served in the Army alone.

Much has been written about National Service[1]; suffice it to say that, in the years of tension following the war, most of the young conscripts found, when they returned home on leave, that it was to the general approval of their fathers and grandfathers who saw such military service as part of the necessary scheme of things. The author benefited in a small way from such national approval when, in 1951, as a private undergoing basic training with the Middlesex Regiment, I travelled by bus between my parental home in Enfield and my new Regimental home at Mill Hill. At no time were the two 'old pennies' I offered for my fare accepted by conductors, either male or female, who seemed oblivious of my presence. Such sympathy, though, seemed to end when the National Serviceman shed his uniform. Perhaps the conventional British never saw him as a proper veteran. A veteran needed some grey hairs and a limp; a National Serviceman joining at 18 would be released before his 21st birthday. With all young men liable for service, everyone shared the same problem of taking up their future careers some two years later than normal. No special arrangement seemed necessary; the final 28 days' leave was considered help enough, but this group undoubtedly lost much time in preparing for their future careers. Some delayed their training, especially apprentice training, until after their military service, others changed direction as a result of their experiences, not always for the better. Realistically it would have been surprising and hardly necessary for National Servicemen to be given comprehensive assistance towards their resettlement. Yet while the Army, for instance, was largely made up of such men, resettlement arrangements as a whole were, at best, neglected. The authorities connived at this in that they were never happier than when some above-average National Serviceman, unable to imagine himself in civilian life, decided to sign on, and many excellent recruits were obtained this way.

That such limited arrangements for helping men re-enter civilian life succeeded as well as they did in 1945 owed more than anything else to the fact that there was little unemployment. This was reasonably satisfactory as long as it lasted, but, as many union representatives could not believe it would, so the great charitable bodies supporting ex-servicemen had similar doubts, both about the present arrangements and what might happen when conditions changed. These were demonstrated in their requests for an Inter-Departmental Committee to consider 'the future objectives of the resettlement service, particularly with regard to employment'. This received a positive and quick response from a Government which, confronted by a national labour shortage, was anxious that all talent, including that of veterans, should not be wasted.

The Wiles Committee's actual terms were "to examine the

problems arising on the resettlement in employment of officers and men coming out of the forces and to make recommendations".[2] Characteristically National Servicemen were not its concern. Its Interim Report came out in 1947 and its main theme was the need for servicemen not just to obtain employment (there was no current problem there) but work commensurate with their ability and experience. The Wiles Committee believed that in order to attract sufficient people of the right calibre into the Regular Forces (a vital need during the Cold War) "potential entrants had to be convinced that they were in no blind alley occupation but enjoyed prospects reaching beyond their term of service."[3]

It divided all ranks into four distinct categories: those with specialist qualifications suitable for civilian employment; those with superior educational qualifications or experience suitable for entry at a senior level into either public service, commerce or industry; those suitable for training in a skilled occupation or profession; those without special skills who needed relatively short training. Each of these categories required different facilities and the main recommendations were concerned with the need for timely and skilled advice during service and short training arrangements for personnel before they left. When training was required after service, an average duration of 6 months was advocated. The Committee counselled that Trade Unions should, after due consideration, recognize officially those trades learnt during military service.

Regarding employment, it recommended that ex-servicemen should have preference in the Home Civil Service, Local Government Services and concessions when entering public bodies such as the Police Forces. It said industry should be made aware of the high ability levels of retiring servicemen.

Special help in employment-finding was proposed by a partnership, the Ministry of Labour working closely with the main voluntary employment body, the Regular Forces Employment Association. Other voluntary agencies were urged to collaborate with the RFEA to avoid an overlapping of services.

This enlightened report recognized officially that those returning needed more than mere employment, they needed employment in accordance with their aspirations and abilities. It reiterated the need for sound advice prior to demobilization. (From 1948 onwards the Army Educational Corps was given responsibility for a Resettlement Information and Advice Service.) for appropriate training both before and after service – in many cases to an average length of six months – and the necessity for special concessions and assistance with employment-finding from both the Ministry of Labour and the Forces' own employment bodies. It put resettlement of the soldier in 'peacetime' on to a new level as a fully accepted responsibility of state.

Unfortunately such recommendations did not lead to substantial improvements in the short term. Under conditions of full employment the official system, limited as it was, seemed to operate adequately enough and ten years were to elapse during which no other memorable developments occurred for British veterans.

The voluntary associations concerned with veterans had good reason to be somewhat subdued at this time since, for all of them, this first postwar decade was one of adjustment to changed circumstances. At the end of earlier wars, in answer to some particularly pressing need, it had been customary for at least one major new body to emerge. This time there was seemingly no crisis that the state and the existing charities could not meet. Undoubtedly the lack of accommodation was a major problem, but it was one that faced the whole country and was far beyond the financial resources of any charity to solve. Within the scope of this book one is bound to pay most attention to the British Legion and other well-established charities devoted to helping specific categories of need, like SSAFA and the SSAHS which after 1948 became the Forces Help Society. There were, of course, others, some representing new military organizations such as the Army's Royal Pioneer Corps Benevolent Trust (1942), the Royal Military Police Association (1946) and the Navy's Women's Royal Naval Service Benevolent Fund (1942). The Army Benevolent Fund (1944) and the Royal Air Force Association joined those already established in the Navy and the RAF and there were new tri-service campaign associations like those of the Desert Rats or the Burma Star.*

This vast mosaic of Regimental Associations, Benevolent Funds and voluntary charities was larger than ever – it now numbered some 600 – but none of the newcomers was formed to meet any single, major perceived need but in the hope that, through judicious co-operation, adequate assistance could be given to all who suffered misfortune. However, with the continued development of the Welfare State, the overriding question was whether such assistance would be a diminishing responsibility; in the circumstances and at a time of relatively full employment it was hardly likely that service charities would adopt too robust a posture.

With the universal membership body, the British Legion, the immediate post-war period was one of strong growth. From less than 500,000 members during the war it passed the million mark in 1947, where it stuck, falling somewhat short of the mandate it needed for negotiating with Ministries of State. True to its traditions, the Legion invariably adopted a polite and measured stance. Unfortunately it was never to have a big enough stick, in membership numbers, to get most of what it wanted by speaking softly and both its very size and elevated position prevented it adopting the blunt tactics possible for smaller pressure groups. For instance, in 1947 it called upon industry "to open the door a little wider to grant more training opportunities". This was hardly likely to make leading industrialists shake in their shoes.

The Legion's activities seemed to stay very much the same as before. The need to press for more 'realistic pension levels and to represent individual cases of hardship' remained. Benevolence was still required for the growing band of ageing veterans from the First World War who found that it was too late for them to benefit from many of the Welfare State's proposals. And while the Legion's own hospital facilities were absorbed into the National Health Service, there were still its disabled industries (despite

---

* The last two were, of course, membership organizations for those who took part in particular campaigns. In the same way Regimental Associations were only open to personnel of the particular Regiment concerned.

REMPLOY), its low-cost housing and a growing need both for permanent nursing homes for the aged and incapacitated and short-stay convalescent accommodation. There remained, also, its responsibility for national remembrance both at home and overseas (although the fight for the traditional Veterans' Day on 11 November had been lost) and it was extending its nationwide social responsibilities through its clubs.

The more pressing single issue then faced by the Legion and the other charities lay in the extreme difficulty experienced by returning men in finding accommodation. Despite representations, no special concessions were gained from governments pledged to provide better housing for all. Typically, the Legion determined both to set an example and to assist as far as it could by offering interest-free loans up to a maximum of £150 to would-be house purchasers, and a limited number of loans for business start-ups, usually for the disabled. By 1958, 769 house loans had been granted to a total of £92,936. While this was undoubtedly an enlightened scheme which helped a significant but small minority, one could argue in retrospect that the Legion might have used the full weight of its lobbying power to obtain special concessions from the Government or to negotiate favourable rates of interest from the City for ex-service borrowers. At no time, however, did the Legion's senior officers consider such arrangements for guaranteed house loans as were available in America possible in Britain. With their experience and in the climate of the day who could deny their doubts?

Despite the extension of the Welfare State, no one could deny that the British Legion was still in business and had every reason to remain so, but with other charities like the Forces Help Society and SSAFA there seemed much more likelihood of their roles being seriously questioned.

In the field of sheltered employment, the Forces Help Society, as the pioneering body, still had its own workshops and the Brookwood Training Centre and Home. For a time these would still be going concerns, whatever facilities REMPLOY might succeed in creating for those disabled in the Second World War. It retained a continuing responsibility for its long-standing workforce and offered opportunities for men choosing to take advantage of its own brand of caring employment. Yet REMPLOY and the compulsion upon normal industry to take a set quota of disabled workers removed the need for expansion and its last new factory was opened by Queen Elizabeth (now the Queen Mother) in Belfast during 1950, after which its workshop capacity showed a steady decline.

The Society's other great work lay in assisting individual ex-servicemen in need. In 1947 it was firm in its belief that the Welfare State would not end this work because "wayward human nature will continue to present problems which only a voluntary society can meet". During 1947 its helpers gave general assistance to no less than 140,000 cases, but this gradually declined until, in 1957, there were 60,613 cases to whom £89,792 was dispensed. With such contraction in its two main areas of work, some form of reappraisal was plainly needed.

With SSAFA the case was somewhat different. The core of its work lay with its 5000 helpers stationed across the country to investigate family problems and then give assistance. If the provisions of the Welfare State were extended satisfactorily, one could expect many of these problems to be relieved by official welfare workers serving the community at large. Yet during its Annual Conference in 1946 Admiral Sir Arthur Power, the Second Sea Lord, denied any likelihood of this. He plainly gave his audience exactly what they wanted to hear, a strong re-affirmation of their importance.

"The Government, by means of insurance and other measures, seeks to control our lives or may I say secure our lives from birth to the grave. That is not enough. . . . The essential required is a generous gift of time and energy by true philanthropists."

During 1946 and 1947 SSAFA investigated no fewer cases than before and dispensed large sums in aid, some £$\frac{1}{2}$m each year from both their own and other charities' funds. During this early period after the war SSAFA naturally also came up against the serious problems faced by families over housing. In 1950 the SSAFA representative at Bournemouth could still say, "Housing, or lack of it, continues to prove itself the greatest evil this island has ever had inflicted on it." The problem was made far worse for ex-servicemen because local authorities demanded residential qualification before allocating homes, something quite impossible for veterans to provide. By 1955 things were plainly improving for many families and the grants paid were only half those of 1946. Indeed, the year before at SSAFA'sAnnual Conference the shrinking requirements of Second World War veterans were acknowledged in the statement that "most of the ex-servicemen of the second World War are established civilians in a prosperous community for whom the war is now a distant memory".

Despite the successful re-integration of so many, SSAFA's helpers now found a different pattern of need emerging as they became more involved with the emotional and social problems caused by modern living than with cases which required financial assistance alone. To help deal with these more complex cases a common form was devised for use by all the charities involved, and a clear desire was shown by SSAFA for further co-operation in casework by their strong support of the Consultative Committee for the Voluntary Service Organizations.

Significant changes in SSAFA's other responsibilities had occurred during the decade. Its Maternity Home at Devonport was transferred to the National Health Service and SSAFA nursing sisters now operated abroad; there were 77 in 1957, still under SSAFA control but wholly paid for by the authorities. The Home for Officers' Widows at Wimbledon continued to flourish but the short-stay homes for children were closed and the secondhand clothing department virtually run down. There was no doubt that SSAFA continued to play an important role but a time for some reappraisal was plainly coming.

At the very time that the main service charities faced a reconsideration of their part in ex-servicemen's affairs, an initiative by the Government spotlighted once more the arrangements made for returning veterans and the future system to be offered by both official and voluntary bodies. With Korea resolved, the Malayan emergency virtually over and the Soviet threat seemingly contained by the Western Alliance, economic factors became the predominant issue in the United Kingdom. The Government released details of a rundown in the Armed Forces over a five-year period, proposing that the Army lose 45% of its strength, the Air Force 35% and the Navy, with more regular personnel than the other two, considerably fewer. Conscription would be ended and voluntary recruitment re-adopted. This first taste of postwar redundancy, the so-called Golden Bowler period, particularly affected Army captains and majors in their 30s and 40s and senior soldiers. While the numbers coming out were small compared with the great demobilization of 1945, they were mostly relatively young men of high calibre who required civilian positions proportionate to their ability and ambitions.

On the face of it a fairly drastic overhaul of the modest arrangements took place, although cynics remarked that the component parts had hardly changed; it remained a partnership between official and voluntary organizations. The presentation, though, was undoubtedly improved. A so-called Forces Resettlement Service was established on a national basis linking the Service Departments (concerned with giving advice and short training courses while men were still serving), the Ministry of Labour (post-release training and employment finding), the Officers' Association (officer employment) and the Regular Forces Employment Association (for servicemen's employment).

A Resettlement Advisory Branch was set up under the chairmanship of Sir Frederic Hooper (Managing Director of Schweppes Ltd and Director of Business Training in the Ministry of Labour at the end of the war) which endorsed principles laid down by the Wiles Committee, its predecessor of a decade before, that service manpower should be used cost effectively to satisfy both the individual's and the national need. The Hooper Board contained representatives from industry, commerce and the Trade Unions as well as from the Ministry of Labour and the Service Departments. As a result, Regional Resettlement Committees were set up throughout the country, and increased, if still modest, grants were made to the voluntary employment bodies.

The main outcome of the Hooper recommendations was that for the first time officers were offered full resettlement facilities, such as they were. Before this officers had had no adequate guidance.

Now in the Army, for instance, Advice Panels were established. These were manned by a senior Educational Corps officer and a representative from the Ministry of Labour and offered advice interviews up to two years prior to an officer's retirement. More emphasis was also placed on improving civilian qualifications before release, either through correspondence courses or through a growing number of month-long in-service courses, taken close to the point of retirement.

The influence of Sir Frederic Hooper was seen in the creation of two courses to familiarize officers and warrant officers with civilian practices. A six-week Business Training Course was offered at selected Polytechnics and Technical Colleges (the extra fortnight had to come out of their leave entitlement) and there was a one-month course actually run by the Ministry of Labour for 'potential supervisors', senior ranks who lacked technical qualifications but whose qualities marked them out for supervisory posts.

Arrangements for employment-finding were improved by the Officers' and the Regular Forces Employment Associations expanding their services, and direct links were now established between the Forces Resettlement Service and the Professional and Executive Register held by the Ministry of Labour. As the Register had never risen to expectations (the vast majority of such posts were obtained through personal contacts or by answering newspaper advertisements) this was not that much of an advantage.

After interviewing some of those about to be made redundant, Sir Frederic Hooper became aware of their great concern over housing. He negotiated with both the Ministry of Housing and with Local Authorities, exhorting them to relax the registration rules for Council accommodation, but by and large he failed to move them. The alternative was, of course, to help veterans buy their own houses and to this end he succeeded in getting relaxations to the immensely complicated rules for commuting a proportion of their future pensions into lump sums. Efforts were made to increase end-of-service grants for long-service personnel. The Army established a "Save while you serve Scheme" which arranged for money to be paid monthly from soldiers' accounts to a building society of their choice, but, apart from the administrative convenience, the only advantage here was that the societies involved were reputedly prepared to advance money on the definite promise of a future civilian job.

Compared with other countries such modified arrangements for British veterans remained unimpressive and the chances of them being improved markedly during the next twenty years or so were by no means favourable.

CHAPTER THIRTEEN

British Veterans in an Adverse World

"Yes makin' mock o' uniforms that guard
you while you sleep
Is cheaper than them uniforms . . .

Tommy
Rudyard Kipling, 1865–1936

Aᴛᴇʀ 1962, when the five-year redundancy period drew to a close and Britain was served by all-regular forces again, arrangements for helping those retiring actually regressed.

Responsibility for this lay in a number of quarters. Within the services themselves the belief endured that undue help for men leaving – certainly those who did so before completing their maximum engagements – was somehow disloyal. The loss of such men only made for increased recruitment problems. The arguments put forward by the Wiles Committee at the end of the war that favourable prospects after service would encourage a better type of recruit had not been generally accepted. More lavish arrangements would have run counter to the spirit of the age. With the ending of National Service there was no longer the same direct interest in the military by the mass of the population. For much of the 1960s and 1970s the mood of the time ran counter to the establishment, of which veterans were undeniably a part. War was seen by many young people in the mid 1960s either in the hideous manifestation of a nuclear explosion's mushroom cloud or the defoliation and random firepower of the much-televised Vietnam

War. This was the decade of the young, the result of that birth bulge in the late 1940s when the men came back. Living under the continued protection of the Western Alliance, they had the luxury of condemning all forms of war and by extension those in uniform who still guarded them. They enjoyed massively increased spending power and were captivated by the music of the Beatles and the Rolling Stones, pro-youth and anti-establishment. Reflecting this craving for change and pleasure, the Beatles' hit "Lucy in the Sky with Diamonds" (the initials of LSD) spelt out the growing use of cannabis and tragically encouraged the sharply increased, if still limited, use in Britain of amphetamines and hard drugs taken intravenously. With fitness a fetish of the services one can well understand the veterans' astonishment and anger over the use of such drugs. As Arthur Marwick put it, the trends in the middle-1960s were notable not just for increased drug-taking but "by resistance to the Vietnam War, with support for peace in general, with transcendentalism and with 'flower-power' ".[1]

The reaction against war was not just among the young, however. 1958 saw the founding of the Campaign for Nuclear Disarmament which, in its early stages, had the support of between one-quarter and one-third of the British public. The 1960s were a time for questioning established customs, including the traditional use of force. In the areas of moral and artistic values, too, permissiveness and defiance prevailed through, for example, the relaxation of theatre censorship, the testing of what constituted obscene literature, and in architecture the building of flat-roofed, box-like constructions that defied Britain's past climatic patterns. This new spirit of questioning was even felt in that most indefinite science, economics, where it was asked why Britain's economic performance had been so poor compared with that of her postwar competitors. Some found the cause in militarism and the large percentage of the GNP spent on armaments in the early postwar years when it should have fuelled expansion.

It is needless to emphasize the effect of such movements on the Defence Forces who found themselves part-aliens in their own country or indeed on the veterans' lobby and its charitable bodies, with their traditional, patriotic attitudes often looking backwards to great deeds and instinctively sympathetic with voluntary initiatives rather than state arrangements. During the next decade there were changes, many hardly favourable to the military establishment. In the middle and later 1970s the optimism and brashness of the earlier decade had given way to a sea of troubles—foreboding of worsening economic conditions; outbursts of industrial militancy on a seemingly ever-ascending scale; corruption in high and other places; violence at home and abroad through international terrorism; in Northern Ireland armed confrontation within the United Kingdom itself; high levels of inflation which threatened the savings and fixed incomes of the thrifty elderly – the very group who tended to support service charities; and a rising graph of unemployment which by the end of the decade had reached the levels of the late 1920s and early 1930s. Before the Thatcher Government's quick correction, such grave economic difficulties had led to the Services falling seriously behind civilian pay levels and much obsolescence and shortages in equipment.

For many reasons during the restless and often adverse years from 1960 to 1980 it would have been surprising if British veterans could have achieved startling improvements either at their point of retirement or in the years which followed. The military establishment itself was rightly concerned with the efficiency of its serving men and was always reluctant to see the causal connection between good resettlement and successful recruitment, while the great voluntary organizations supporting British veterans were struggling for their own survival.

The period is marked by relatively few major initiatives within the military establishment. An exception occurred in 1967 when a combination of changing threat perceptions and economic necessity brought further and larger reductions in the Armed Forces over the next five years or so. Accordingly Hooper's machinery was revived and dusted down, with some small improvements being effected. Advice interviews prior to retirement were supplemented by one-day briefings. Some of these briefings discussed the prospects of joining particular occupations while others helped men learn the civilian skills of making job applications. Training during service was expanded with more varied short courses at Polytech-

227

nics and Technical Colleges. Yet, while there might now be more choice, their length remained the same, i.e. to coincide with the basic grant of 28 days. This 28-day period applied to all who completed their service, whether on a 3- or 30-year engagement.

The situation in the Federal Republic of Germany was far different, where in 1969 men who had served 6 years were granted 12 months professional training while those with 12 years' service qualified for 36 months. For the whole period of such training they were to receive at least 90% of their pay during the last month of active service.[2]

In Britain, when longer training before retirement appeared to be a non-starter, the three services started pressing for realistic monetary grants towards worthwhile training courses afterwards, the option taken in most other countries. Their representations failed due to their concidence with a grandiose scheme for national retraining. The politicial 'buzzwords' at the time were that all citizens should have at least two careers in their working lifetimes. If so, ex-servicemen could hardly argue that they were that much different from others. In fact, most of the Government's proposed courses were inappropriate to midlife students like ex-servicemen, and the national subsistence grants inadequate for men with families. With the implementation of these central arrangements, later to evolve into the rather ill-starred Training Opportunities Scheme (TOPS), all chances for regular British veterans to receive extended training grants, like those in other countries, disappeared for at least 20 years.

If the 20 years to the beginning of the 1980s saw no breakthrough in central provisions for veterans, it was hardly likely that the period would be one of startling success or exciting developments in the voluntary sector either. For some the ability to continue with their traditional work was success enough. Much depended on the nature of their original purpose. The British Legion, as the self-acclaimed body representing all veterans, not just those on its active membership roll, would expect to suffer from adverse changes in the national attitude towards the military but with the Forces Help Society and SSAFA, non-membership bodies devoted to relief, the effect might not be so marked.

In the event both improved welfare arrangements and societal changes were clearly felt by the Forces Help Society. Two of its three main responsibilities, i.e. those of helping older ex-servicemen who got into financial difficulties and of providing sheltered employment for the disabled, both contracted markedly during the period 1960–80. Through honoured practice, its assistance to individuals was granted for compassionate reasons and was given on the advice of helpers who never consciously set themselves up as judges. The recipients were either soldiers old in years struggling to cope or 'old soldiers' who found difficulty in becoming part of normal society. For much of the time a job-finding service of no ordinary nature was offered at its Headquarters. This Employment Branch was set up to help itinerant ex-servicemen and women of no fixed address. In 1973 its users were described as "varying little down the years, usually footloose, with no dependants, unskilled and in poor shape physically". By 1980 this generation had gone, many had died and the small number of men still seeking such assistance over employment were passed to the Regular Forces Employment Association.

Where general assistance was made through small cash donations, the number of cases steadily declined: the total of 60,000 in 1957 had shrunk to just 13,000 in 1979. This decrease could legitimately be seen as something for celebration, marking, as it did, a reduction in the numbers of indigent old soldiers. In the Forces' Help Society there were naturally mixed feelings. Over the years it witnessed both a diminishment of role and a numerical falling away among its dedicated volunteers countrywide. Through its Annual Reports there ran the understandable conviction that, while the work might be reduced in scale, it was still vitally important to relieve human misery—and that such help voluntarily given was unquestionably more praiseworthy and of a different quality than the more comprehensive aid dispensed through Government officials. The Society's lack of innovation, deliberate or not, assumed great merit with its members in an age when past standards were challenged ever more frequently. In 1964 the delegates at its Annual Meeting were told that belief in the "aims and objects of our Society remain steadfast despite the fact that cynicism is fashionable now". Two years later they heard that "Change is a fetish of our age often misrepresented as progress. Sometimes people advocate change when they fail to appreciate the particular strength which exists in tradition and stability". In 1972 the platform went further: "The larger, the more faceless and impersonal that the centralized institutions of the State, Local Government or Welfare Services become, the deeper necessity there is for the familiar organizations such as ours to provide the help and compassion that best comes from friends and neighbours, for we were born of and are sustained by voluntary effort."

By the late 1970s a more pragmatic tone prevailed. The Society saw its primary role no longer in just giving physical aid but in helping "ex-servicemen secure the social security benefits to which they are entitled, in addition to the wide range of services provided for them by the local authorities". The Society's volunteers had always considered themselves as friends, people whom old servicemen could trust. Now their best contribution could come through skilled and sympathetic advice.

The pattern of a reduced workload was repeated with the Society's Sheltered Workshops. Despite periodic attempts to modernize them, their workers declined in number while their average ages rose. In times of slackening trade they became highly vulnerable and of the eight factories extant in 1960 only three survived 20 years later, at Dundee, Edinburgh and Liverpool. Dundee was receiving substantial assistance from its local authority; Edinburgh was a very small unit which owed much of its survival to its healthy investment income; while Liverpool gave serious concern as to its continued viability. The 1977 Report envisaged closure of them all within the next ten years or so as their workforces reached retirement age. In contrast, towards the end of the 1970s its Homes at Brookwood and in the Isle of Wight were flourishing and new purpose-built cottages for the disabled were being constructed. With changing needs and some diminishing responsibilities, it was plain that fundamental reassessment of both role and structure was imminent.

SSAFA faced new challenges too. With its responsibilities for the families of serving men as well as those of veterans, its continuing role was guaranteed. A percentage of service families would always get into difficulties, but, while problems continued to occur, they were not like those of past years. In 1958 its Chairman observed that "as poverty in the old sense was relieved, other social ills have developed. It seems as though some spiritual price is being paid for material progress in the alarming neuroses among the population since the war. Our present problems are . . . the mishandling of money, insecurity and loneliness, emotional immaturity and inadequacy in human relationships." He went on to say, "The problems we were founded to deal with are disappearing and others quite different have taken their place."

During 1958 SSAFAs Married Families Club and its large Children's Home closed, but the Wimbledon Home for Officers' widows continued to be in great demand and the case work endless. Many argued that relaxing moral standards would only guarantee an increase in such work. In 1959 its distinguished President, General Sir Gerald Templer, restated SSAFA's role as that of "helping men and women in adversity of some sort, keeping a regular bond with wives and children who are separated from their husbands and ensuring there is no overlapping with SSAFA and other voluntary organizations".

Overseas, its nursing sisters, with their District and Welfare Duties, had become an essential part of the system. At home, its welfare service relied on its wide-flung band of volunteers across the face of Britain. For SSAFA the challenge was certainly not one of a diminishing role but whether its workers at home could become professional enough, in an age when social workers took prolonged training, to retain its traditional responsibilities which remained heavy. In 1960 its caseworkers dealt with no less than 87,000 problem cases and made 22,602 grants totalling £178,717. While by the late 1970s the number of grants had dropped to some 15,000, the amounts authorized had risen sharply to over £600,000. In the 1980s both the numbers interviewed and the amounts distributed would rise.

No less important than numerical comparisons was the fact that the nature of the advice given became more complicated because of the ever-increasing range of state allowances and with new problems – including neuroses – which no longer centred on poverty alone. In 1976 SSAFA's Report gave as prime causes of such problems "affluence, ignorance and permissiveness".

Such demanding skills required prior training. In 1960 a training course was developed for new caseworkers and two years later responsibility for it was placed under a Training Adviser who was upgraded to a Training Director in 1977. Courses run both at Headquarters and in the provinces increased in number, but by the end of the 1970s they were still not compulsory. Herein lay the challenge to SSAFA – whether it would recognize the need for its voluntary workers to be formally trained. If it did not, there was a growing risk that its fitness for such a specialized role would be questioned. If it did, retraining would be a painful process which would lead to many resignations among its 6,000 helpers and create a major requirement for training their replacements.

While it procrastinated, the organization avoided criticism because so many of its voluntary caseworkers were of high calibre, without formal training but setting themselves demanding targets both of knowledge and interviewing techniques. Inevitably there were some exceptions, 'amateur' caseworkers who were by no means as conscientious or effective as they might have been. SSAFA was also saved possible embarrassment by the very conservatism of the Armed Services. Traditionally, the overall control of welfare matters fell upon Commanding Officers and such men felt a natural empathy with SSAFA representatives, either retired personnel or the wives of such. But, like the Help Society, formidable problems faced SSAFA as it entered the 1980s.

The British Legion, as the only general membership body and national leader of ex-service affairs, also found the 1960s inimical both towards its members as old soldiers and some of its aims. In the climate of a Welfare State any special lobbying was bound to raise questions in certain quarters about whether its members should be given singular privileges. If this privileged group was seen as men who re-enacted battles long past or glorified militaristic values in their remembrance ceremonies so much the worse. In short, during much of the 1960s and early 1970s British veterans suffered the age-old fate of their class, wide indifference tinctured with strong antipathy from certain elements, both among the young and, of course, from the anti-war campaigning movements.

Such carping had little effect on the Legion's First World War veterans who had been through the fire of the interwar period. These men would stoically put on their medals and march to their local war memorials paying homage to old friends regardless of the animosity and ignorance of those young enough to be their grandchildren. In many cases this would make them even more determined to do so. Many must have shared the thoughts of Canon Powell when, in 1971, he addressed the old contemptibles of the Marlborough British Legion as they laid up their standard in the parish church. Paying tribute to their dead comrades he said:

"I wonder what those men would think of the moochers and loungers, the Spivs and lay-abouts, the fiddlers, the purveyors of pornography, think of our modern highwaymen who hold the community to ransom, caring nothing if old people shiver in their houses and all of us stumble in the dark."[3]

For veterans of the Second World War it was rather different; they came from a generation less keen to march behind their banners in public and, with the more favourable economic conditions of the time, they needed the assistance of an organization like the Legion that much less. Some, too, were more liable to be affected by the anti-war feelings of their children. Such men would not participate in Legion activities. The Legion's membership reflects this. By 1960 it had settled at around the million mark, if one included in the total the Women's Branches, numbering some 250,000. And in that year, of the 724,000 male members, 105,000 could hardly be called active, being at least 12 months in arrears with their subscriptions. Three years later the male membership had fallen to 486,108, its low point for the decade. In succeeding years modest net increases were recorded. By the mid-1970s ordinary membership was given as 477,600 and the Women's Section as 160,000. This level was more or less maintained until the end of the decade, although there was a growing tendency for associate members (servicemen's children, etc) to increase, while ordinary membership continued to fall.

Given the general climate of the time, to hold the membership at these levels was no mean achievement. In this respect the scale of the continued loyalty and selflessness shown by the Women's Section, often given scant recognition, was outstanding. Notwithstanding, it would be wrong to call the British Legion a highly dynamic and vibrant force during the 1960s and much of the 1970s, hardly surprising considering that the organization was ageing and had attracted fewer men from the Second World War than it might have expected. If in Britain there was a national feeling – and there seems no doubt there was – that after their great and successful exertions during the war people might now begin to relax a little and enjoy the fruits of greater national prosperity, how much more justifiable would such a feeling be among those who had done most to win that war? The whole current of the time seemed to be moving against the stern if praiseworthy ideals of their austere founder. Why should members not also be influenced by the hedonism of their age?

It was, of course, immeasurably more complicated than this, but the period, certainly during the 1960s, was one where rather less emphasis was given to aid and more to the perfectly legitimate social relationships provided by the clubs. To some senior members of the National Executive there were simply no fresh windmills to tilt at: the benevolent system was in place and apparently working well, pensioners' grievances were well and energetically represented at Head Office, the residential and convalescent homes were full, the disabled industries and their own Village flourished (although they would probably become less important as time passed), a great new initiative on housing had been taken in the shape of the Housing Association and the sacred trust of Remembrance was paid annually. This thinking is seen in the 40th Annual Report of the National Executive Council in 1960:

"Conditions today are vastly different from those which faced an older generation of servicemen. Most of the injustices and anomalies which ex-servicemen had to fight between the wars no longer exist, thus, while the service and benevolent work of the British Legion will continue for many years to come, this will of necessity occupy the time and energy of but few members in our branches."

With hindsight it was, of course, a most optimistic statement made at a time when expectations were far lower than they were to become in the last two decades of the century. It was made when the scale of the problems facing veterans and their dependants of the First World War were not fully realized and before those facing Second World War veterans developed. Like the other voluntary organizations, the British Legion found that many of these were not dependent on financial difficulties alone. Such a statement in the 1960 Report did not anticipate the need for increasing assistance nor the greater demands on residential and convalescent homes.

Having partly disposed of benevolence, the Report went on to say, some might think with breathtaking arrogance, that "We must find different ways of providing a creative incentive for the present-day rank and file to grasp. To this end greater emphasis is being placed upon what can be done for the youth of this country . . . for there is a very real need at the present time to further the interests of youth and it is in this direction that the Legion can play an important part". When one pauses to consider that the strength of any veterans' organization lies in its caring aspects, in mobilizing the idealism and generosity of its members, the statement assumes a truer perspective. Yet in the 1960s and part of the 1970s such an aim ran directly against the current of the time, when many young people were antipathetic to any connection with an ex-servicemen's body, however distinguished, and it is no wonder that results were not dramatically successful, although about one-fifth of the Branches associated themselves with youth clubs. But there seemed little prospect of winning large numbers of young people over to the veterans' arena at this time, although more tangible results would become possible in the next decade.

The first half of the 1960s were very difficult years for the British Legion, as with other veterans' bodies. Within, its membership showed little sense of urgency, while without, voices challenged its founding principles. In 1962 its then National Chairman, Roy Bucher, warned against the enemy within:

"Most certainly any organization which is too discreet, is over-defensive of its record and is inward rather than outward looking, will make less and less impact on the general public and especially on the younger citizens." The members' sense of casualness was again referred to in 1964/5 when the Executive Council's Report felt "bound to express some concern at the fact that there does appear to be considerable unawareness, even amongst our own Members, about the aim and objectives of the British Legion".

Declining interest was demonstrated in the sharply lower numbers of both legionaries and the general public who attended Remembrance Ceremonies compared with ten years before. It was seen in the poor support for its in-house publication, *The Journal*, which had a circulation in the 1960s of no more than 55,000. The very lifeblood of the Legion was threatened by the decline in public support for its Annual Poppy Day. In 1966 the net total contributed was just £150,000 higher than in 1945, despite the serious reduction in the buying power of the pound due to inflation. During the 1960s the average annual increase in poppy donations was 1%, while the average increase in the cost of living was $7\frac{1}{2}\%$.

There were, too, sporadic attempts from without at discontinuing the traditional form of the Remembrance Ceremonies. The Legion's 1963/4 Report referred to a sermon on Remembrance Sunday by Canon Carpenter, Archdeacon of Westminster, which expressed the view that "Remembrance Sunday should be linked with the hopes of peoples throughout the world and become a day of dedication to idealism". "Time for a change" was also the theme of a sermon that year by Canon Collins in St Paul's Cathedral who, in a thinly veiled reference to the Legion, said, "We continue to look backwards, to think too much of our finest hour, and too little of the purpose for which the sacrifices had been made".

In 1967, two weeks before Remembrance Day, the Bishop of Birmingham moved a Resolution in the Church Assembly calling for thought to be given to the future form and purpose of Remembrance Day. This caused many papers to comment adversely on the traditional form of Remembrance Day as a "pathetic formality" or as "glorifying war", to which the Legion's President wrote a rejoinder in *The Times*.[4]

Along with critical comments from trendy churchmen, not above courting publicity themselves, the Legion faced a considerable challenge from new charities with their sophisticated publicity and more easily understood appeals to younger generations, charities whose aims often cut across the work of the ex-service bodies. Paramount here was Oxfam (1941), but other significant members joining the field were Age Concern (1940), Help the Aged (1961) and SHARE (1970).

In retrospect the Bishop of Birmingham seems to have done the Legion no harm. What the old soldiers needed most was an overt challenge to what they held dear and by the late 1960s there were a number of heartening signs that the Legion was fighting back with renewed belief in its purpose. Its Annual Report for 1967 carried a more confident tone: "It might be thought that improvements in the social welfare system would appear to make redundant certain aspects of the work of the British Legion. This is not so, but has added to, rather than lessened, the great benevolent work for which the British Legion has been renowned for nearly half a century."

And in 1968 the National Chairman could write to his members: "Without attempts to forecast the future, your Council is confident that for many years hence the British Legion can continue to play an increasingly important role in the community."

In 1966 a firm of Public Relations Consultants had been appointed to mastermind an educational campaign to let young people know that, while there had been no major wars for over 20 years, the care of those still suffering as a result of past service relied on the income derived from the Poppy Appeal.

Another sign of new determination in the same year came with the ambitiously-named "Operation Supercharge" which was launched "to bring the organization up to the highest degree of efficiency and membership" for the Golden Jubilee in 1971. The early results were most disappointing: at the end of the financial year 1970 the membership showed an actual decrease of 7.54%, but within this smaller membership significant changes were taking place and not a moment before time. The younger veterans of the Second World War were beginning to dominate the management of affairs.

One activity which certainly flourished over these years was that of the Legion's social life. On 30 September, 1964, the total of fully recognized clubs was 1003 and in 1970 there were 1024, for the most part representing social activities with a conscience: charitable donations during 1970 totalled £456,700.

Things were by no means easy over these years. At first the better publicity arrangements which came from the partnership of the newly-appointed Public Relations Consultants with a more active internal Press Department seemed to be bearing fruit. There was a marginal increase in Poppy receipts, which totalled £1,272,000 in 1968, although they still fell short by £163,000 of the Legion's expenditure on benevolence alone. Disappointingly, the upward trend was not maintained, 1969's take being £43,000 down, but a positive result of the better publicity during 1969 was that many more young people were apparently attending the Remembrance Day Parades and Services, something undreamt of five years before.

Much of the Legion's immediate attention was now directed towards its 50th Jubilee celebrations. Among other publicity arrangements, the journalist Antony Brown was commissioned to write a book, *Red for Remembrance*, in time for sale at the Annual Conference. The coming festivities certainly gave the organization a much-needed uplift. There was a Royal Garden Party at Buckingham Palace and a service at St Paul's Cathedral, followed by a March Past before the Lord Mayor of London. Above everything else was the honour of having the prefix Royal conferred upon it.

These celebrations helped to create renewed enthusiasm among its members. The Annual Conference for 1971 attracted over 1000 delegates (and 2000 guests). Poppy receipts exceeded £1,300,000 and the membership increased by nearly 9%. (Annual wastage from death and other causes ran at about 5%.) The National Chairman was able to say in his Annual Report: "(Your Council) sees a new spirit running through our movement. It sees the Legion as one of the greatest driving forces of this country and an organization that will be at all times an upholder of the British way of life."

The prefix Royal helped to lift the Legion above some of the criticism which it had had to endure and the Jubilee Festival of

Remembrance, broadcast in full colour, attracted more public viewers than ever before, followed by large numbers attending the Cenotaph Ceremony the following day. It had truly become one of the nation's great institutions surmounting the waves of anti-war feeling recently directed against it, although this, of course, brought about the problem of having to live up to its new-found stature. Yet another factor was working in its favour, namely the reflected benefits which came from the outstanding demeanour of the nation's dedicated professionals who served in Northern Ireland: The officers and soldiers illuminated by television's powerful gaze turned out not only to be competent and thinking men, but also remarkably young, the same age, indeed, as the members of the RBL when they had taken part in earlier conflicts.

The harvest from better publicity and changing public attitudes began to come through in 1972 when, for instance, the number of requests received for information about its work from both schoolchildren and students at Higher Educational Establishments was markedly higher.

But to give the impression that the rest of the 1970s were fat years for the service charities or for the military establishment would be quite wrong. The curse of rapid inflation both in Britain and in much of the industrial world caused many severe economic problems, compounded in its later years by serious industrial strife. As a result the Armed Services suffered reductions in both pay and equipment budgets. Many private soldiers in Northern Ireland and elsewhere found that their income was below subsistence level and they were qualifying for income support. Equipment became obsolete and had to be cannibalized to retain front-line efficiency. But, due to high civilian unemployment, recruiting was not a major problem and any proposals for improved resettlement measures had to remain on ice, the obvious priority being to keep the fighting machine as efficient as possible.

Along with everyone else, the great charities wrestled with the financial problems attendant upon galloping inflation. They made Herculean efforts to increase their income from donations but, at best, these only enabled them to maintain their services. In any case many of their strongest supporters were of advancing years and living on fixed incomes, and were thus hardest hit by the times.

In many respects, though, the Royal British Legion maintained a certain air of serenity through the upheavals of the decade. Its position was now assured in public life and its bureaucracy was well-skilled and long-practised at conducting its traditional responsibilities. Like all other organizations, continued existence relied on its ability to meet the two fundamental problems of manpower and money. Regarding the first, there was deep concern that not enough young ex-servicemen were joining, although increases in the number of associate members helped to slow the downward trend. With respect to income, the annual collection campaigns, orchestrated to reach their climax on November 11 each year, were now far more sophisticated. By 1979 the Appeal succeeded in raising almost £4.5 million compared with the £1.3 million of Jubilee Year. Put into context, this remarkable achievement only just succeeded in keeping pace with inflation and did not make up for the erosion which had occurred in earlier years. At this time, though, the move for covenanted subscriptions also began to gather momentum.

In 1980 the RBL felt its financial position sound enough to mark its 60th anniversary, due the following year, by sanctioning the building of a Rehabilitation and Assessment Unit for the disabled in its Village at Maidstone, to be named after Winston Churchill. Other indications of continuing confidence were seen in the modernization of its Headquarters Building, due to be opened by the Queen in 1981, and the reversal of the disastrous decision which had changed its mouthpiece, *The Journal*, into the form of a tabloid newspaper.

At its Annual Conference in 1980 the National President, Sir Charles Jones, in what was to prove his valedictory address, was in combative and confident form. He thundered against the contemporary mood in Britain: "We are lacking the will to work and are undoubtedly without influence in the world. . . . There is a great lack of aim and purpose in our minds today; we have neglected the old virtues of hard work and prudent living within our incomes." He was particularly vitriolic about a recent BBC Television programme, "Gone for a Soldier": "I have never seen such anti-British and Anti-Army propaganda"; nor did he spare those in the Legion who were quite content to let things continue as they were. Sir Charles saw the Legion, if it chose to stand up, as an important counterpoise to some of the more divisive elements of the time. To combat such attitudes successfully it must increase its membership, money and spirit. "We must continue our good work but adjust to the needs of the times."

This was, of course, just what many delegates wanted to hear, their gallant leader railing against the alien, distinctly non-military, elements which were bedevilling their society and more gently telling them not to be idle men themselves. What had yet to be seen was the continuing impact of such words beyond the Conference Hall. After the celebrations of 1981 would legionaries and their leaders be willing to adopt a higher profile and change past patterns by moving, for instance, towards greater professionalism and integrated action with other charities over benevolent work? Would the Branches have sufficient appetite and drive to go out and find ageing veterans and their dependants in their community areas? On the Branches discovering injustices and instances of unhappiness, would the leadership then be prepared to pursue, with the necessary energy and determination, the long and difficult process of persuading Governments to change their regulations?

Formidable problems assailed the military establishment, the RBL and other ex-servicemen's organizations as the 1980s opened, ones which in the past they had not always been best equipped to grapple with. Unknown to them, certain circumstances were unfolding which were favourable both to serving and retired men and to their representative bodies.

CHAPTER FOURTEEN

The 1980s: New Hopes, Fresh Plans

"Friendships of the Battle-line . . .
Those friendships that are fast and fine,
That never, ever wane
I wonder where he will be now,
I wonder if, and where, and how
We'll ever meet again."

Ian E. Kaye,
Pick and Shovel Poems

THROUGHOUT the 1980s the political stage had been occupied by a reforming right wing Government which began by making savage cutbacks in public spending to help create a base for lasting economic reforms. These, of course, were not made for economic reasons alone; from the beginning Margaret Thatcher stressed the primacy of individuals over Government bodies and the finite nature of public expenditure. She looked to a new age where the continuing growth of central agencies since 1945 would be halted and indeed reversed through placing new responsibilities upon private enterprise and committed citizens. As she put it, "The Balance of our Society has been increasingly tilted in favour of the state at the expense of individual freedom."[1]

The outcome of the new political mood was soon felt by both the service charities and the military establishment itself. For the charities, who for 25 years had been adapting their roles against a backcloth of the state assuming ever growing social responsibilities for all, including veterans, it came as a considerable shock. The combination of new ideas and recession caused the unthinkable, an actual retraction of benefits with the State no longer meeting the full range of health, welfare and social demands upon it. It could only mean increased demands on the charities' voluntary workers. Ironically opportunities which in 1945 would have been greeted with great enthusiasm did not meet with the same response in the 1980s. There were fears that Government economies would leave areas of need far beyond the ability of voluntary resources to meet and, although these proved largely groundless, there was a sharp apprehension over the huge and comforting safety net being reduced.

At the same time it was becoming apparent to the charities that, as the great majority of ex-service personnel, certainly those of the Second World War, entered their retirement years both casework loads and expenditure would inevitably increase. The prospect of expanding responsibilities was to concentrate the minds of their leaders towards reforms which had been looming, but were postponed, over the last 20 years or so.

There were changes for the active military establishment too. Against a background of seemingly renewed Soviet challenges, notably through the invasion of Afghanistan, new emphasis was placed on defence. The 1980 Defence Estimates expressed the Government's fundamental belief in maintaining strong military forces: "Without the national security which defence capability provides, plans to contain inflation, restore incentives, secure economic growth, improve on health care and our children's education rest on sand; for the national life in which these objectives can be pursued in peace and freedom may disappear beyond recall."[2] This was not just rhetoric, for, while other areas of Government expenditure were being strongly pruned, Defence was given increased funding. Service pay, which had fallen seriously behind civilian levels, was swiftly restored and an undertaking was made to keep it there, involving an average increase in pay for all ranks of some 32%. The effect was immediate: in 1980 recruiting was 17% higher than in the same period for 1978 and, more significant still, the Armed Forces felt their role was once more being appreciated.

In John Nott's 1981 review of defence, "The Way Forward", he could say that expenditure was already 8% higher in real terms than three years before and that it would be increased by a further 3% annually up to 1985/6. By that time the Defence Budget (excluding the Falklands additions) was nearly 20% higher than in 1978/9 and the longest period of substantial growth in defence expenditure for more than 30 years had taken place.

Such increased priority helped to raise service morale to an extent undreamt of in the late 1970s. This was, of course, a matter for congratulation by the service charities too. Yet, with their responsibilites for veterans they could not allow defence euphoria to blind them to possible problems caused by the Government's new stance. In particular they remained convinced that the proposed cutbacks in public expenditure would expose the old, the sick, the disabled and those in real need to new uncertainty, despite Government assurances to the contrary. In 1980/81, for instance, the Government reduced its expenditure by $5\frac{1}{2}\%$. Cutbacks were particularly heavy in the housing programme and these, together with such measures like increased charges for prescriptions, were expected to act against many poorer veterans. Geoffrey Howe's Budget Speech of 1980/81 included the chilling remarks: "Social security is now one quarter of total public expenditure and still growing. It cannot be exempt from measures to restrain its growth when these can reasonably be made."

Such fears and the expectation of increased demands from their ageing ex-soldiers stung the service charities into new action. At the same time the Government sought to encourage such voluntary initiatives: Geoffrey Howe introduced substantial new tax relief for covenanted donations, he doubled the tax-free capital sums which could be authorized within one year of death and extended VAT relief for disabled people and the charities supporting them. To embark on ambitious new plans required confidence on the charities' part. This was not very high in the early 1980s when, in the face of a host of challenges, public support for the Government seemed to be draining away. A new Government would be likely to reverse the new social policies and Defence might again take a lower priority both in Governmental and, by extension, public esteem.

Public regard for both the Thatcher Government and its military forces received an immense boost from a remarkable and utterly unexpected occurrence, the Falklands War. Since the end of the Second World War the role of the services had been to stand guard to prevent a future war either by means of the largely conventional forces in BAOR or through nuclear forces, mainly located in submarines. At the same time they had been involved with security problems within the Commonwealth (chiefly concerned with terrorism). Then out of the blue the Dictator of a major South American country ordered the invasion of British sovereign territory, the windswept Falkland Islands, just 400 miles from Argentina but some 8000 miles from the mother country amid the massive rollers of the cold and inhospitable South Atlantic.

After a war of $2\frac{1}{2}$ months which required a naval task force of over 100 ships, British troops from units which were legendary for their bravery and fitness, the Marines, Paras, Guards and Gurkhas, recaptured the islands, triumphing against defending forces more than three times their number. It was a war for everyone to savour. The technological buffs could watch planes, missiles and helicopters which had never been deployed in battle tested to the limits of their capability, while the veterans of previous wars could learn of infantry actions reminiscent of the two World Wars. Through this campaign no British citizen, however opposed to the use of force he might be, could doubt the immense bravery, professionalism and self belief of the British Armed Forces. As *The Times* put it:

"Modern man has come to be overawed by a sense of the big battalions' statistical enormities, the dimensions of the mass. . . . The invasion of a small community in the middle of the South Atlantic by the mass forces of a dictatorship somehow exposed all those deep feelings which had been suppressed in Britain and perhaps explains the vigour with which the nation responded to an invasion of its spirit. . . . Certainly that invasion and the war to recover the islands has stirred emotions which have been sunk deep within the spirit of Britain. That spirit has been rediscovered as people have rediscovered something about themselves and their country."[3]

The war was small enough, and modern communications quick enough, for the nation to have instant heroes: Lt Col "H" Jones, Major Chris Keeble who took over from him in battle, that great character Major Ewen Southby-Tailyour, expert on Falkland bays and more besides, the amazing helicopter crewmen, bleak-faced captains who had lost their ships, guardsmen lying in their sleeping bags before the final offensive for Port Stanley listening on the world service to their brother regiments marching down the Mall for the Queen's Birthday. Ordinary people came to be filled with both admiration and sympathy for these young professionals and possibly understood a little better, in a way unknown for many years, the awesome responsibilities of their guardians.

As the ships and men returned great crowds unheard of since the Boer War met them at both docksides and airports, singing 'Rule Britannia' and waving Union Flags while their children carried patriotic balloons. There the ubiquitous cameras captured unashamed tears from the 'strong' men who returned and delirious public embraces. The effect went beyond Britain. A day after the fall of Stanley, Sir Anthony Parsons, Britain's Ambassador to the United Nations attended a party where he was surprised to find glasses being raised in his direction from the most unexpected quarters, with such words as "Congratulations, Sir Anthony. Well done. . . . I drink to you, sir. . . . This is a fine day for your country".[4]

Such rejoicing could not last, of course, but the Falklands Factor changed the current of national feeling. It could be seen in the vast subscriptions to the South Atlantic Fund and in November of 1982 the British Legion's Remembrance Day services and ceremonies were better attended and by more young people than for many years, despite notably bitter weather and driving rain. Ever since, the survivors of the Second World War have attended in growing numbers, their self-consciousness gone and past remarks about warmongering men largely absent too. There is universal recognition that these ageing men who served their country meet to renew old comradeships and to remember a time of challenge to those democratic values which now stand supreme in the contemporary world.

Through the resources of the South Atlantic Fund which were, of course, additional to any central grants, widows and other next of kin came to be better treated financially than at any previous time. Each widow received £10,000 from the Fund alone and next of kin of a single soldier £2,500. In the months which followed, the British tendency to forget and denigrate their fighting men, both serving and discharged, began to reassert itself, although, for some years, particularly after the recent Gulf War, things can hardly revert to the depths reached on occasions during the 1960s and 1970s. The Falklands War and the continuing emphasis during the 1980s on the need for Britain to maintain strong and efficient armed forces gave the service charities both the external support they needed, not least through public contributions, and a new confidence to initiate measures to help veterans. One can argue that there is still a good way to go but they are on the march again and during the decade self-doubts were noticeably fewer.

Within the military establishment itself, while its fighting efficiency rightly took pride of place, there were indications of changing attitudes towards resettlement and veterans' concerns, although, even in the early 1990s, these have not brought the positive results needed.

At the very end of the 1980s there was dramatic proof of what could actually be achieved by charities who worked together and adopted highly professional methods. This came with the success of the campaign to bring the pensions awarded to war widows before 1973 into line with those granted afterwards.

The story can only be told in outline but the triumph over a tough Government determined to hold down public expenditure needs no exaggeration. After the concession of £40 a week more for the 53,500 remaining war widows there were even some who expressed surprise that it had taken so long to obtain. Realistically such a small number of elderly ladies would never have obtained near parity without a most skilfully conducted campaign on their behalf.

A central role here was played by the RBL and its pension branch, which, under its head, Mike Day, exerted significant and growing pressure for reform. More than anything else, though, success was due to the skilled and determined advocacy of a relatively small body, the Officers' Pension Society, and its General Secretary, Major-General Laurie Gingell. As a charity dedicated to pensions issues alone, it had more freedom of action than a massive organization like the Legion. Moreover, it was Laurie Gingell who conducted things in the manner of a classic military campaign and who had the courage to engage a firm of communication specialists. Their fees, inclusive of newspaper advertisements, exceeded £250,000, but Vera Lynn, the 1939–45 "Forces' sweetheart", gave her enthusiastic and valuable endorsement by inviting donations and pledges of support. The operation was scheduled to reach its climax at the time of the annual Remembrance ceremonies and was to be short and sustained, starting in earnest on 30 October, 1989. Accordingly, journalists were alerted, sympathetic MPs from all parties briefed and more than 100 parliamentary questions tabled. Features and editorials on the so-called "Debt of Honour" increased to a climax around 11 November, but the *Daily Mail*, which in the past had been a champion of soldiers' families by sponsoring collections like that for Kipling's Absent-Minded Beggars' Fund was quick to make the subject its own campaign. (It was followed in this by the *Daily Mirror*, the *Daily Star* and the *Sun*.) As early as 27 October the *Mail* carried an article about 83-year-old Ivy Cowan who had been widowed in 1943. For 45 years her life was a desperate struggle. She had brought up her daughter (and supported her father whose health had been shattered in the previous war) on an initial pension of £1.6.8. (£1.33) a week, taxed as unearned income, plus 11/- (85p) for Jean, her daughter. Jean was compelled to leave school at 15, when the child pension stopped, although she was quite capable of benefitting from further education and subsequently qualified at night school. It was a powerful account of Government miserliness and the heavy economic and social price paid by three generations of the Cowan family.

On 1 December the same paper cited arrangements in other countries. In West Germany a widow received three-quarters of the average industrial wage, together with a rent subsidy equivalent in UK prices to £167 a week. To give the newspaper campaign its initial impetus, before such articles as the *Mail*'s were appearing daily, Laurie Gingell, on his professionals' advice, recruited the aid of the ex-Chiefs of Staff and all six of them joined together to write a powerful letter to *The Times* which was published on 2 November. Public support was strong throughout and it kept on growing. This was demonstrated by a flood of donations ranging from £1 to £10,000.

Continuous pressure was kept on the Government, notably at Prime Minister's Questions, and on 4 December a second full-page advertisement appeared in the national papers. This was more aggressive than the first and demanded "How Much is a Man's Life Worth?" It went on to say that, of course, human life was priceless, yet the Government refused £160m for the fair treatment of those whose husbands had sacrificed their lives for their country. The seemingly universal and growing support for the campaign, including those who gleefully joined any anti-Government measures, could only have one result. On 11 December, six weeks after it had started, the concession was announced. By any standard it was a notable victory and one which gave notice of a new level of determination about a subject of deep concern to veterans.

On learning of the climbdown, Major-General Gingell kept to the jugular by commenting that the Government "would not only be repaying the nation's debt of honour – it would also be targeting resources to a particularly deserving group". However much the Government tried to ring-fence widows' pensions as a once and only concession, the precedent opened up the possibility of further concessions for other deserving groups. This concerned the whole field of service retirement pensions, including those for the war disabled, while the aggravation of old injuries, either through increasing age or for other reasons, offers almost limitless debate. As medical science progresses more is learnt too about the mental effects of active service, particularly those resulting from trauma and shock.

This was demonstrated in 1989 after the tragic sinking on the Thames of the pleasure boat *Marchioness*. It was soon found that as a result of the disaster extensive therapeutic treatment for post-traumatic stress disorder was needed, not only for the survivors but for spectators on the river bank who watched helplessly as the horror unfolded. In this context the imagination baulks at an account given by a First World War veteran, Charles Austen (91) as he revisited the site of Passchendale (1917) in November, 1989. He joined his company of the 60th Rifles as the junior lieutenant; within half an hour of the battle opening, he was its only officer. Shattered and depleted as the battalion was, it was ordered to dig in some 200 yards in front of the unbroken enemy positions. This, he explained, was virtually impossible, due to the remains of those with whom they had advanced shoulder to shoulder that short time before. Detached heads, limbs and broken corpses obstructed and sickened them. Austen himself plainly came to terms with these horrors, not, it must be assumed, without subsequent traumas of memory, but many other participants would hardly have coped so well. One needs no reminding either that during the Falklands War the fire on the *Sir Galahad*, described so vividly by Simon Weston, seared not only bodies but minds and personalities.

Apart from stress-induced disorders, medical science is only now learning about the full effects of prolonged malnutrition, as suffered by many prisoners of war, on both the endocrine glands and on the brain itself. Sadly, in the case of so many it is already too late for special help and compensation. Unlike the veterans' movement in the United States, there is little chance of British organizations being able to sponsor research into physical and mental disorders following service experiences. The success of the widows' pensions campaign, though, gave new heart to veterans' watchdogs and will surely cause succeeding Governments to be more cautious before neglecting deserving cases.

In other areas the veteran bodies showed rediscovered vigour and belief. The 1980s were dynamic years compared with other post-war decades, but, because of different perceptions about how such changes could best be implemented, they have hardly been free of controversy.

During the next 25 years, at least, Service charities saw themselves facing their greatest challenge from the very large numbers of ageing ex-service personnel. Veterans of the Second World War now have a median age of 69 years and over 14 million people are eligible for assistance. It was estimated that by the year 2000 68% or 3.3 million of the survivors (apart from their families) would be over 60 and that over half the nation's very elderly, that is people of 75 or over, would be ex-service or their dependants. In welfare terms the service charities looked to establish a truly national network capable of giving practical as well as financial help. Those requiring assistance were expected to include "the proud and would-be independent who have outlived their resources but fail to claim their entitlements to DHSS benefits or those whose very ethos makes them shy away from normal charity".[5] More than anything else, some would be desperately lonely. The helpers would need publicity services and an "intelligence network" to seek out the needy without affronting their dignity or pride. Such representatives would have to be trained, sensitive people who, above all, had a strong sense of obligation and loyalty to those who served their country.

Quite apart from such welfare work, the charities had to undertake massive improvements to their residential accommodation and the facilities they offered for short periods of rest and convalescence.

If one were asked to summarize the decade as far as the voluntary bodies were concerned the answer would be in their search for greater unity and increased professionalism. Greater unity was desperately needed. It still is. The very multiplicity of the charities involved demonstrated this. In addition to the "Big Three", among whom the RBL and RBL Scotland were undoubtedly the largest, with wide-ranging areas of responsibility, there were also about 140 Regimental Associations. These varied considerably in both size and levels of activity. There were, too, the massive Trust Funds of all three services, the foremost being the Royal Naval Benevolent Trust, the Royal Air Force Benevolent Fund and Association and the Army Benevolent Fund. Other organizations represented special groups like St Dunstan's and BLESMA and there were residential homes/hospitals like the Royal Star and Garter at Richmond and the Erskine Hospital near Glasgow. There were many more besides.

Admittedly Service charities had a co-ordinating body, the Council of British Service and Ex-Service Organizations (COBSEO), but inevitably with so many participants it was very large! Unanimity was difficult to achieve and quick decisions well nigh impossible. If this were not enough there remained, and continues to remain, no central Government Department with whom the charities could negotiate. The Pensions Branch of the RBL, for example, had to work with no less than twelve branches of State. To sum up, the veterans' support system was typically British in that it was immensely complicated, had grown up over many years and contained a large number of proud organizations each with its own charter. How it worked so comparatively well was something of a mystery, attributed by some to a mixture of good British common sense and shrewd eccentricity.

New urgency for reform was evident from significant initiatives taken by each of the 'Big Three'. The twin goals of greater unity and increased professionalism were sought with rare determination by both SSAFA and the Forces Help Society. Since 1985 these two charities worked towards the integration of their casework for both ex-servicemen and their families. In 1988 this resulted in a memorandum of understanding and the network of voluntary helpers concerned with welfare became a joint responsibility of both organizations. All aspiring caseworkers were trained and refresher courses were given to those with experience. Both charities expressed their strong satisfaction with the strengthened and unified service nationwide.

With respect to SSAFA, the period 1984–90 confirmed the anticipated growth in its casework responsibilities, the number of cases more than doubling from 33,323 to 72,369. Financial assistance also increased markedly from just over £1m in 1981 to £1,700,000 in 1984 and £4,039,000 in 1990. The move to professionalism was seen in the growing emphasis on training, from 481 workers in 1984 to 1746 in 1990. From 1986 all intending caseworkers were obliged to do training and from 1984 there was a large turnover of personnel, with many older workers retiring, but even more coming forward to replace them. By 1988 the total of 5500 volunteers was 1000 higher than four years earlier. In addition to its much extended casework SSAFA still retained control over its nursing sisters overseas and its sixty full-time social workers, together with its Wimbledon Home for Officers' Widows.

For the Forces Help Society reform and change did not stop with the reorganization of its casework. Other services were amended to serve contemporary needs more effectively. By the end of the 1980s the workshops were down to two, at Dundee and Edinburgh, and, with current emphasis on the disabled working alongside the able-bodied, this function was expected to diminish further. On the other hand strong growth had taken place in its Retirement and Convalescent Homes and in April, 1990, a holiday complex was opened where disabled men and women, and those looking after them, could take short breaks. The conversion of its Woking homes into a care unit for the frail and elderly was in progress and due for completion in 1993.

With the largest of the "Big Three", the very range and scope of the Royal British Legion's activities made it far less amenable to adopting radical changes like those implemented by SSAFA and the Forces Help Society. Many of its services had steadily evolved into an effective form for the 1990s and in any case major proposals affecting policy took time to pass through its procedural chain. They then had to be agreed by National Conference, a massively loyal and patriotic assembly, but one hardly renowned for its radical ideas or strong sense of adventure. The early 1980s saw successive Presidents and National Chairmen chiding their members for a "tendency to resist changes even when the need for change is irresistible".[6] At the 1984 Annual Conference General Sir Patrick Howard Dobson said:

"Frankly, I believe that we could do with some revolution. There are in my opinion far too many sacred cows, too many things which are holy writ simply because we have always done things that way."

In the following year its National Chairman, Windsor Spinks, reminded delegates that "The Legion must learn to change with this ever-changing world, setting targets anew, whilst remaining true to our basic aims and principles."

Such words did not appear particularly welcome to delegates

who felt their august body *was* the ex-servicemen's organization – dignified, comforting, almost beyond contemporary upheavals.

Whatever opportunities it might have missed, the Legion, with its reputation standing as high or higher than ever, was seen as a responsible and caring organization which operated on a truly national scale. The leviathan cannot change direction as quickly as lesser fish – nor need it – but, like all such swimmers, it must respond to sea changes. For the RBL the decade had been marked by solid achievement. Like other charities, it benefited from the Falklands War. Poppy contributions in November, 1982, reached a record £6m and, to the credit of its collectors, it more than maintained this level in succeeding years. In addition to founding the Churchill Centre, there was a massive refurbishment and extension programme to its residential Homes. A programme on this scale could only be adopted by an organization confident of its financial soundness; the new Lister House was opened in 1988 after no less than £2¼m had been spent on it and more homes were scheduled for the 1990s. The Legion's major Housing Association continued its work despite a financial disaster in its leasehold housing activities, due, in large measure, to the slump in the housing market at the end of the decade and to penal interest rates. Its Attendants Company had been revitalized and directed on to modern lines, while a one-time job creation scheme established at Ellesmere Port in 1976 had developed into a thriving Training Centre for both business and trade skills. The Pensions Department took a leading role in the victory for widows' pensions and its welfare commitments showed an ascending graph. National ceremonials were conducted with unrivalled skill and the 1989 and 1990 Festivals of Remembrance reached new heights. During the Annual Conference of 1989 (the liveliest one for some time), after an inspiring address from the President, delegates reaffirmed their agreement to the computerization of the membership figures and the reinvigoration of *The Journal*. They agreed that henceforth this should be sent to every active member.

Such developments would seem an impressive catalogue for any body and so they were. Yet there was another side to the story, namely the strongly conservative attitude of its members to any new initiatives. This had been apparent when the question of membership arose. Despite a shrinking and ageing membership, delegates at National Conference showed a continued reluctance to extend the rules of eligibility. It was only in 1981 that serving members of HM Forces and ex-members of the Home Guard came to be made eligible for ordinary membership. Proposals for family membership "to encourage the children of ordinary members to play an active role in its future" were rejected by the 1986 National Conference.

Such checks were not limited to matters of membership. Plans put forward by the National Executive Committee for streamlining its cumbersome decision-making structure were drawn up in 1985, but they were shelved by Conference until 1987. Discussion documents on training took years to be implemented, despite Headquarters' money being made available for county training schemes. Whilst a commitment to young people was enthusiastically agreed at successive Conferences, something of rare importance during the unemployment of the early 1980s and a means of breathing fresh life into Branches and Clubs, by midway through the decade only eighty-four of its 3400 Branches had actually formed youth sections. In 1988 there were still only 104 and by 1990 114.

North of the Border love of the pipes and enthusiasm for martial music generally led to the creation of many youth bands. This musical activity culminated in annual competitions for both individuals and their bands and in a remarkable, magnificently staged celebration held each year on the ramparts of Edinburgh Castle where up to 400 young people took part. In England too Festivals of Youth and Music were held but much scope remained. With the notable exceptions of such tattoos, Outward Bound schemes and other physically demanding experiences like sail training, young people associated with the Legion during the 1980s were probably not yet given sufficient responsibilities. They could, for instance, have taken part in the mammoth task of identifying needy veterans and their families among the community at large. Their very presence would have been of inestimable benefit to old people, for more than the other demons of old age, it is probably loneliness and the sense of having no purpose which outweighs any humiliation from increasing dependence.

Overshadowing all the Legion's work was the need to recruit new members to offset the annual loss of 10,000 men and women which had occurred regularly since 1945. Among such recruits there was a pressing need for younger men and women who had recently left the services and for a greater proportion of ex-officers and warrant officers, men with the appetite and ability to assume management positions.

It was difficult, though, to see people about to leave the forces joining the RBL in the numbers required without some change of image. This needed to be a change rather than a transformation – the traditional functions were clear enough – or the older members would feel betrayed. Among such changes was the need for a new sense of mission in many branches – the urge to seek out local veterans and their families with a determination not always displayed in recent years. This need not apply to benevolent cases alone. Many men and women would not need monetary assistance but help in being made to feel part of their local communities, and encouragement to participate in communal activities, including, where appropriate, those sponsored by the Legion. Even with injections of new recruits, it seemed doubtful whether some branches, as constituted, would be equipped to take on such increased responsibilities. In certain cases they would require professional support at the local level. Unless they were to respond positively, however, they were unlikely to retain any younger members from either the regular or territorial armies. While the latter were enthusiastic and knowledgeable about military matters, they were also established and successful citizens who would not be satisfied with second-rate facilities nor with being excluded from office. To cater for such new members many branches and clubs, in particular, would have to change their image, on the one hand through undertaking increased welfare work, and on the other by instituting wider para-educational activities and more active sports. For instance more soccer teams could be formed where, if required, associate members might be welcomed. There was clearly a need to extend such activities beyond the inevitable darts and bowls, however popular they might be with the older generation.

To this end, at the Annual Conferences of 1990 and 1991, the Legion's President, General Sir Edward Burgess, gave notice of developments which would offer prospects of greater efficiency and lead to a renewed sense of purpose, including the creation of a fast promotion stream for younger men of obvious ability and an extension of the Legion's nursing home facilities. Notable also was the appointment of external consultants to examine its management structure. In 1991 they proposed, among other things, the appointment of paid officers at county level (to give further support to the branches) and at senior management level the setting up of a relatively small Management Board to be supported by a Larger National Advisory Council (which was to include outside experts from fields such as management, law, finance and medicine). To their credit the response from the assembled delegates towards such potentially disturbing ideas was a prolonged and standing ovation in 1990 and their assent in the following year for further consideration of the proposals leading to their possible implementation after the 1992 Annual Conference. 1991 will surely see more animated discussion about the Legion's structure and role than in any other year since its foundation seventy years ago.

During 1989 the RBL had already taken the important decision to establish a recruiting department which specifically targeted the regular and territorial armies. Its timing was fortunate for the Gulf War led to a new warmth in the relationship between serving personnel and veterans. 25,000 parcels were sent through the RBL to the British Forces in the Gulf, and Brigadier Patrick Cordingley's visit to its 1991 Annual Conference plainly delighted the assembled delegates. He thanked them and said how much their support was appreciated and that their example had been an inspiration to those presently serving. Both he and his men in the Gulf felt that "we could not let down those who had gone before us".

There now seems a real prospect that RBL recruiters might attract a good proportion of the young people so sorely required. The next challenge is to persuade them to stay. Unlike the vast numbers who came out after the two world wars anxious to retain their wartime associations, the more affluent, ambitious and critical young people of the 1990's will only do so if they find the organization and its work eminently worthwhile.

Within an organization of this size the full effects of the reforms presently being implemented and those about to be undertaken will only become fully apparent by the mid-1990s.

It has to be acknowledged that, with respect to service charities as a whole, the initiatives taken during the late 1980's did not lead immediately to common action. Understandably, by flexing their muscles, organizations tended to heighten their own sense of identity. In this context some attempts to achieve greater unity in the Welfare field have met with distinct reservations from the RBL. During 1986, in a demonstration of renewed confidence, SSAFA and the Forces Help Society developed a joint concept which they called "Forces Care". This nominally proposed "an equal partnership of tri-service ex-service organizations to co-ordinate casework by setting up a network of local workers who could act as agents for any Service or ex-service charity". The aim of the new network was to provide a genuinely comprehensive service, with increased numbers of caseworkers ensuring that needy veterans and their families, wherever they might be, could be given rapid help, while through a co-ordination of all financial sources grants could be made on an adequate scale. It was hoped that this integrated service would prevent any veterans being able to play off one charity against another and reduce duplication of effort, another longstanding problem.

The sticking point, of course, was over who would be the senior partner. The proposals originated from SSAFA, an organization whose major commitment had always been benevolence. It was made with the fresh confidence which arose from the new team of revitalized, trained caseworkers. In the RBL where many had not yet embarked on such a programme of universal training they viewed the approaches as something akin to a reverse take-over. It must also be said that it was not just the largest organization, the RBL, which reacted with some apprehension; other proud and independent charities were similarly unenthusiastic. Apparently the wooing had been somewhat roughly done (to some it would never be gentle enough where their future independence was concerned) and expressions were used of approaches akin to a rogue elephant in an orchid garden. As a result of the furore aroused COBSEO agreed that Forces Care would not be pursued but that another attempt would be made to investigate how further improvements could be made to the joint welfare arrangements. This resulted in the setting up of a formal committee, an initiative common enough in the Ministry of Defence but much rarer in the world of independent voluntary charities. Colonel Sir Greville Spratt, a noted industrialist, recent Lord Mayor of London and past Commanding Officer of the Honourable Artillery Company, was asked by COBSEO to carry out such a study, the RBL providing his Secretarial support. His terms of reference included the words "to consider whether there is a need for improved co-ordination of the (welfare) effort involved; if so, to make appropriate recommendations".

It was no great surprise that the Committee's recommendations, made in July, 1989, did not turn out to be very radical ones; after the commotion constructive compromise was the order of the day. It came out against further merging in the welfare field on both grounds of practicality and feasibility but proposed the setting up of Committees at County level to bring about closer and practical co-operation among all the voluntary bodies, including co-opted members such as those from the Citizens' Advice Bureau. The Spratt Committee plainly showed its support for some of SSAFA's reforms by recommending effective publicity and the need to recruit and train further caseworkers. A novel recommendation made was for encouraging those still serving to carry out welfare work on behalf of both the services and ex-services community. This was, in fact, already being done in the Royal Navy, which had the advantage of its recognized home ports, but in the Army's case where personnel moved about much more freely the prospects for success were far less certain.

Whatever the outcome of the Spratt Committee's recommendations, the fact that it was convened represented a significant step forward, and the level of discussions aroused during its visits over the country have tended to lead towards further co-ordination in the medium term. Yet in essence it observed a system which remained diverse, a number of separate voluntary organizations working to a considerable number of sections both within the Ministry of Defence and the Departments of State. With respect to official resettlement arrangements the Committee made one strong and unequivocal recommendation, namely that a Veterans Department was required "to enable ex-service associations to approach Government through *one* recognized Department and Minister". This last recommendation hardly came as a surprise to any working in the ex-services' field. It had been taken up repeatedly by the RBL in recent years and the campaign, including the sponsorship of a Private Members' Bill in Parliament gathers pace in the 1990s. By highlighting it, though, the Committee performed a most important function, for it seems virtually inconceivable that in Britain, with its immense military involvement throughout the 20th century, no political department has been established to meet the needs of veterans as, for instance, in Canada, Australia, New Zealand and the United States. In the US the Veterans Department is considered so important that it was recently elevated to Cabinet status and is in fact the second largest of the fourteen Cabinet Departments. Surely it is no coincidence that Veterans' Day in the US is given the highest profile, while in Britain, taken as it is with Remembrance Sunday, the impact is considerably less.

That American veterans, and even those of our Second World War adversaries, enjoy a wider and more generous range of benefits than British ones is unarguable. This cannot be due solely to the different political cultures of other countries; the administrative advantages of a system where veterans' affairs are considered as a whole must be a powerful reason too. If the charities could have lobbied a single Department of Veterans' Affairs it is difficult to believe that British War Widows would have been compelled to endure such anomalies for so long. While the United States Legion and its Veterans of Foreign Wars are both powerful organizations, they surely enjoy no greater stature than the RBL. Yet through the American system they are able to bring more pressure and influence to bear when addressing particular issues of veterans' concern. This in turn develops greater confidence in their ability to get things done. Another noteworthy actor on the American scene is the Reserve Officers Association, with George Bush and Ronald Reagan as its current senior members. All veterans' organizations in the US have the advantage of being able to direct their advocacy on one clear target.

While Britain's ageing veterans are unquestionably a major concern, there are also those who continue to re-enter civilian life. Through lack of a Central Department and because undue reliance is placed on voluntary bodies, and their ability to cope somehow, official arrangements for British personnel presently leaving the Services remain deficient.

Prior to completing their engagements all are given **advice** on whether an extension of engagement is possible, or, if they are definitely leaving, which civilian career seems best suited to their requirements. Yet the current system of individual interviews and one-day briefing courses seems barely adequate, especially for junior ranks, bearing in mind that commanding officers are not yet obliged to let servicemen attend anything more than the basic interviews. A not inconsiderable number do no more than this.

Arrangements for advice appear positively lavish compared with those for **training** before the end of service. All personnel on the completion of their service, regardless of its length, are eligible for just 28 days' training in which to prepare for the quite different competitive climate of civilian life. This is the same arrangement which applied to those leaving at the end of the Second World War, but in the earlier period between the two world wars some long-term personnel were able to take trade courses of up to 6 months' duration prior to their release. This system involving longer pre-release training has never been revived. There seem to be good reasons for this. Any increase in pre-release training would cause serious manpower problems for the Ministry of Defence, since men could not take such training and remain at normal duty. It would also run counter to the practice of most other western countries, where the solution is for generous post-service training grants over periods up to three years or more. (Such grants would enable mature students to maintain their families.) At the top end a degree course (or its equivalent) could be taken at a University or Polytechnic, although many would, of course, not require such protracted training.

No equivalent grants presently exist in Britain and the Government Training Agency is not geared to helping anyone taking training beyond twelve months. In recent years the range of shorter courses leading to artisan and technician status have actually been reduced in number. Courses for which many servicemen are considered suitable attract grants which are too low for family men. In 1989 the rate of allowances in the United States ranged from no less than $376 a month with no dependants to $510 with two dependants. A veteran who had served for a continuous period of not less than eighteen months after February, 1955, was entitled to up to 45 months full-time educational assistance.[7] The low levels of allowance over relatively short periods reflects failures on the part of the veterans' lobby to gain preferential treatment for those leaving and the lower priority on training/retraining in Britain compared with other western countries. A wider range of appropriate courses with adequate allowances seems long overdue.

With respect to the essential aim of successful resettlement, suitable **employment**, British veterans suffer a major disadvantage when compared with countries like West Germany, France and the United States. Very few concessions are given to ex-servicemen for subsequent Government employment. For serving personnel seeking posts in the open market employment arrangements are the concern of both official and voluntary agencies. Within the Ministry of Defence separate, and by no means comprehensive, employment facilities are offered by each of the three services while outgoing men and women also come within the umbrella of the Government's Employment Service and are entitled to help from voluntary agencies such as the Officers' Association and the Regular Forces Employment Association. But it is still an untidy system which needs major modification. At present many look to the option of self-employment for which there is limited Government support over the first two years, and the British Legion offers an interest-free loan up to a maximum of £3000. While undeniably useful, the latter is by no means sufficient to finance any sizeable venture. In other countries aid is more wide-ranging; US veterans, for instance, have preferential rights when tendering for all Federal Contracts of $10,000 or less. In sum the treatment of British veterans on their release and afterwards shows startlingly few advantages over the years. While some improvements have been made in the **advice** they receive, the **training** offered is still inadequate for many wanting to achieve posts commensurate with their levels of responsibility whilst serving, and **employment finding** remains largely uncoordinated.

As for that other great concern, the need to find suitable accommodation, the story remains a familiarly depressing one. While the Army and the RAF sponsor schemes to encourage saving, only the Royal Navy offers a loan system, which personnel can take advantage of after twelve years' service. Something more is urgently required. By the very nature of their life, servicemen are required to move across the world at the shortest notice. During the normal tour of two years or so, it is important for both personal and morale reasons that their families accompany them. Furnished housing is therefore made available which they vacate on being posted away. This system both enables the Forces to preserve the essential mobility of their members and to encourage the special qualities of adaptability and mutual comradeship so important in military life. Yet, with inflation leading to steadily increasing house prices, despite the pause over the last eighteen months, many men conclude they must buy a house as soon as possible. Soon they tend to develop a pride in it and become reluctant to move. In many cases the decision is made to leave their families behind with all the ensuing complications.

This situation is fully understandable when they are given no preference by many local authorities for accommodation nor offered loan facilities. In the United States at the end of the Second World War, the American Veterans' Association guaranteed about 5.9 million home loans totalling more than $50.1 billion and the arrangement continues. The present system in the United Kingdom leads to less efficient armed forces and is a powerful disincentive to recruiting.

A number of possibilities have been considered in recent years by the Ministry of Defence to amend it, the most promising of which appears to be the option of allowing personnel to pay rent as if for a mortgage. At the end of their service they would receive the notional capital sum realizable on their married quarter at current market rates. Due to its expense this has remained in Ministry Defence "In Trays" but the price would be relatively small in terms of more contented, more efficient armed forces.

While the 1980s saw some positive achievements in the system of support for British veterans, particularly in the voluntary field, much still needs to be accomplished before the traditional problem of neglect can be put to rest and it can be fairly said that Britain offers its outgoing servicemen a range of facilities comparable with those of other western countries. In fact the minimal advances in official arrangements for ex-servicemen during the 1980s have meant that in international terms they have continued to lose ground.

With the onset of the 1990s western military establishments face challenges quite different from those during the previous ten years or, for that matter, at any time since the Second World War. The onus is back on the Ministry of Defence to take its responsibilities for outgoing servicemen – including those who are likely to be made redundant – more seriously than it has in the past. It can hardly fail to do so if it wants to achieve success in a major reorganization of our defence forces.

CHAPTER FIFTEEN

End of the Cold War

"Everlasting peace is a dream"

Moltke 1800–1891

As its third year ends, we can see that the last decade of the twentieth century has already established a character of its own. With Germany reunited and the Berlin Wall a memory, the Warsaw Pact dismantled and Soviet forces withdrawn from most of eastern Europe; with communism discredited in the Soviet Union itself and collaboration having taken place between the Americans and the Soviets during the Gulf War; with the need for the West to provide economic and food aid for a Russian Empire seemingly sliding into greater chaos as each month passes, the world is indeed changed. Both Ronald Reagan and Margaret Thatcher, the two leaders whose foreign policy was ever underpinned by strong defence forces, have left the stage. The ten years which saw the longest period of sustained growth in British Defence expenditure since the war have been succeeded by a decade where defence cuts are assured. In May, 1990, three former Service Chiefs declared the Soviet threat to Europe negligible and other authorities have harked back—prematurely as it turns out—to that time of international stability which followed the Congress of Vienna.[1] If this were the case, so the argument went, both Britain's and NATO's defence postures required their most fundamental reassessment since the war, with movement away from primary emphasis on British forces stationed in Germany, relying on main battle tanks together with their artillery and long-range air support, to lighter, flexible, home-based defence forces. These could meet the additional requirement for possible challenges arising outside rather than within the NATO area. Such is the unpredictability of world politics that just seven months later, in addition to large naval and air detachments, a British land contingent was sent to the Gulf, spearheaded by main battle tanks and supported by artillery and air/detachments.

During 1990 there was much talk of defence economies with some estimates of savings up to £100 billion over a ten-year period. In the House of Commons during July Tom King, the Secretary of State for Defence, outlined the government's definitive thinking here with his so-called "Options for Change", which proposed a reduction in total service manpower of some 18%. The bulk of this was to fall on the Army and lead to the contraction of its forces in Germany from three armoured divisions and Corps headquarters to one armoured division with a further armoured division and an air mobile brigade held in Britain for rapid deployment overseas. Such cuts have now been confirmed at 8200 men for the Royal Navy (13%), 44,400 for the Army (28%) and 14,700 for the Royal Air Force (16%). With economic concerns again pressing they could eventually be larger still. The bulk of the cuts relate to the Army and have caused much grief in that arm. Mergers must take place among the Household Cavalry and Royal Armoured Corps units and more proud infantry regiments have had to go. The number of support corps has been reduced from 18 to 10.

Inevitably over the last eighteen months some voices counselled caution in reducing the shield. During June, 1990, former Chief of the General Staff, Field-Marshal Sir Nigel Bagnall, concluded an article in the *Daily Telegraph* with the words that in matters of defence "history clearly shows that it is almost invariably the unexpected that occurs".[2] And during the "Options for Change" debate Tom King showed his awareness here by referring to the "unexpected and irresistable claims on money and manpower which had faced the Armed Forces from the time of the Korean War onwards". He went on to say, "We certainly hope that we shall not face anything like that again. My job is not to take risks but to ensure that, if what we do not want to happen occurs, we can defend ourselves".[3] In the following month Saddam Hussein made the unexpected happen but "Operation Granby" was never likely to give the Army the last-minute reprieve which the Falklands campaign offered to the Royal Navy.

Reductions on the scale agreed by Parliament in July, 1991—and certainly more extensive ones still—have a significance for the veterans' establishment which is not hard to see. Despite earlier assurances from the Ministry of Defence that they would be achieved by natural wastage, such statements could never be taken seriously. Tom King himself was always much less categoric during the 1990 "Options for Change" debate: "I am not hinting at natural wastage. I regard the opportunity to ensure that we make a proper, orderly and planned change as a virtue. . . . That is a duty we have to those in the armed forces, and it is one that the Government are determined to discharge."[4]

Belatedly it has been acknowledged that such reductions cannot be accomplished by natural wastage alone and a process of demobilization has to be devised for what will almost certainly be the last —and, given the present unemployment levels, possibly the most painful—of the post-war redundancies. There are good reasons to hope that the redundancy terms should be fair, even generous. For no professional British Army has achieved a higher standard than the present one, nor deserved fairer treatment. As the Gulf crisis demonstrated, despite the unsettling effects of discussions about cutbacks, its members continued to meet their defence responsibilities with a degree of flair and selfless commitment largely unknown in civilian circles. In any case, with demographic patterns indicating a national shortage of young people, it is in the country's best interests to make full use of such an invaluable resource, highly-trained vigorous people whose leadership qualities and communal sense of responsibility have been honed both by out-of-theatre operations and through anti-terrorist duties in Northern Ireland.

The present minimal resettlement arrangements have to be amended for those made redundant and it is hoped that most of the extended provisions will become the standard for servicemen subsequently retiring. The redundancy, for instance, seems to offer an ideal opportunity for the long-delayed creation of a single Veterans Department to oversee it. Improved resettlement arrangements will not benefit veterans alone, they can contribute directly to greater military efficiency, particularly in respect of future recruiting. For, even at a time of force-shedding, a young man's profession still needs regular intakes of suitable recruits. Hopes that the Ministry of Defence might be paying rather more regard to their eventual return to civilian life have been raised by the announcement of plans to help increase the proportion of soldiers who own their own homes and new arrangements to enable servicemen to have the best possible insurance cover against injuries suffered both on and off duty.

Such assurances are necessary, for Britain's professional forces face not only a necessary reconsideration of their role but a major crisis of confidence. Despite the recent Gulf War and serious unrest within the Soviet Union, the previous pattern of East/West confrontation which resulted in the so-called Cold War seems a thing of the past. This is not all. Influential voices have been raised over the extent of the commitment to "Operation Granby" and against Britain ever again taking such a degree of military responsibility without greater European support, particularly from Germany. In the short term one effect of the Gulf conflict will surely be to make both the United States and Britain less inclined to take on such major military commitments. With such factors in mind, while the level of our forces must still be high enough to meet the unexpected, the prospect of fewer military challenges to the present generation of dedicated, ambitious men and women is undeniable. The limited number of overseas stations will be reduced still further with more time being spent in mainland Britain. In the aftermath of the Gulf operation such considerations are likely to make many would-be recruits conclude that soldiering cannot offer them the same attractions as before.

However powerfully Major-General John Strawson might argue that military life can still be made challenging and exciting by imaginative training and enhanced pride in one's unit (many of which are to lose at least part of their identity in the reductions) major difficulties clearly lie ahead for the recruiters.[5] One certain aid—if not the major one—towards recruiting high-quality men and certainly one way of avoiding detrimental publicity is through good resettlement. Young men should not normally think of their retirement but their parents do and in the services this comes early enough for them to pursue another major career. With changed circumstances many might opt to spend a still shorter time in the services before taking up a civilian career. But in an age of unparalleled civil liberties those who choose to voluntarily surrender theirs and put themselves in a position more hazardous than that of any of their fellows must be given positive and advantageous facilities to establish themselves afterwards. After the Gulf war, with continuing instability in the Middle East, new unrest in the Balkans and major political convulsions in the Soviet Union, who could be blind enough to bank on a future free from unexpected upheavals and danger? Britain must therefore continue to attract men and women of high calibre into its defence services. This will hardly happen if they find themselves seriously disadvantaged at the end of their engagements.

With the general public, perhaps it is not too fanciful to hope that, in the last years of the 20th century, now the mushroom cloud of nuclear weapons appears to hang less heavily over them and the sacrifices made by generations of servicemen seem finally to have borne fruit, the sterling qualities of British servicemen, serving and retired, might at last be better appreciated. Is it not time that cult images of the past, of blimps or mindless psychopaths, should fade before the bravery of such as Simon Weston who talked of the modern fighting man's self belief during the Falklands War. "If we believed in freedom ourselves we had no choice."[6] Fortunately, with the higher profile now taken by veterans' associations for both serving and retired personnel it is likely that more people might come to appreciate the contemporary serviceman's responsibilities, that even after the Gulf War they are still awesome, and that even now some of those returning to civilian life will do so with their bodies maimed by bullets or bombs. Most are the result of terrorist activities in Northern Ireland and on the mainland, but not all.

Corporal Simon (Nobby) Clark BEM of 3 Para left the Army in the Autumn of 1989 still short of his 30th birthday. He, along with five others of his section, had been wounded by Argentinian sniping on Mount Longdon, when all but the first got hit, he said, helping each other. Due to the continued accuracy of the fire, they were forced to lie out in numbing cold (two subsequently died) before being piggy-backed off by mates who risked their own lives in doing so. Nobby was wounded in an ankle and after 17 operations, followed by ceaseless pain and frustration, his lower leg was finally amputated. In physical terms he defies the odds. Despite his disability, as the goalkeeper in an able-bodied soccer team he holds his place on merit. He is a keen sub-aqua diver and motorcyclist. Unlike many others from his regiment, as a qualified design engineer he has clear civilian skills. Nobby acknowledges that his injuries and sufferings have led him to realize how precious life really is and, partly because of those friends of his who lost theirs in the Falklands, he is determined to live his to the full.

Even so, the cost of his service, the shock of injury and the intense physical pain, followed by subsequent amputation and rehabilitation over an eight-year period, has hardly been a light one. Even in a world now seemingly freed from conflicts on the scale of those of the early twentieth century but when in the Gulf upwards of 40,000 British troops stood ready again to fight brutal aggression, is it too much to hope that the great majority might still concur with the Rt Rev John Eastaugh's message of homage in 1982 to those who served in the Falklands campaign:

"If there is to be peace, freedom or justice, if the world is to be transformed there must always be those who are prepared to guard that freedom on our behalf."[7]

One might add that they must continue to be given the necessary weapons and remain at sufficiently high force levels to safeguard the nation's security, for in the sophisticated conditions of modern violence they need both the traditional bravery and patriotic spirit of their forebears allied with high levels of intelligence and training. From the skies over Iraq and among the special forces, in particular, new heroes have emerged to join those past generations of serving men to excite the marvel and deserve the homage of those in the home country. There will surely be others in future crises as yet unknown and doubtless like the Gulf and the Falklands in wars wholly unexpected.

In this book we have seen those who stood up returning from the wars over a period exceeding 500 years, who with their collective valour and blood have saved their country from foreign invasion and allowed it to develop its own unique parliamentary traditions and national character. We have seen them poorly rewarded and soon forgotten as is the way with democracies and their fighting men. Let us hope they will, in future, gain just recompense. It is unlikely to be lavish for ordinary men can never forgive missing the unique experience which is given to those who have served together. This form of envy is described by William Shakespeare;

> We band of brothers:
> for he today that sheds his blood with me
> Shall be my brother; be he ne'er so vile,
> This day shall gentle his condition
> Shall think themselves accursed they were not here
> And hold their manhoods cheap whiles any speaks
> That fought with us upon Saint Crispin's day.[8]

But their recompense should not be inadequate nor markedly inferior to other Western States. Along with their proud memories a nation's veterans should, by right, have the chance to reintegrate successfully with civilian society. For any state which shortchanges its guardians deserves neither liberty nor safety.

CHAPTER ONE

1 Arthur, Max, *Above all Courage* (1985), 112/113.
2 Lord Moran, *The Anatomy of Courage* (1945), X.
3 The Comments of Flight Lieutenant David Morgan, Captain Samuel Drennan, Captain Ian Gardiner, Major John Kiszely and Major Chris Keeble all come from *Above all Courage*.
4 Interview with the author, 30/12/88.
5 Ecclesiastes iii, 1–8.
6 Chaney, Otto Preston, *Zhukov* (1972), pp. 346–358.
7 Hopkins, H., *The Strange Death of Private White* (1977), 19.
8 Carew, Tim, *Wipers* (1974), 116.
9 Hopkins, H., op cit., 245.
10 Braddon, Russell, *Cheshire VC* (1954), 13.
11 Henry Williamson's book, *The Patriot's Progress*, written in 1930 from his first-hand knowledge of the trenches, was one of the most shocking and powerful anti-war books of his age.
12 *The Times*, Wednesday, November 9, 1988.
13 Royle, Trevor, *The Best Years of their Lives* (1986), 196.

CHAPTER TWO

1 Hewitt, H. J., *The Organization of War under Edward III* (1966), 34.
2 Macaulay, Thomas Babington, *History of England*, Vol 1, 91.
3 Grose, *Military Antiquities* Vol II (1786), 180–181.
4 Roxburghe, *Ballads* VII, 647.
5 Fortescue, J. W., *A History of the British Army*, Macmillan (1889), Vol 2, 561.
6 Fortescue, op cit, 896.
7 Harries-Jenkins, Gwyn, *The Army in Victorian Society* (1977), 84.
8 Shipp, John, *The Path of Glory*, Chatto and Windus (1969), 229.
9 Bond, Brian, *The Victorian Army and the Staff College* (1972), 17.
10 Jackson, Robert, *A View of the Formation, Discipline and Economy of Armies*, 3rd Edition (1845), 189.
11 Fortescue, J. W., op. cit. 403–4.
12 Skelley, Alan Ramsay, *The Victorian Army at Home* (1977), 29, 33.
13 Laffin, John, *Tommy Atkins* (1977) 124.

CHAPTER THREE

1 British Library CAL S.P. Dom, Charles II, Vol CIX, No 104 CAL, 466.
2 Dean, Captain C. G. T., *The Royal Hospital, Chelsea* (1950), 23.
3 op. cit., 35.
4 PRO, WO 23/1 Chelsea Reports.
5 PRO, WO 97/1387, 1389.
6 The story is well told in a book by Philip Newell, *Greenwich Hospital, a Royal Foundation, 1692–1983* (1984).
7 PRO: *Instructions in Drill for the Use of Enrolled Pensioners* (1844), 3.
8 PRO HO 50/439 Extract of Christie to Torrens, 5 August, 1819.
9 Hughes, Robert, *The Fatal Shore* (1987), 2.
10 Fortescue, J. W., op. cit., Vol II, 268–9.
11 *London Gazette*, 4–8 October, 1763.
12 PRO WO 43/542, 1.
13 PRO WO 43/542, 65.
14 PRO WO 43/542, 528.9.

15 Costello, Edward, *The Peninsular and Waterloo Campaigns* (1967), 15.

16 PRO, WO 6/112, 174–184.

17 Dalhousie Commission on Recruiting, 1866, Minutes of Evidence, para 4410–4456.

18 Annual PMG Reports, 1856–62. Appendices.

19 Fifth Report of the Select Committee on the Army before Sebastopol (1855), 23.

20 Woodham-Smith, Cecil, *Florence Nightingale* (1950), 208.

21 Aldershot, *A Record of Mrs Daniell's work amongst Soldiers and its sequel* (1879), 42.

22 Dunant, Henri *A Memory of Solferino*, Washington (1950), 60.

23 Reese, Peter, *Our Sergeant* (1986), 25.

24 General Annual Return of the British Army, XLIII, LIII.

CHAPTER FOUR

1 *Hansard*, Third Series, Vol III, COLS 445.6.

2 War Office Library (WOL); Annual Report of the Inspector General of Recruiting for 1871 (1872), 1 (General Clement A Edwards).

3 RA ADD MSS E1/10679, Lt-Col L. V. Swaine to HRH, 10 March, 1884.

4 PRO Middleton Papers 30/67/3, C-in-C to St John Brodrick, 12 December, 1887.

5 RA ADD MSS E1/10607, Sir Donald Stewart to HRH, 23 June, 1884.

6 Archives RFEA: Typewritten copy of original letter.

7 *Brigade of Guards Magazine*, Vol V, 1892, 99, Vol X, 1898, 98.

8 Fraser, John, *Sixty Years in Uniform* (1939), 50.

9 First AGM, SSFA, 8 May, 1886.

10 Laffin, John, Op cit, 163.

11 Price, Richard, *An Imperial War and the British Working Class* (1972), 64.

12 Annual Report of SSFA for 1899, 6.

13 SSFA HQ *Short History of SSAFA from 1902*, 106.

14 Oliver, Dame Beryl, *The British Red Cross in Action* (1966), 86.

15 Butler, Sir W. F., *An Autobiography* (1911), 191.

16 WOL Annual Report of the Inspector General of Recruiting for 1902, 28, 29.

17 Amery, L. S., *The Times History of the War in South Africa 1899–1902* (1902), pp. 2–47.

18 Commentators like Waters, W. H. H., *The War in South Africa* (1905), and Conan Doyle Sir A., *The Great Boer War* (1901).

19 WOL Pedley A. C., *Notes on the Days that are Past*, (unpublished autobiography) 116.

20 Edwards J. E., *Military Operations, France and Belgium 1914*, 1925, Vol 1, 10–11.

21 Hansard Debates: Questions on Army Affairs, Session 1910, Cols 360–370; 413; 257–8.

CHAPTER FIVE

1 *Statistics of the Military Effort of the British Empire, 1914–1920*, HMSO, 1922.

2 Clarke, I. F., *Voices Prophesying War 1763–1984* (1966), 1.

3 Charteris, Brigadier-General John, *Field-Marshal Earl Haig* (1929).

4 Cooper, Duff, *Haig* (1935) Vol 1, 131.
5 Magnus, Philip, *Kitchener, Portrait of an Imperialist* (1958), 279.
6 De Groot, Gerard J., *Douglas Haig* (1988), 126.
7 Terraine, John, *Impacts of War 1914–1918* (1970), 75.
8 Tuchman, Barbara, *August, 1914* Constable (1962), 123.
9 Barker, A. J., *The West Yorkshire Regiment* (1974), pp. 52, 53.
10 *Sussex Life*, May, 1985.

11 Atkinson, C. T., *The South Wales Borderers, 24th Foot*, CUP, (1937), 433. (A company totalled about 120 men).
12 Beckett, Ian F. W. and Simpson, Keith, *A Nation in Arms* (1985), 10.
13 There were 7,808 women in Queen Mary's Army Auxiliary Corps on 3 August, 1918, and 1,094 women as nurses or others with the British Red Cross Society. *Statistics of the British Army*, op cit. 93.

CHAPTER SIX

1 HQ SSFA, Proceedings of the 30 Annual General Meetings, 13.
2 Select Committee on Naval and Military Service (Pensions and Grants), 1914–16.
3 Select Committee, op. cit., 207, 8.
4 HQ SSFA: Proceeding of the 31st Annual Meeting, 14–22.
5 Select Committee on the Training and Employment of Disabled Ex-servicemen 1922 vi, 425.
6 *Statistics of the Military effort of the British Empire during the Great War 1914–1920*, HMSO, (1922), 741.
7 Select Committee op cit, 269–272.
8 Select Committee op cit, viii.
9 Interim Report of the King's Roll National Council on the Employ-

ment of Disabled Ex-Servicemen, (1923), 10.
10 Select Committee on Naval and Military Service (Pensions and Grants) 1914–16 op cit, 487.
11 Report of the War Cabinet for 1917, XIX.
12 Report of Annual General Meeting of NAERDS for 1920, 3.
13 Terraine, John, *Douglas Haig, the Educated Soldier* (1963), 483–4.
14 *Statistics of the Military Effort of the British Empire 1914–1920*, Demobilization, 684.
15 Claxton, Major-General P. F., *The Regular Forces' Employment Association 1885–1925*, 21.
16 Claxton, Major-General P. F., op cit, 22/23.

CHAPTER SEVEN

1 Terraine, John, *Douglas Haig, The Educated Soldier* (1963), 483.
2 Charteris, John, *Field-Marshal Earl Haig* (1929), 388.
3 Secrett, Sergeant I., *Twenty Years with Haig* (1929).
4 Sixsmith, General E. K. G., *Douglas Haig* (1976), 181.
5 Duncan, G. S., *Douglas Haig as I knew him* (1966), Preface.
6 *The Private Papers of Douglas Haig, 1914–1919*, Ed. by Robert Blake (1952), 208.
7 G. S. Duncan, op. cit., 49.
8 *British Legion Magazine*, March, 1928, p. 266, quoted by G. S. Duncan.
9 *Private Papers of Douglas Haig*, 349.
10 NLS Haig Papers 3155/221a *Liverpool Echo*, 20.7.1919.
11 Letter of Haig to Lady Haig 4 Oct.

1918 cited by Gerard de Groot in his book *Douglas Haig*, 398.

12 Haig, Countess, *The Man I Knew*, Moray Press (1936), 242.

13 Letter of Haig to Elibank of 27 July, 1919, cited by Gerard de Groot, op. cit., 400.

14 Wootton, Graham, *The Official*

History of the British Legion (1956), 30.

15 This has been done in able fashion in Graham Wootton's book, although his diminution of Douglas Haig's role seems inexplicable.

16 Wootton, Graham, op. cit., 34.

CHAPTER EIGHT

1 Wootton, Graham, op. cit., 31.
2 'Soldier's Booklet' AB 472.
3 National Library of Scotland, Haig Papers 349(2) 29.3.20.
4 Haig Papers H 236d. *The Times* article of 4/8/1921.
5 Haig Papers H 328g. Letter of 5/4/1930.
6 Wootton, Graham op. cit., 42.
7 IWM Library: Diaries of Capt (later Brigadier) Hodgkin, A. E.
8 IWM Sound Records, 36/06 2/Lt Thorpe-Tracy, R.
9 IWM Sound Records, 318/08 Sapper Neyland, B.
10 IWM Library: Clegg, Harold, unpublished historiography.
11 *Legion Journal*, July, 1921, 5.
12 Haig Papers H 235a.
13 Haig Papers, 349(2). Address at Central Hall, Liverpool, 5/4/1922.
14 *Legion Journal*, October, 1921. 76. Article by Chistopher Addison, MP, (late Minister for Health).
15 Haig Papers, H 227d. Speech of 25/9/1925.
16 Haig Papers, H 326d. New Zealand Repatriation Scheme.
17 Haig Papers, H 236d. *The Review*, (1922).
18 Haig Papers, Haig to Crosfield, 20/4/1923.

19 Haig Papers, Haig to Crosfield, 3/11/1923.
20 Wootton, Graham, op. cit., 76.
21 IWM, Sound Records, 212/14, Sgt Painting, Thomas Henry.
22 IWM, Sound Records, 8946/18, Pte Pickard, John Joseph.
23 IWM Library: Pte Taylor, Henry, *One Poppy Spared*.
24 IWM Library: Clegg, Harold op. cit.
25 IWM Sound Records, 4977/03. Pte Claydon, Walley.
26 IWM Sound Records, 375/06. Pte Clarke, Walter Ernest.
27 IWM Sound Records, 9756/04. Pte Manton, Horace Charles.
28 IWM Sound Records, 10404/04. Pte Tolley, James William.
29 IWM Sound Records, 212/04. Sgt Painting, Thomas Henry.
30 IWM Library: Sgt Simpson T. J. *On Three Years' Captivity in the Hands of the Bulgars*, 1915–18.
31 IWM Sound Records, 8849/08, L/Cpl Edmed, Thomas Henry.
32 IWM Sound Records, 327/08, Pte Fagence, Victor Edgar.
33 IWM Sound Records, 554/18, Pte Quinnell, Charles Robert.
34 IWM Sound Records, 31/02, Dvr Lock, Ernest Walter.

CHAPTER NINE

1 Haig Papers, 3155 H 227d. Letter of Haig to Crosfield, 3/9/1921.

2 Haig Papers, *Our Empire*, Vol I, No 10, June, 1926.

3 Haig Papers, H 227d. Letter of Haig to Crosfield, 20/7/1921.
4 Wootton, Graham, op. cit., 47.
5 BL Comd 317, xxx, 139, Inter-departmental Committee on TB (1919).
6 NLS, Haig Papers, H 227. Haig to Crosfield, 24/3/1926.
7 Menett, Stephen, *State Housing in Britain* (1979), 31.
8 SSAFA 39th Annual Meeting 22/6/1925. Statement of Mr Willoughby Cole.
9 Stevenson, John, *British Society 1914–45* (1984), 130.
10 British Legion HQ pamphlet surveying activities during 1925.
11 WEA Western District: Crudge, H. G., *Fifty Years in the Life of a Voluntary Movement*.
12 Haig Papers H 227j; letter of Crosfield to Haig of 17/10/1927.
13 A good account of the provisions made in New Zealand is that of N. P. Webber, *The First Fifty years of the New Zealand Returned Services Association, 1916 to 1966*, 3.
14 *BL Journal*, Sept, 1922, Article of P. A. Tixier.
15 *BL Journal*, June, 1924, Members of the FIDAC—Italy.
16 *BL Journal*, June, 1924, Members of the FIDAC—The American Legion.

CHAPTER TEN

1 *British Legion Journal*: President's Report during the 9th Annual Conference, July, 1930.
2 *British Legion Journal*, July, 1935. Annual Conference.
3 Sekuless, Peter, and Rees, Jacqueline: *Lest we Forget 1916–1986* Rigby NSW.
4 op. cit., p. 85.
5 Severo, Richard & Milford, Lewis, *The Wages of War*, Simon & Schuster, 1989, pp. 264–279.
6 *BL Journal*, July 1935, Proceedings of the Annual Conference.
7 Wootton, Graham, op. cit., 178.
8 *BL Journal*, August, 1935, Reception of the Austrian Chancellor.
9 *BL Journal*, Annual Conference, 1937.
10 *BL Journal*, 1936, 409.
11 *BL Journal*, March, 1937, 319.
12 PRO CAB 23/96. Cabinet Meeting of 25/9.1938.

CHAPTER ELEVEN

1 Goralski, Robert, *World War II Almanac, 1931–1945*, 1981, 425–428.
2 British Library, COMD 6415 (1942–3) VI, 67.
3 Robertson Andrew: *REMPLOY, We have a part to play*.
4 British Library, COMD 7822 XVII, 567. Ministry of Labour and National Service Report for Year 1948.
5 British Library, Comd 7822 XVII 567 (Ministry of Labour and National Service Report for the year 1948. G. A. Isaacs Minister).
6 British Library, Comd 7076, X, 693 1946–7 (Hancock Report).
7 Tomlinson, George, *A Short History of War Pensions* (Talk given at BLESMA Conference, 1989).
8 Parker, H. M. D., *Manpower. A Study of Wartime Policy and Administration*, HMSO, 1957, 199.
9 op. cit., 503.
10 Jary, Sydney, *18 Platoon*, 1987, 129, 130.

CHAPTER TWELVE

1 Notably in Trevor Royle's book, *The Best Years of their Lives*.
2 Named after its Chairman, Sir

Harold Wiles, from the Ministry of Labour and National Service.
3 Wiles Report, 3.

CHAPTER THIRTEEN

1 Marwick, Arthur, *British Society since 1945*, 147.
2 Paper for the Fifth anniversary of the Federal German Armed Forces Advanced Vocational Training

Service by Ministerialrat Dr Emil Tuschhoff.
3 *British Legion Journal*, Jan, 1971, 3.
4 *The Times*, 20 October, 1967.

CHAPTER FOURTEEN

1 Conservative Party Manifesto for 1979.
2 Defence Estimates 1980, 2.
3 *The Times*, 16 June, 1982.
4 *Sunday Times* Insight Team, The Falklands War, 262.
5 HQ SSAFA: Paper on SSAFA and

the Forces Care Concept of 8 June, 1987.
6 *British Legion Journal*, Opinion Article, March, 1983.
7 *Guide for Service Officers, Veterans Benefits, Veterans of Foreign Wars of the United States*, 22nd Edition 1989.

CHAPTER FIFTEEN

1 *Daily Telegraph* 17 May, 1990.
2 *Daily Telegraph* 26/6/1990.
3 Hansard 25/7/1990, Pg 80.
4 Hansard, Options for Change 25/7/1990, 73.
5 Strawson, John, *Gentlemen in Khaki*, 1989 pp 277–84.

6 Weston, Simon, *Walking Tall*, (1989) 284.
7 Rt Rev John Eastaugh, Bishop of Hereford, *Daily Telegraph* 15/11/1982.
8 Shakespeare, *Henry V*, Act 4, Scene 3.

Index